Also by Renée Richards

Second Serve

NO WAY RENÉE

The Second Half of My Notorious Life

RENÉE RICHARDS
with JOHN AMES

SIMON & SCHUSTER

New York   London   Toronto   Sydney

SIMON & SCHUSTER
Rockefeller Center
1230 Avenue of the Americas
New York, NY 10020

This work is a memoir. It reflects the author's present recollection of her experiences over a period of years. Certain names and identifying characteristics have been changed.

For information about special discounts for bulk purchases,
please contact Simon & Schuster Special Sales:
1-800-456-6798 or business@simonandschuster.com

Designed by Jaime Putorti

Manufactured in the United States of America

10   9   8   7   6   5   4   3   2   1

Library of Congress Cataloging-in-Publication Data

Richards, Renée.
    No way Renée : the second half of my notorious life / Renée Richards
with John Ames.
        p. cm.
    1. Richards, Renée. 2. Transsexuals—United States—Biography.
3. Transsexuals—Identity. 4. Transsexualism. 5. Gender identity.
I. Ames, John. II. Title.

HQ77.8.R52A3 2007
306.76'80973—dc22   2006052252

ISBN-13: 978–0–7432–9013–5
ISBN-10:   0–7432–9013–5

No Way Renée *is dedicated to all those people who must struggle to figure out who they really are.*

No man, for any considerable period, can wear one face to himself, and another to the multitude, without finally getting bewildered as to which may be the true.

Nathaniel Hawthorne
The Scarlet Letter

Contents

Author's Note xi

Preface 1

CHAPTER 1
The First Half of My Notorious Life 7

CHAPTER 2
Mother, Father, Sister, Brother 35

CHAPTER 3
Then and Now 61

CHAPTER 4
They Called Him Rastaman 91

CHAPTER 5
An Adolescence for Renée 121

Contents

CHAPTER 6

Renée and Martina 149

CHAPTER 7

The Doctor Is In Again 177

CHAPTER 8

Country Retreat 205

CHAPTER 9

The Physical Side 231

CHAPTER 10

Sex, Love, and Romance 249

CHAPTER 11

Was It a Mistake? 277

Acknowledgments 293

Index 295

Author's Note

NO WAY RENÉE EXPLORES new territory. To my knowledge, no other transsexual has written about the long-term consequences of a sex change, probably because postsurgery life for a true transsexual is in many ways one long sigh of relief, and relief is never as riveting for readers as anguish. However, my case is different. Because of my notoriety, people continue to be curious about me, and for better or worse, my tendency to stumble into intriguing situations did not diminish as I built my life as Renée Richards. So, I offer this account in part because it may help promote a better understanding of transsexuality, but mostly because it is interesting in its own right.

In organizing *No Way Renée*, I was inspired by the questions people ask me. They want to know how my family (especially my son) has adapted to my situation, what it was like playing and coaching tennis as a woman, how I managed to resurrect my medical career, if I ever found romance, if I am healthy, if I am encouraged by society's growing acceptance of transsexuality, and if I regret my choices. As I address these questions, I move backward and forward in time, so *No Way Renée* is only roughly chronological. My goal is to paint an entertaining picture of how I solved my problems and found an honorable place in my culture.

Few readers will be surprised to discover that I have a complicated view of myself, but they might be surprised at how that view affects my expression. Although I am not one of those pompous people who refer to themselves in the third person, I sometimes do so because of the several incarnations I have gone through. I occasionally speak of Richard Raskind in the third person, especially when I want to emphasize the split in his personality. Dick was plagued by an entity named "Renée." That Renée and I are not the same. She was a desperate creature who destroyed Dick's life, and I always refer to her as "Renée," never "I." Furthermore, Dick's sex change did not bring into being an entirely new person. People called me Renée in those days; however, it is hard to say exactly who I was, but I was surely not who I am now. I sometimes refer to this emerging person as Renée, especially when I want to emphasize her maturation process.

My use of terminology differs a bit from the current trend. I prefer "transsexual" to "transgendered," and "sex change" to "gender change." I consider "sex" to be a much more concrete word than "gender." I definitely had a sex change, but even so I have a mixture of gender characteristics. This is true not just of transsexuals, but of all people. As a physician, I am serious about accuracy in medical matters, and I use the terms that I consider most clearly descriptive. In general, I have tried to use as few medical terms as possible, and when I do, I usually provide a short explanation of them. Occasionally a term cannot be accurately condensed, so rather than insert a lengthy definition or use an imperfect layman's term, I let it stand alone.

Wherever possible in *No Way Renée*, I have disguised private people who might be embarrassed by my remarks. Their names, origins, places of residence, and other details of their lives have been changed. In every other way, I have been truthful; however, I realize that others may recall or interpret events differently than I do, and I respect their right to do so. *No Way Renée* is not out to settle any score; quite the contrary, it is a work of reconciliation that I hope shows clearly that I hold no grudges. Readers of *Second Serve*, the account of the first half of my life, may notice that I have altered some of the interpretations I offered twenty years ago and have corrected some errors in my reporting. *No Way Renée* is as accepting and accurate as I can make it.

No book, however well-meant or carefully stated, can truly sum up a life, especially one as unconventional as mine. I don't expect my readers to close *No Way Renée* and say, "Now I understand Renée Richards." The best I can hope for is that they might say, "Renée has had an interesting life, even if you ignore the sex change."

No Way Renée

Preface

IN 1976, I WAS one of the most famous people in the world. The paparazzi were on my trail twenty-four hours a day, hungry for any photo, the less flattering the better. The mainstream press was better, sometimes. *People, Time, Newsweek, Sports Illustrated*—I was featured in them all, an international phenomenon. Once, at the height of my notoriety, I found myself in Uruguay, where I had gone beyond the urban centers like Montevideo and was walking down the beach at Carrasco, a tiny coastal village. I was enjoying a welcome sense of anonymity, but a man in a little kiosk pointed to my picture on a magazine and with much excitement asked me to sign it, which I did. Recognizable even in the countryside of Uruguay: that sums up the Renée Richards phenomenon at its zenith.

During that time I was deluged by a myriad of television opportunities. All the major figures wanted to interview me:

Phil Donahue, Tom Snyder, Howard Cosell, and many others I can't recall. I was on the *Today* show, *Good Morning America*, and a host of other major shows. I was even invited to do *The Hollywood Squares*, but I declined. I had my limits.

And what had I done to merit this interest? Perfected an organ transplant procedure? Gone over Niagara Falls in a barrel? Neither. Simply put, I had undergone a male-to-female sex-change operation and then had the temerity to play in an amateur women's tennis tournament. Of course there was more to it than that, but basically that was the source of my infamy. To compound my audacity, I had not hung my head and apologized. I had gone to court, won my case, and played professional tennis as a woman.

The story of how I got into that situation was told in my autobiography, *Second Serve*. Born Richard Raskind. Raised a nice Jewish boy. Educated at Yale. Tournament tennis player. Top surgeon. Lieutenant-commander in the Navy. Married to a beautiful woman. Father of a wonderful son. But compelled by a secret drive that could not be suppressed, even with years of psychotherapy and every trick in the book. Another entity, Renée, kept growing stronger and stronger until she eventually took over.

It was a long nightmare for Dick, and just when it seemed to be over, another one started for Renée. She had to walk onto a tennis court and endure the intense scrutiny of thousands of people. It was a choice, yes, but not a happy one and not made out of a desire to show off. I took a stand on principle, but it exacted an emotional and financial price. When I left the tour, I was very tired of the fishbowl.

But I have had more than twenty-five years to get my second wind, so I want to respond to the question I hear so often: "What have you done lately, Dr. Richards?" One answer is that I have been doing what I always wanted to do in the first place: live a private life. Yet I remain a subject of interest and live in the memories of the many people who followed my adventures years ago. Unhappily, their mental image of me is too frequently tainted by grainy tabloid photographs and sensational headlines. I don't deny that my life has been strange, but strangeness is only part of a complex whole that is not well understood.

I have practiced a highly specialized form of eye surgery for forty years, and I am still operating every week. I am also an educator, having served as a clinical professor, first at Cornell Medical School and later at New York University, where I continue on the faculty to this day. I have instructed and influenced hundreds of residents and postgraduate fellows who are out in the world putting my lessons to work. They think of me as a distinguished mentor, not a curiosity. In 2001, I received the Helen Keller Services for the Blind Award, Manhattan Branch, given yearly to an outstanding ophthalmologist.

Many people know that I coached Martina Navratilova to two of her Wimbledon championships, but few know about the many lesser-known players, both professional and amateur, whose skills I have helped improve. They have gone on to become ambassadors for the game I love. This behind-the-scenes contribution is at odds with the picture of Renée Richards as an unbalanced, publicity-crazy flake. I am not despised by the tennis community. I am a respected figure, despite my notorious past, and in 2000 I was inducted into the Eastern Tennis Hall of Fame.

And I am seldom given credit for all that I have done in the area that has made me notorious, transsexualism. I'm the first to admit that I have not been an avid ambassador for transsexuals. I do not think of myself primarily as a transsexual. In fact, I fought for my rights largely because I was personally affronted that a medical operation could overshadow everything else I was as a human being. But there is no denying that when I retired from tennis, the world was much more aware of what a transsexual was, and that familiarity, not to mention my success as a professional coach, dispelled a lot of the condition's scandalous overtones. I opened doors for those who came after me, and I am a hero to many of them.

But I have not written *No Way Renée* as a justification of my life; rather, it is a look at the second half of a life that I hope no longer needs justifying. It is the story of how I thought through and reconciled my bizarre family life; how my son and I coped with my changed persona; how I gave my new incarnation an adolescence; how I restored my medical career; how I searched for understanding, stability, romance, health, and a sense of my place in a changing world. It answers the question in the minds of so many, "Was your sex change a mistake?"

When I first exploded on the scene, I was in my early forties but was nevertheless a newborn who hardly knew how to respond when asked, "How does it feel to be a woman?" Thirty years later, I have enough experience to at least say something about how it feels to be a particular woman: Renée Richards. Why bother? Well, somewhere along the line, I became something I never imagined I would be, a notable part of America's social history. So, *No Way Renée* completes the record of my unusual pursuit of the American Dream, an ideal that encourages us to make of ourselves the most we can. It is a dream my immigrant family embraced and realized. I continue to believe in it.

CHAPTER 1

The First Half of My Notorious Life

O N AUGUST 18, 1934, my mother began to hemorrhage. This was inconvenient because she was determined to give birth in a hospital for women, with a woman physician in attendance. However, she was in Queens, New York, and the hospital and doctor she had picked were in Manhattan. In typical fashion, Sadie Muriel Baron refused to bow to circumstance. Bleeding all the way, she drove to Manhattan where she could have things as she pleased. It was a blighted birth from start to finish. The placenta was in front of my head. My mother had lost too much blood. In the end, however, Mother risked her life to bring me into the world through a Caesarean section, and on August 19, my life as Richard Henry Raskind began.

I was known to friends and family as Dick. The irony of that nickname has haunted me for most of my life, but at first little Richard Raskind—named after Richard the Lionhearted—enjoyed the position of favored son in a Jewish household: the *puritz,* or prince. It was clear that I was to carry the family banner. In that regard, I took over from my sister Josephine, Jo for short, who was five years older than me and had been acting son before my appearance. She grew up a raging tomboy who might occasionally be coerced into a dress, though she sometimes screamed for hours in indignation.

Jo simultaneously despised and loved me, and these mixed feelings drove her to be both physically hurtful and loving. She sometimes played a game with me that reflected the source of her conflicted attitude. After pushing my penis into my body, she would say delightedly, "Now you're a little girl!" The penis game was strictly a private matter between my sister and me, but Jo was sometimes present on the rare occasions when my mother would dress me in a slip, which I assume was done for the seemingly innocent purpose of making me look cute. At these times, Jo would join my mother in praising me, and in this situation I felt they most approved of me.

How my mother, one of the few women psychiatrists of the time, managed to reconcile this behavior I cannot say. It seems to me that she practiced psychiatric insight only at work. By contrast, she governed the Raskind home by a shallow set of rules based on a Victorian idea of family relationships and above all on what the neighbors would think. She wanted us to give the appearance of a perfect family, right out of the Gilded Age. This was most evident when we sat down to eat in the evening, my father in his smoking jacket and my mother in dressy attire, most often a low-cut dress that emphasized her bosom. Dinner would consist of seven courses and would last

two hours. Often it was two hours of arguing that would occasionally escalate until two or more of us were screaming at
the top of our lungs. The sources of this friction were the endless contradictions in our household. My father, apparently the
elegant master of the house presiding over his table, was actually more the argumentative wife who never won an argument.
My mother, seemingly the refined lady of the house, was more
the dictatorial husband. My sister, clearly a girl, just as clearly
wished herself a boy. And then there was me, a little boy trying
to figure out what was what.

More than anything else, high-volume arguing characterized the Raskind household. So many matters, even minor
ones, seemed to come down to a contest of wills. The will that
prevailed was my mother's, not that the rest of us didn't try. I
protested loud and long every time she administered my weekly
enema, but I always got one just the same. My father put on
the best show of all. He was gruff, physically intimidating, and
could shout with the best of them, but he never stood a chance
against my mother. This was not lost on me, and I felt great dis-
dain for my father because of that weakness. When my mother
or sister sought to dominate me unreasonably, my father was
the natural person for me to look to as protector, but his efforts
were all show. When the crunch came, I knew he would fold.

No wonder my father was so often gone from the house.
I imagine it was a tremendous relief for him to be someplace
where he could occasionally win. One such spot was the Sunrise
Tennis Club, which consisted of a row of dirt courts by the Long
Island Railroad tracks in Sunnyside, Queens. The clubhouse was
a shed with an aluminum roof, which served as everything from

office to locker room. Here my father could meet other men on more or less equal terms, though he was never a highly competitive tennis player. For him, tennis was more an occasion for socializing, and probably for winning an argument now and again. I spent many weekends at the Sunrise Club, shagging balls for my father. It was a welcome release for both of us, and my interest in tennis was born on those shabby courts.

In one area, my parents shone brightly: They were excellent providers. By the time I was five, they were able to buy an expansive Colonial-style house in Forest Hills. It had fifteen rooms and gave us all a little breathing space. Even so, on a typical day the house was full of people. My mother worked at home, and my mother's spinster sister, my mother's mother, and our housekeeper were usually around. There was just as much yelling in the new house, but I got my own room, where I could get away from it and escape my sister's sneak attacks. Thus began a new phase in my development.

At about age nine, I was alone in my room one day and got the unsettling urge to reenact the dress-up sessions but without my sister or mother. A change in Jo's attitude may have prompted this. When I reached the age of five, she began to insist that I be completely masculine in both behavior and dress, the tougher the better. In one way this was welcome, but I missed the feelings of warmth and approval that had come with the dressing up as a girl. It had been several years since we had gone through such a session, and perhaps I was emerging from the latency period described by Freud as occurring between five and eight. Whatever the reason, the idea that I might dress as a girl on my own was both exciting and terrifying. I crept to the door and listened. I could hear muffled sounds from the rest of the house but nothing near my room.

I took a breath and, pulse racing, scuttled down the hall. I opened Jo's dresser and with trembling hands picked up a pair of her panties. This was as far as I had intended to go, but a sudden impulse seized me, and I grabbed a skirt, a blouse, shoes, some stockings and a garter belt, even a hat. With these items draped about me, I ran stealthily down to the bathroom where I could lock the door. Inside, I threw off my boy's clothes and stood naked, and then with a mixture of anxiety and anticipation, I quickly dressed myself in Jo's clothes. As young as I was, I still realized that I looked pretty bad. The clothes were too large, but even as I was wondering if I would ever have the nerve to dress that way again, I was thinking that there were things in her closet that she had outgrown, and they would fit me better. And there was something else. My anxiety level had gone down tremendously. There was no denying that dressing in this fashion felt good.

Unfortunately, as I disrobed, my feeling of well-being faded and was replaced by self-loathing. I hastily replaced Jo's clothes in her closet and drawers, retreated to my room, and closed the door. There, in my nine-year-old way, I mulled over the giant leap I had taken. Something that had previously been out of my control, I had just instigated in my own behalf. It seemed wrong in a nasty way, but there was no denying the satisfaction I had taken in doing it. How could something be wrong and right at the same time? It was a question with which I would struggle for the rest of my life.

My first fifteen years were a terrifying mix of triumph and failure. I became a star athlete with a circle of male friends who never suspected me of much other than being a little more sensitive than the usual jock. For the most part, we were all typical teens of the time. We double-dated, made out with girls in lovers' lanes—never getting much further than first base—and felt pretty rakish to have done that much. But under this veneer of normality lurked my terrible secret: the desire to transform myself into a female. Though I was close to my friends in the manner of young buddies, I never revealed this perverted longing to any of them. I feared that if I did, my world would come crashing down around my ears. Many times I promised myself that I would never let my female side out again, but it was a promise I could never keep. By this time I had named her Renée.

However, as I got older, the obstacles for Renée were greater than ever. I was no longer a fuzzy-cheeked child. I was a sizable man with a beard, body hair, and fully developed genitals. To top it off, I was a trained athlete with the muscles to match. I was no weight lifter but no sylph, either. The transformation that had been so simple just a year or two earlier was now a complex task. First, I shaved my face carefully. My beard wasn't heavy, and close shaving and makeup did a pretty good job of removing its traces. I also had to shave my legs, even if no one would see them. Renée was beginning to demand as much authenticity as possible. When she was in command, my male genitals had to be eliminated as much as possible. This started with the uncomfortable process of shoving my testicles up into my body cavity. For most men this would be impossible, but in my case, the inguinal ring through which the testicles had first descended was larger than normal. It was painful, but I could push my testicles through that ring. I kept them elevated with a crosshatching of adhesive tape. To minimize my penis, I stretched it backward and used more tape to stick it down. Renée was then as smooth as she could be. This distortion of delicate tissues grew less comfortable as the hours went by, and much of my time as Renée was excruciatingly painful. In later years, I devised a more brutal method of minimizing my penis by knotting twine around the head, stretching it backward between my legs, and knotting the string to a rope around my waist.

This behavior ebbed and flowed during my years at Yale University and later in the medical program at the University of Rochester. Dick Raskind had meaningful love affairs with women and starred as a tennis player. When he was in love or in heavy athletic training, Renée would seldom emerge. When she did come out, however, she came out with such a vengeance that afterward Dick found himself nursing serious bruises and tears to his genitals. On one occasion, my right testicle swelled to twice its normal size. I began to worry that out of frustration Renée would do me permanent harm, perhaps even commit suicide and take Dick with her.

Once while in medical school, I grew despondent. I had broken off a significant love affair the previous year, and two years of psychiatric analysis had done nothing to ease my problem. Desperate for some masculine validation, I called up a girl with a loose reputation and went to her house. She was pleasant and willing, but I couldn't perform and left humiliated. On the way home through a Rochester blizzard, I was distractedly mulling over the incident when suddenly I became aware of two lights in the darkness ahead of me, and a split second later my face crashed into the steering wheel. I escaped death by inches, but my jaw was horribly smashed and hours of surgery were required for reconstruction. It was wired shut for eight weeks and immobile for another four. Even though the other driver was drunk and charged with the accident, I couldn't help wondering if Renée were somehow at fault. In her frustration, was she trying to kill Dick? There was no knowing for sure, but I began to trust myself less and less.

During this period, I probably would not have survived without tennis. I can't emphasize enough how important it was to me. Athletics was the one constant in an otherwise uncertain world. I understood it and thrived on it. The companionship of my tennis buddies was as important to me as the tennis itself. Thoroughly masculine, uncomplicated, and sometimes a little crude, they provided a strong aura of testosterone that helped counteract Renée's influence. But in spite of every effort to stifle her, Renée remained lurking in the background, coloring every aspect of my life.

In 1959, I started my medical internship. At first, the crowded schedule worked in my favor: I was too busy and tired for Renée to emerge. The worthwhile work was enjoyable, and I felt fairly normal for a change. At the end of a demanding year of internship, I began therapy with the renowned Dr. Bak, one of the premiere Freudian analysts of the era. Each day I would hurry to my 6:00 P.M. appointment and stretch out on a black leather couch, staring at the ceiling and occasionally glimpsing a billow of gray smoke from my psychoanalyst's cigar. Dr. Bak was an arrogant and intellectually intimidating man, so when he eventually proposed his theory of my neurosis in his Viennese accent, it sounded like gospel.

Dr. Bak held that I had no desire to be a woman. Quite the contrary, I was afraid of losing my penis. The effort I expended to make it go away when I became Renée was a symbolic castration, which I went through only so I could experience the satisfaction of turning into Dick again. Dr. Bak brilliantly explained what he considered the origin and development of the problem, and it certainly was an attractive hypothesis. If what I liked was being Dick, it should be possible to get me to be permanently satisfied with what I really liked. Case solved. But it didn't happen. Despite Dr. Bak's brilliance, my case proved so thorny that by the end of our association, he had abandoned his Freudian method and just started telling me what to do, often in a loud angry voice. When I brought up the possibility of a sex change, Dr. Bak warned me that it might drive me mad, but shortly after my mother's death, I broke with him and sought surgery through Dr. Harry Benjamin, who had treated Christine Jorgensen and had coined the term "transsexual." By that time I was serving a stint as a Navy lieutenant-commander.

Dr. Benjamin's waiting room was not a reassuring place for a young fellow who had been warned by his psychiatrist that he might go mad if he became a woman. In one corner, a six-foot-six-inch black man in a blond acrylic wig and a miniskirt was putting on red lipstick. Another man in a button-down shirt was rhythmically rubbing his breasts. He told me that they had recently begun to itch, and during the night he was scratching them raw in his sleep, so he had come in to see if that was normal. In such an environment, the word "normal" seemed out of place.

Some of Dr. Benjamin's patients were, to be frank, grotesquely ill-suited for womanhood. Still, once I settled down and could tear my eyes away from them, I saw that there were some attractive women in the room. I hoped they were transsexuals, not just friends or relatives. I found out later that everyone in the room was a male-to-female transsexual at some point in his treatment.

Eventually I was called in to see Dr. Benjamin, who was not an impressive-looking man, especially compared to the overpowering Dr. Bak, but I soon realized how well he knew his business. Dr. Benjamin was short, wore thick glasses, and spoke with a heavy German accent. As I detailed my lifetime of shame, self-abuse, failed therapy, and broken resolve, I occasionally groped for words, which he would gently supply in such an easy manner that it took me half the conversation to notice he was doing it. He listened kindly until I completed my history, and then he became brusque. He warned that a sex-change operation was not a cure-all. It was an experimental technique that might solve some problems but would create others. I said I was ready for what might come. He nodded noncommittally and abruptly thrust two large photographs into my view.

"Do you want to look like that?" he asked gruffly.

The photos were of two old men, nude to the waist, slack-skinned and unhealthy-looking. They had both facial hair and breasts. Repellent. I lost my composure for a moment, but I rallied quickly.

"I can't believe I'll wind up like them," I replied.

With that, his tone softened. I had passed the first of many tests, and after a thorough psychiatric evaluation, I was scheduled for my first hormone injection. On the appointed day, Dr. Benjamin unceremoniously instructed me to drop my pants, after which he jabbed a needle into my ass and sent me home with a handshake. A sense of calm settled over me, not through the action of the hormone shot but because I had taken the first step toward something better.

My hormone therapy went beautifully. I took a few pills every morning and returned to Dr. Benjamin once a week for a shot. For six days, I felt nothing, but then I began to experience an elevated mood, probably like the effect of an antidepressant drug like Prozac. As the treatments progressed, I felt increasingly better. Conveniently, my hitch in the Navy was up before the changes in my body became too noticeable. Everything seemed to be falling into place.

Then Dr. Benjamin stopped my treatment. I was devastated and pleaded with him to let me continue, but he had gotten cold feet. Dr. Benjamin's rather vague explanation was that he and his associates had reviewed my case and found too many troubling factors. I was heterosexual. I was a successful professional. He had a litany of excuses. I've always had the feeling that my sister intervened, but if she did, I am not clear how she found out. Possibly she confronted me about my physical changes, and I blurted out the cause, but if that happened, I have repressed the memory. She may have taken a look at the changes in me, deduced what I was doing, and discovered who was treating me. Jo had the knowledge and resources to do it.

I fell apart. There was no residency, no internship, no Navy, no analysis, no hormone treatment, nothing to give my life order. I went home to my old room in the Forest Hills house and sat there. My father fussed over me but I wondered where all this solicitude had come from and thought it might be the result of a guilty conscience. He had probably been a partner with my sister in destroying my new life as a woman. We never discussed it. I was thirty-one years old with a trunk full of trophies, degrees, and licenses, all made out to me, but I didn't know who I was. I thought about going to Europe and continuing my treatment, but I had heard horror stories about botched surgery in Casablanca. Sex-change surgery is complicated, and I had been counting heavily on American medical expertise to improve my chances of a good result.

After a month, I decided to continue my education, a familiar endeavor that might provide me some comfort. During my medical residency, I had become interested in strabismus, a complicated field and little understood at the time. Here I could be in the vanguard. I took advantage of a fellowship offer that allowed me to follow my interest. In the next year, I learned a lot about ocular motility but little about myself. In my off hours, I did a lot of fast driving in my Shelby Cobra and engaged in other flamboyant and dangerous behavior. Suffice it to say that during that year I used my .38 revolver to stop a mugging in Oregon, did a striptease in a transvestite nightclub in Kansas City, and nearly killed myself learning to fly an airplane in Iowa. I cared about my patients, but I didn't care about myself. However, as I returned to New York to take over the ophthalmology residency training program at Manhattan Eye, Ear and Throat Hospital, I resolved to put my life in order. I was on track for a career that would give me financial security, power, personal satisfaction, and prestige. I would take those assets and make Renée a reality.

During my second year back in New York, I took a trip to

Copenhagen and met with Dr. Christian Hamberger, one of the physicians who had attended Christine Jorgensen in the fifties. He listened kindly to my story and with no further questions prescribed a course of estrogen. Even before I returned to American soil, I could feel the familiar changes beginning in my body. However, the surgical options in the United States remained closed to me. Dr. Benjamin was the top man in the field, and my being turned down by him made all the others leery. In desperation, I decided to go to Casablanca for my surgery after testing myself by living for a year in Europe as a woman.

The year went well, and I eventually found myself standing in the hot Algerian sun with four thousand dollars in hundred-dollar bills in my purse. Inside the clinic, the money would do the talking: no endless questionnaires to fill out, no forms to sign, no recourse if something went wrong. I told myself it didn't matter, but a knot of fear formed in my stomach. Every step I took toward the building was agonizing. Dr. Bak's predictions of madness rushed back into my mind. Suddenly, I felt as if the successful months I had spent in Europe, the months I thought proved that Renée had a fighting chance, were nothing more than a bizarre vacation. I had proved nothing except that I was a confused and disgusting creature. Trembling, I turned away from the clinic and walked back to my hotel. For several days I tried to figure out what kind of monster I was. I dressed in an androgynous fashion. I hung out with two gay men I met at my hotel. I was the subject of a failed seduction by a Moroccan man. I hated what I was doing. I returned to the clinic, but again I could not go in. Two days later, I was back in New York.

Despising myself as a coward and a half-creature, I went

off the hormones and started working sixty hours a week. I regained the use of my genitals, but otherwise my body remained womanish. This did not hinder my love life. I had girlfriends again, but I began showing up at the apartments of friends dressed as Renée. I took a perverse pleasure in their confusion and embarrassment. After seven months in New York, I went back on the hormones. I was worse off than I had ever been. My depression deepened. Well into my thirties, I felt I would soon be too old for surgery, but if I kept taking the hormones, I would certainly suffer irreversible effects. I might wind up like those old men with breasts in the photographs Dr. Benjamin had thrust under my nose years before.

During the holiday season of 1969, I was feeling especially low, so I went to see my friend Josh. He had a date but that never mattered. I had been a third wheel many times with him, and sometimes the threesome was actually set up so that he could dangle yet another beautiful woman in front of me. He was convinced that all I needed was the right girl. As I sat in Josh's apartment feeling sorry for myself, in walked the most beautiful woman I had ever seen. She turned me on, and the feeling was mutual. By June we were married. My friends were flabbergasted. It seemed that one week I was sashaying around in a frock, and the next I was smoking a pipe and wearing a tweed jacket with elbow patches. Josh was ecstatic and took all the credit. He told anyone who would listen that he had cured me, and for all I knew, he had. Renée was in remission and possibly gone for good.

Meriam was as ambitious as she was beautiful, and she encouraged me to take on more private patients to raise my income and my status. I didn't protest. We embarked upon a lifestyle that included dinner out several nights a week at top New York restaurants like La Côte Basque and frequent trips to luxury destinations like St. Moritz. Meriam was one of two women in New York who had a sweater in every color from the exclusive boutique Veneziano. The other was Jackie Kennedy. Our apartment was undergoing constant redecoration. This pace went on for months, and as I look back on it, I can see that it was really a cover-up for what was happening in our private life. Though I had been an ardent lover at the start of our relationship, I had become much less so after our marriage. I made love to Meriam only occasionally and not very vigorously. She tried to understand, but she couldn't help being hurt. I went to see an endocrinologist, and he was not encouraging.

In his view, years of female hormone therapy had permanently compromised my male potency. He doubted I would ever regain it, but he prescribed pituitary hormones to stimulate my testicles and testosterone to enhance my masculinity. This therapy went on for several months, but there was no improvement. My libido remained weak and my breasts were as large as ever. They were a minor matter in the greater scheme of things, but they took on great importance because they were a reminder of my tortured past, and they were a continuing embarrassment to both Meriam and me. When I played tennis, I had to wear bulky attire; even so my breasts were noticeable—naturally, they drew stares.

As if to make up for my failures as a lover, I became something of an arrogant bastard in my professional life and toward Meriam as well. I was an odd fellow to be sure. I swaggered like a macho man, but I jiggled when I did so. At length, I sought a remedy: breast reduction surgery. It was surprisingly simple to arrange. Everybody thought cutting my breasts off was a terrific idea. When I came out of the anesthesia, I was flat-chested, but I felt strange, like an amputee. I began to wonder if somewhere inside me, Renée was in pain.

My more masculine appearance brought some improvement to my married life but not much. The strain between Meriam and me continued until, in another bizarre twist of fate, the unthinkable happened. Meriam got pregnant, a possibility that had been all but ruled out by the endocrinologist who had treated my low sex drive. Relations between us improved for the period of her pregnancy and shortly thereafter, but once the flush of excitement over the baby died down, we went back to our old pattern of behavior. It was not a matter of infidelity on either of our parts. We were just misfiring.

In spite of the downturn in our relationship, we never let little Nicky Raskind hear us argue. Our son brought out the best in us, and though we were cold in our bed, we could be genuinely warm in his presence. Nicky made me feel manly—not just because I had managed the masculine trick of impregnating a woman and having her bear my child, but in another way that is hard to understand. I loved being with him, protecting him, rocking him to sleep. I never felt more masculine than I did when I tended my son. But that masculinity did not spill over into my relationship with Meriam, except maybe to make me more arrogant and unreachable. I fell increasingly silent, and finally she ordered me out of the house. I didn't blame her. I would have thrown me out, too. It wasn't entirely my fault by any means, but the situation was intolerable for both of us. Shortly after we broke up, Meriam met a man whom she eventually married.

I started my single life sleeping on the couch at the office. As it had so many times before in my fractured life, tennis gave me some solace. I was still competing regularly and had recently turned thirty-five, so I was one of the young lions of the junior veteran's class. The year I broke up with Meriam, I reached the finals of the national championships. Nicky would often come to the tournaments with his nanny. Those were wonderful moments that made me feel that my marriage had produced at least one worthwhile thing, my son, and I worked hard to keep a close relationship with him.

Meanwhile, my practice flourished, and I was in charge of my life, but freedom spelled trouble. Renée wanted to come back. I tried to suppress her, but I felt I would go mad or commit suicide if I continued masquerading as Dick, and then of what use would I be to my son? My only option was to let Renée out, and my dressing as a woman began again. Not long after, I went to see Dr. Benjamin again and found that his practice had been taken over by his associate, Dr. Ihlenfeld, though Dr. Benjamin was still in the office. To my great relief, both were sympathetic and put me on hormones. Within three months, I was as womanly as I had been at any time in my life, with the exception that my surgically reduced breasts showed only moderate improvement. However, that detail did little to diminish my satisfaction.

On a spring day in 1975 I entered a hospital under an assumed name, and after three and a half hours of surgery, Renée became a reality. As I lost consciousness under the anesthetic, I thought about my new name. Little Dick Raskind had chosen it without knowing its meaning. Renée: reborn. Renée Richards: Richard reborn. I didn't know what lay ahead for Renée, but at least Dick's sufferings were at an end. The operation eliminated Dick's penis and used some of it to create the lining of Renée's vagina. I awoke in a haze of pain, but after a little over a week in the hospital I was discharged. One of the first things I did was to call Nicky. He jabbered away and called me Daddy, just as if nothing had transpired. This was immensely reassuring. Of course, I understood intellectually that he had no way of knowing what I had done, but somehow a nagging doubt had plagued me until I had that conversation. There was much ahead with Nicky, but speaking to him so naturally on the phone made me feel that we would prevail. I called Nicky every day.

In three months, I was essentially healed and ready to concentrate on the rest of my life. For a while, I continued to work in New York, dressing as a man during the day and as a woman in the evenings. I considered trying to carry on in New York as Renée, but try as I might, I could not think of a way to shift from a male to a female doctor without creating a flap. I couldn't bear the idea of trying to speak individually to all my patients and colleagues. I suppose I could have designated a representative to explain my situation, but who besides me could do it justice? Or I could have sent out announcements. Or I could have tried completing business as a man one Friday and then showing up as a woman the next Monday. Or I could have gradually changed from masculine to feminine attire over a period of months, hoping no one would notice. Every tactic I thought of was more ridiculous than the last. In the end, I just decided to get as far away from New York as possible. Renée would live and practice medicine in California.

Through a stroke of fortune, I was able move into a situation in Newport Beach in Orange County. The area was a bit conservative, but I had a sympathetic contact there, and I was promised a place on the staff of a top eye specialist once I had built a local reputation. I settled into a nice apartment with a Pacific view and joined the nearby John Wayne Tennis Club, but this blissful period of anonymity was brief. The thing that tripped me up was the thing that had saved my sanity so many times before: tennis. The better you are, the more you want to play at a high level, which means playing against the best competition, and when you are the best player at a club, the only way to get real competition is to play against the best players from other clubs. That's what tournaments are for. And everyone at the club gets a boost in status if one of their members wins a tournament, so everyone wants a potential champion to play. Club managers are also fanatical about tournaments because they are great recruiting tools—new members not only mean more money for the club but also fresh opponents for the old members, which means that they stay members. So it was no surprise that I was soon asked to play for the club in a tournament.

At first, I said that I was concentrating on my medical practice and wanted to play tennis only for recreation. For a while this worked, but the more the members and staff saw me play, the more pressure they put on me to compete. I tried to hold firm, but they good-naturedly wore me down. It didn't take a lot of wearing because I wanted Renée to have everything Dick used to have. After all, she was competitive, too, and a damn good player. Why should she have to deny herself? That was my train of thought, so when I was asked to play in an unofficial local club match, I thought, "Why not?"

That was the beginning of a slippery slide. I played and so enjoyed myself that I agreed to play in more small fun events. And nothing happened. But without my noticing, the scale of the events was increasing, even though I always asked the staff, "Is this tournament anything major?" and they always replied, "No big deal." Eventually, they asked me to play in an out-of-town tournament. They hadn't had a winner in a big tournament in La Jolla for at least two years, and Newport Beach was looking for a way to restore some civic pride. As usual, the people around the club downplayed the tournament's importance, calling it strictly local amateur stuff. I wanted to believe them, so I did.

When I arrived at the tournament, I was surprised at the number of spectators and a little shaken by the nightly television reports on the progress of the event. If this tournament wasn't a big deal, it was uncomfortably close to one, but I was playing and winning in a pleasant environment, so I settled down. Then somebody figured out who I was. It was a woman who didn't actually know me but who had heard a story about a prominent East Coast tennis player, a doctor, who had undergone a sex-change operation and secretly moved to California. She went to the extent of checking in Newport and discovered that I was a doctor and had lived there only a short time. Convinced I must be the party in question, she started blabbing. The story may have been fairly accurate when it left the lips of my discoverer, but soon the tournament grounds were crackling with half-truths.

Still, I played on, but now the crowds who had been polite and enthusiastic were just polite. Nobody was rude, but nobody seemed especially interested in the tennis. Rather, the focus was on my frame and how its present form was related to what it might have once been. After I won the semifinal, I decided to withdraw. The tension was reaching unbearable levels, and I thought it best to end the melodrama. As fate would have it, my phone call to the tournament office was answered by an official who had known me from my tennis life before Renée. She had actually umpired my semifinal match the day before, and to my surprise she counseled me to stay in the tournament. Her father was African American and her mother Filipino. She had experienced the distressing feeling of being considered neither one thing nor the other. Her approach had always been to stand up and show them who she was. She urged me to do the same.

I stayed in the tournament and won it. I felt sorry for my opponent, who seemed so unnerved by the atmosphere that she couldn't play her best game. But I was relieved that the match ended quickly and even more relieved when the posttournament interviews passed with no mention of my origins. I fled back to Newport vowing to stay out of the limelight forever. I went to my office the next day still under the delusion that I had dodged a bullet. What I couldn't know was that a San Diego reporter was checking into my background. He looked into Dr. Renée Richards' schooling, which is an important matter of record for any physician. As he did his research, my old name kept appearing in one way or another. Finally, he called me and asked if I recognized the name Richard Raskind. I panicked, said, "No," and told him not to call me again. But he did, and each time he did, he had another piece of information linking me to Dick. Finally, he asked outright if I had once been Richard Raskind.

At that point, I ceased my denials and tried appealing to his better nature, pleading that I hadn't done anything illegal or immoral. I reminded him that I was a private citizen and described how much my son would suffer if I were exposed. I couldn't make a dent. He felt that I had lost my right to privacy when I appeared as a contestant in a public tennis tournament, and added that he would not be doing his job as a professional if he did not fully report a public event. With that, he hung up.

That night the story broke on the eleven o'clock news. I couldn't watch. Naturally, the tabloids jumped all over the story, but it was also featured in the so-called reputable press. Virtually no news agency bothered to fully check the facts, and it was not until after several days of contending with the paparazzi that I held a press conference at the John Wayne Tennis Club to get the truth out. More than a hundred reporters attended. Afterward, I was approached by Dick Carlson, the man who had broken the story. He thanked me for inviting him to the press conference. I responded, "Mr. Carlson, we couldn't have had it without you."

Following this humiliating experience, I might have tried to go back to my private existence if I had not been insulted by some of the very people whom I felt I could trust most, the tennis community—not so much the players but the tennis governing bodies, the United States Tennis Association and the Women's Tennis Association, who for reasons I have never understood, declared that I would not be allowed to play professional tennis as a woman. Since I had not asked to play professionally, this ruling seemed unnecessary, and I resented the implication that Renée Richards was not really a woman. The New York City Health Department had issued me a document specifying that I was a woman. What more did they need? Their action made me angry, and it made a lot of other minority representatives angry, so with the support of groups ranging from the disabled to the Black Panthers, I decided to make a stand.

I had my first chance when Gene Scott, an old tennis friend, invited me to play in an important tournament that he had run for years in Orange, New Jersey. Gene was ready to go against the tennis establishment because he believed in me personally and in the stand I had taken. Three weeks later, I arrived in New York amidst a new frenzy of publicity. I was glad that Meriam had sent Nicky to Ireland for the summer as a way of protecting him from the scene. The days before the Orange tournament passed in an exhausting round of interviews, during which I kept emphasizing that I was fighting for a principle. I had an official document saying I was a woman, and thanks to hormone therapy and expert surgery, I was pretty close physically as well. Over and over I asked, "Why should I be barred from playing in women's events?"

By the day of my first match, I was exhausted. I arrived at the tournament venue to find that cars were parked on the roadway a mile from the tournament site. Reporters crowded into the little dressing room I had been assigned and peppered me with the same questions I had been answering all week. When the first wave finished, a new one came in, and then another. I eventually escaped through the dressing room window to try to get in some practice time on an out-of-the-way court, but the crowd discovered me and came pressing forward against the fence begging for autographs.

Finally, Gene Scott arrived and escorted me to the stadium. The atmosphere grew ever more oppressive the closer we got to the entrance. Waiting for my introduction, I had to stand in a solid, stifling mass of humanity. When my name was called, I pushed onto the sidelines where I could breathe, but barely. Thousands of people filled the seats rising up on all sides of the court. The aisles were choked with the overflow. Everywhere there were photographers, the flashes going off continuously. I looked into the crowd, where I could make out an occasional friendly face, but for the most part everything was swimming.

As we warmed up, my opponent, Kathy Beene, started missing quite a few balls. The poor woman had signed up for a tennis tournament, not a circus, and she was facing an unknown and possibly scary creature across the net. She knew nothing of me other than what the papers had been printing, and some of that was awful. I sympathized with her, but I vowed to blot out everything and concentrate on one tennis move at a time though I felt almost too weak to make any move at all. My energy was spent before the first serve. On the other side of the net, I saw the same signs of nervous exhaustion in Kathy. Both of us could have used a week's rest, but we were more than tired women: We were competitors. So we took our places in the hundred-degree heat and staggered through a match that was less a sporting event than a test of fortitude. I won, but it was an ugly thing, and I nearly passed out several times in the second set.

Following the match, I faced an equally daunting trial, being interviewed by Howard Cosell. Despite my fears, this turned out to be one of the best things that ever happened to me in my public life. Though Cosell is remembered by many as an obnoxious character, he treated me respectfully and like a lady, and for that I will always remember him kindly. The day wore on with more interviews, but eventually the crowd diminished, and I went back to my Manhattan hotel room. There I found I was in the headlines: RENÉE ROLLS IN NEW JERSEY OPENER. On the streets, people yelled encouragement. I felt as if the tide was turning. But at four o'clock in the morning, I was still awake and cried uncontrollably for two hours.

The tournament ended for me with a semifinal loss to Lea Antonoplis. I played hard, and it was a close match, but she beat me fair and square, going on to win the Wimbledon Junior Championship the following year. I cried afterward, more out of relief than disappointment. I thought my performance at the tournament must have crystallized some issues for the governing bodies of tennis. They now had proof that as a woman I was just as responsible and well-behaved a player as I had been as a man. Perhaps even more important for their peace of mind, the results showed that a woman could beat me. Surely these facts would count for something.

They didn't. No matter how often I pleaded my case over the next months, they refused to reconsider. Meanwhile, without my physician's income, my debts continued to mount. I barely kept up with the help of tournament organizer Gladys Held-man, who bucked the establishment and invited me to play in a couple of events. But when I returned to Newport Beach, my financial situation grew ever worse. I could have caved in, but after a lifetime of self-absorption, I was caught up in a fight for principle, and I liked it. This was Renée's fight, something to give her validity.

The tennis powers stood firm, though they did offer me the option of taking a chromosome test. This test had been available for ten years, but they had not used it even once. They had taken every other player's word that she was a woman, but Renée Richards, the only applicant who had a legal document stating she was a woman, would have to take the test. They knew I would fail. Over the next few months, I saw the best and worst of women's professional tennis. I received great support from important people like Billie Jean King, who offered to play doubles with me. I thought, "If the most influential player in women's tennis will accept me as her partner, governing bodies cannot reject me." Wrong. No matter how often I pleaded my case, they continued to hide behind the chromosome test. I am not proud to say that I submitted to it on several occasions. The first time, I actually passed, undoubtedly due to a lab error, so they made me take it over again. As far as I know, no one who has passed the chromosome test has ever been required to take it again, except for me.

I endured one humiliation after another and grew listless and despondent. Then I received an offer to play professionally for the Cleveland Nets, which I gratefully accepted, staying with the team when it became the New Orleans Nets and later the Sunbelt Nets. At last I was playing tennis regularly in front of appreciative fans. In general, I was well received, and I developed lasting friendships with some of my teammates. Finally, Renée had received some official recognition and acceptance, and she was succeeding on both a professional and personal level.

Playing for the Nets was a joyous experience, and the more I savored it, the more I brooded about my rejection by the USTA and the WTA. My work with the Nets should have made it obvious to them that the world did not fall apart when a transsexual played professionally. Nevertheless, they continued to insist that I pass a chromosome test. It seemed that I would face this stone wall as long as I continued to ask nicely. After more than thirty years of apologizing to myself and to the world in general, I was through apologizing. It was time for a savvy lawyer.

Roy Cohn was more than a savvy lawyer. Some people said he was the meanest man in New York, if not the whole country. He certainly was controversial, always embroiled in something, most famously as chief counsel for Senator Joseph McCarthy's House Un-American Activities Committee. Humorist Alan King recommended him, and I took his advice. I didn't know if he would accept my case, but Cohn seemed to like controversy, and I was certainly controversial. Our first meeting was in the Manhattan brownstone that served as both his office and his residence. Cohn was in his bathrobe. I walked into his presence and opened my mouth to speak, but he cut me off.

"I know. You want to play in the U.S. Open. I'll take the case."

And that was it. We had another meeting, but again Cohn did the talking. He understood my case better than I did, so I went home to the Raskind house in Forest Hills and waited, sleeping once again in the room where Renée had first emerged. A few days later I got a phone call. I had won my case. The two prestigious Wall Street law firms representing the USTA and the WTA had been overmatched against Roy Cohn. It was as simple as that.

Yet as I gathered my things for the short walk from our house to the U.S. Open grounds, I wondered if anything in my life would ever be simple. I glanced at Dick's trophies and thought, "Now it's Renée's turn." But as I remembered Richard Raskind, poor haunted creature, I knew that he lived inside me. I was Renée, but not entirely reborn. I was the sum of all that had ever happened to me and all that would happen in the future. Renée could never be an entity entirely to herself. I was naïve to have entertained the notion.

Out in the neighborhood, people crowded around, wishing me well on the same streets over which I had skulked thirty years before, wearing my sister's clothes. A man rushed up and said, "God loves you, Renée." He disappeared before I could ask him how he could be so sure. My life had been in so many ways a narrow struggle. What would a higher power think of me and the things I had done? Would my suffering and humiliation offset what I had done to my family and friends or what they had done to me? Would Renée Richards be allowed her portion of happiness? And Nicky. He was my life's greatest gift, but what was his future?

All these thoughts I put aside as I reached the U.S. Open complex. There was tennis to be played. My heart lightened at the prospect. I was about to do the thing that had saved me so many times before—and on the greatest stage in the world, I would do it as Renée. They had tried to deny her, just as I had tried to deny her, but she couldn't be denied.

CHAPTER 2

Mother, Father, Sister, Brother

THE SETUP IS CLASSIC: dominating mother, subservient father, jealous sister. Surely this dynamic was a crucial factor in bringing Renée Richards into existence, though genetics cannot be eliminated from the mysterious cocktail of causes. I spent years analyzing my relationships with my immediate family, but it took me a surprisingly long time to see that each was struggling with his or her personal set of demons, not as spectacular as mine, but overwhelming just the same.

My mother, Dr. Sadie Muriel Baron, has always been a mystery to me, but her environment twisted her just as surely as mine twisted me. Her father was in a sense two people. For the first half of his life, he was a drunk and a reprobate; for the second, an ascetic, celibate recluse. He died before I was born, and there were no pictures of him. On the day of my graduation from medical school, my mother pointed out one of my classmates and said, "He looks like your Grandpa Baron." The man she indicated was a little scary. He reminded me of Rasputin, and I gather that, like Rasputin, Grandpa Baron was also crazy. Nonetheless, my mother loved him.

He was by far the more interesting of her parents. Sadie's mother was a tired and humorless woman, whose life changed little whether her husband was screwing a good portion of Bryn Mawr's Jewish women or studying the Torah in his room. Grandma Baron spent her days behind the counter of the family candy store that funded Grandpa's exploits both sacred and profane. I surmise she liked him better in his religious phase because she was religious herself.

Later in life, when she lived with our family, Grandma Baron went to shul every Sabbath, walking from our home. She was, in her own words, the "antique" of the congregation but was in her nineties before she agreed to be picked up from services by car, finally defeated by the problem of crossing busy Queens Boulevard. However, only Dick was allowed to drive her home. I called her Little Grandma to distinguish her from my father's mother, who was known as Big Grandma.

By contrast with this conventional little woman, my grandfather must have seemed the picture of energy and life to my mother. Whatever his faults, he was not boring, and young Sadie was smart enough to be bored with a great many of the people in her circle. Grandpa Baron seems to have treated Sadie more like a young son than a daughter. He encouraged her to learn Hebrew, though he tried to hide her secular schoolbooks from her. In an odd twist, she also attended classes at the Women's Christian Temperance Union on how to be a cultured young lady. I doubt Grandpa Baron ever heard about that. The Temperance Union lessons apparently worked. Mother spoke beautifully, with no trace of her Ukrainian Ashkenazi Jewish background. A brilliant student, she was the valedictorian of her high school class and was awarded a scholarship to Bryn Mawr, where she was also valedictorian. Obviously, Sadie was better at finding her textbooks than her father was at hiding them.

When my mother announced her plans to attend the Women's Medical College of Pennsylvania, Grandpa Baron protested, but by then she had somehow developed the capacity to dominate her surroundings, even her wild father. I suppose she used the same tools that she used on her family later in life— lung power and strength of will. At a time when most women were sentenced to lives as housewives and second-class citizens (my mother was an adult before women won the right to vote), she was headed toward a medical career. On the other hand, my mother's sister, Molly, prepared to be a housewife, though she never succeeded in attracting a marriage proposal and died a spinster, dependent on my mother's emotional support during her whole life. Well into middle age, Sadie maintained the fiction that Molly was much younger than she in the vain hope that her sister would snare a man sooner or later, but to no avail. In all the time I knew Molly, I do not remember one suitor. Sadie may have escaped the narrow traditional woman's role, but she paid the price of assuming the responsibilities that are usually loaded onto the eldest son in a Jewish household, which is how she wound up figuring prominently in my grandfather's death.

Grandpa Baron developed a lump on his back. My mother, who was then a medical student, examined him and observed that the lump seemed to be attached to one of his ribs. This was serious. She arranged to have him seen by the best doctors at her school, and they decided to operate as soon as possible. My mother insisted on the best surgeon, and she herself suited up for the operation. She was present when the surgeon cut into the tumor and unleashed a torrent of blood that could not be stopped. Another woman might have looked away, but Grandpa Baron died under his daughter's unbelieving stare. Sadie carried that sight with her for the rest of her days, though when she spoke of the event she used a distanced, professional voice. She had done all the right things, but I think she left the operating room feeling responsible for her father's death. And perhaps she was angry with her father for dying and leaving her alone. Maybe she got the notion that since she had been instrumental in taking a man out of the world, she owed it a replacement, but a better one than her father, an improved type. She certainly hungered for a son to raise. Of course, this is only speculation. Mother and I never exchanged truly personal information, at least nothing emotionally revealing. There was always something standing between us, something perhaps connected to Grandpa Baron's death under the surgeon's scalpel.

Sadie continued at medical school. One of her classmates described her to me as "a good student and a good person. Quiet." This is an accurate description of the professional demeanor that my mother developed. She was impressive to all of her medical associates, and I myself used to marvel at her calm in dealing with patients in crisis. However, her behavior in a family crisis was different. Then her calm broke, and she became another person, irrational and unreachable. Almost every evening after her office hours, I would hear my mother on the phone, gently talking patients through their problems, using what I felt should be time spent with me.

Even in her physical appearance, she was a contradiction. She had a splendid womanly body, lavishly so. Her skin was exceptional, fine and creamy. She was vain about her figure and loved to wear low-cut gowns that emphasized it. From the neck up she was not a beauty: her face was plain and her thick glasses added to that impression. But she did have an enviable crown of rich black hair, which fell to her waist when loose. She brushed it often to improve its luster. As a child, I would often wander down to my parents' room in the mornings and wedge myself between them. I would entwine my fingers in Mother's hair and breathe in the faint smell of her Arpège from the night before. She was warm and responsive in her half-awake state, which was when I found her most loving and motherly. She remained that way for the first part of the morning, but almost every day I would watch with fascination and a little dread as she went through a transformation.

After washing and dressing her hair, she powdered and perfumed her body and put on frilly women's underthings. Thus far, all was right in my world, but the next phase was sobering. Over this feminine core went a severe woman's business suit, which made her the picture of a Susan B. Anthony suffragette. She pulled her beautiful hair into a tight bun and powdered her face to a pale hue, effectively covering the natural glow of her skin. Horn-rimmed glasses, a no-nonsense hat, flat-soled shoes, and a large leather bag finished the job. I always wondered where my soft, feminine mother had gone.

In her place was the rigorous Dr. Baron, dictatorial, unbending, and certain of her rectitude. With Dr. Baron, there was no appeal either to reason or compassion. She once forced me into a Halloween outfit so perfectly female that the parents who gave the party inquired discreetly why the pretty little girl was not in costume. My hysterical screams of protest were unavailing. What she mandated was always what happened in the Raskind house, though it might take a lengthy shouting match to finally get it in place. My mother and I clashed many times but never directly over my gender confusion. She was too much the psychiatrist to recriminate against me or to see the problem as more than a challenge for the Freudian analytic technique. She came as close to an apology as she ever did when she said, "It was my fault. You must have identified with me instead of your father."

Mother died before Renée became a reality. If she had been alive when I made my decision, I think she would have done anything to keep her son intact, including physically attacking my surgeon, if need be. I feared her reaction more than anything. There is just the smallest chance she might have realized that there was no keeping her son intact. She was capable of that kind of distance with her patients, but I would not have taken the chance. She exerted a powerful influence over me, and my conviction that it was counterproductive never diminished its power.

My most emotionally rewarding moments with my mother came near the end of her life, when she was in the last stages of

Mother, Father, Sister, Brother

a losing fight with colorectal cancer. She was only sixty, and it was shocking to see her slowly turn from a vigorous and commanding woman to a frail and dependent one. Yet in caring for her, I finally felt an emotional connection that had previously been missing. Nothing dramatic happened, but on occasion, when I would anticipate some small desire, like a glass of water, and would bring it to her without being asked, I saw on her face an expression of gratitude that meant so much more than her "Thank you." At some point in my mother's decline, I let go of my long-held resentment, but her attitude remained as it had always been. She was saddened by my personal torment, even chagrined at the part she had played, but that issue was never confronted directly. Still, we never abandoned one another. And even if I had somehow found the courage to become Renée while Mother was still alive, she would never have disowned me, though there would have been a tempest of monumental proportions. It's probably good that she did not know Renée.

On the other hand, my father, Dr. David Raskind, who lived to be a hundred, spent more than twenty years with Renée, though he never directly acknowledged her existence. We created our own version of the "don't ask, don't tell policy." I had seen him handle many situations in this way, most notably my mother's terminal illness. Of course, he was aware of her decline, but he essentially refused to discuss the situation. If he was worried by some development in her case, he would not refer to it directly but would complain bitterly about some trivial matter like bad traffic. We could only know he was worried about his wife because the traffic on that day was no worse than on any other.

The first time I appeared before my father dressed as a woman was not too long before my surgery. He had surely noticed that I had gone through several odd physical transformations in my life, but he had never acknowledged them. Perhaps I hoped to pierce this veil of silence by suddenly appearing before him in women's clothes, though I would never have conceived such a plan on my own. At the time, I was under the influence of an acquaintance, a fellow doctor, who was also a budding transsexual. It was he who convinced me to go to the house in Forest Hills dressed as Renée.

My father didn't show any sign of surprise; in fact, he didn't say much to me to all. He spent the hour or so talking to my friend, Franz. While they talked, I sat quietly in an armchair, smoothing the wrinkles out of my conservative blue skirt, which I had paired with a sweater, stockings, and shoes. I had on a little makeup but not much. I probably looked a bit like a serious-minded college coed. Over my skirt and sweater, I wore, of all things, a silver mink coat. I can't remember what prompted this choice, but I do know that I could never afford that coat today. I ended up years later giving that mink to my mother-in-law. She looked better in it than I did. Anyway, Franz and Dad talked, mostly Franz, who was anxious to clarify issues for my father.

"Obviously," he said with a gesture toward me, "Dick has become Renée or is at least well on the way to becoming Renée."

My father rolled his eyes.

"This is a woman!" Franz barked.

"Listen," my father replied, "I've known women all my life." Gesturing toward me he added, "This is not a woman."

Apart from being the object of much gesturing, I had nearly nothing to say during their conversation. When it was obvious both of them had run out of gas, I picked up my purse and quietly followed Franz to the car, mumbling a good-bye to my father. Several days later, I saw my father again. This time I was dressed as a man. I expected some comment on the odd fact that I had been dressed as a woman, but he made no mention of it. Rather, he focused on Franz.

"That guy that you brought around on Sunday, he's got some tic!"

This was true. Franz did have "some tic," an unconscious vocal mannerism that caused him to take a funny breath and utter a strange sound before the next phrase. My father observed that this tic was evidence of something seriously wrong with Franz, and this was also true. For one thing, Franz was a closet transsexual, quite willing to expose me but very paranoid about his own condition. On trips to New York, he used to go about dressed like a German hausfrau. I never thought he was a true transsexual, and I thought surgery would be a terrible mistake for him. I once met his wife and urged her to discourage him as much as possible. I lost track of Franz once I became famous. He didn't want to be found out through association with me. So my father's instincts about Franz were correct, and I was sorry that I had agreed to have such a neurotic person plead my case.

My father was perceptive in many ways and, despite his shortcomings, there was much to admire about him. I had to keep reminding myself of that as I tried to determine his place in the influences that shaped me. When the blame game begins, it is all too easy to see family members only in light of their failings. My father was considered argumentative and contentious by some people, but he was also generous and steadfast, a great lover of life.

David Raskind was born in 1900 in Russia's Ukraine, specifically in Ekaterinoslav, which later became Dnepropetrovsk when the Bolsheviks threw out anything that had the name of the royal family attached to it. In 1905, with his younger sister, Olga, and my grandmother, Anita Litofsky, he set out in steerage on a boat from Hamburg, arriving in New York to be picked up by his father, Joseph Raskind, who had come over earlier. Shortly after his family cleared Ellis Island, Grandfather moved them to Bridgeport, Connecticut. He was a tailor and my grandmother a dressmaker, and there was work to be done in Bridgeport, much of it connected to the Ringling Brothers and Barnum & Bailey Circus, which had its headquarters there.

That is how my father happened to escape growing up on Manhattan's teeming lower East Side, where so many other immigrant kids landed. In this relatively benign environment, young David flourished. He was an excellent student at Bridgeport High School and within ten years of his arrival was awarded the Fairfield County Scholarship to Yale, quite an achievement for a sixteen-year-old tailor's son who started out in a shtetl under the thumb of Czar Nicholas and his Cossacks. After six years at Yale, my father graduated with a degree in medicine. In many ways, he was a perfect example of an American success story: immigrant boy rises to a high station through hard work and education. Incidentally, he never forgot what Yale did for him, and he donated thousands of dollars a year to the medical school for more than half a century.

But there is another side to this American Dream, one that was especially true in my father's era. It is possible to rise high in America without losing the sense that one is not quite as legitimate as one's colleagues. Dad went to Yale, but he was an immigrant Jew with no prep school finish. While most of his fellow students were young men of leisure, he had to supplement his income with a variety of odd jobs—some very odd, like feeding ice cream to the professional boxers in downtown Bridgeport; his favorites were Knockout Brown and Battling Levinski. While his classmates were cashing bank drafts to fund summers on Nantucket, Dad was touring Maine on a bicycle selling maps to the farmers.

He never complained about this difference. He was deeply grateful to America for the opportunity to better himself, but I've always wondered how much better Dad believed he had become. He was a gregarious man and tremendously affable, once you got past his gruff exterior, and his classmates liked him, but how completely he was accepted is an open question. Dad played lacrosse at Yale, and his manner of joining the team is revealing.

One of his jobs was waiting on the training table, and when a member of the lacrosse team was injured, the remaining team members requisitioned him and taught Dad how to play. I still occasionally look at a picture of him with his teammates, all of them holding their lacrosse sticks and standing behind a sign saying, "1919: Yale 3, Harvard 2." If you look closely, you will see that he looks a little out of place among these WASPy gentlemen athletes. Like them, he is handsome, but in a slightly foreign manner, his dark hair and serious mien in contrast to their easy lightheartedness. Did he always feel a bit of a foreigner? Did he bluster to cover his insecurity? Did he cave in so often at home because at heart he didn't believe he was good enough?

Even my mother showed my father a tinge of condescension due to his background. They met when they were both interns at Harrisburg Hospital in Harrisburg, Pennsylvania. He was the only Jewish male intern. At first, she paid no attention to the fellow she spoke of as the "little Jew boy." She was, of course, Jewish herself but quick to dismiss anyone who resembled what she considered an embarrassing stereotype. But when my father achieved some notoriety in town by saving a dog who had been hit by a car and setting his fractured limb (his first foray into orthopedics), my mother took note. A romance blossomed. They got married after graduation, and they loved each other until her death thirty-four years later. She would write letters to him that began, "My Beloved David Dearest." She was, to him, "Sweetheart Sadie." In perhaps the ultimate act of deference, my father gave up his own advanced training in orthopedics in order to allow my mother to take a residency in psychiatry. In that era, it was almost unheard of for a husband to make such a professional sacrifice for his wife. These things cross my mind as I look back on the father whose behavior so disappointed me as a youth. I ask myself, "What difference would it have made if I had seen him win a few arguments with my mother? Would I really have been turned down a different path?"

Though my father never could bring himself to discuss my problem openly, he did offer a great deal of support in his way. After I was unmasked in California, there was no longer any need for the type of masculine charade I had practiced on my trips back to New York. Aside from that one unannounced visit I had paid him dressed as Renée, he had never dealt with me as a woman, and I wondered what his attitude would be. I found out when I came back to New York to play in the Orange, New Jersey, tennis tournament that became such a circus. I was literally headline news and hardly had time to practice between interviews before the tournament began, but on the evening of my first match I put on jeans and a warm-up jacket and drove to Forest Hills, where I surprised my father in the kitchen of our old house.

"Good," he said, "you're just in time for dinner."

So, I sat down at the kitchen table and ate with him, just as I had done countless times before. And just as we had always done, we talked about medicine and about sports, except no mention was made of a certain physician tennis player of peculiar genesis who was the biggest sports story of the year and maybe the biggest medical story, too. Still, I thought he was probably pleased that I had temporarily turned my back on glamour and notoriety in favor of dinner with him in the kitchen.

"I have to go," I said after a couple of hours. "I'm playing in a tournament over in Orange."

"Well, good luck," he replied.

I thought that our little dinner in the kitchen might be the extent of my father's participation in my life at that time.

I had tried hard to keep him out of my comments to the press. I thought surely he must be deeply mortified by all the lurid fuss surrounding me and would rather be skewered than identified as my father. Still, the man loved his tennis and he loved me, so I was not completely surprised when he showed up in New Jersey to see my third match. Dad had always loved to watch me play. To the end, it never seemed to matter whether I was playing as a man against men or as a woman against women. Anyway, he was immediately recognized because he knew everybody in the New York tennis crowd, and somebody pointed him out to the press. He was quickly surrounded by newshounds who didn't know what they were in for.

"You take a picture of me," he said menacingly, "and I'm going to break your camera over your head."

And that was the last time they attempted to get near him.

At the end of the match, one of the photographers said to me, "There's a man here who says he's your father."

I came out of my dressing room and there was Dad. We hardly said anything to each other, but instead of going back to Long Island with "Rolls" Levy, the friend who had brought me, I got into Dad's car and we drove to Forest Hills, where I had dinner and then stayed overnight. The next morning at the breakfast table we talked about the tournament and who I would probably have to play. We didn't say a word about the emergence of Renée, the media frenzy, or the fact that much of the population of the world had my name on their lips. It was as if someone had dropped an atom bomb, and we talked about whether or not to have French toast. The closest he came to recognizing the situation was to ask me if I would be returning to my medical practice in California.

"I don't know," I answered. "I think I might play tennis for a while."

Amazingly, he did not blink an eye. My whole life had been devoted to becoming a top eye surgeon in a very specialized field, and now I was talking about playing on the women's tennis tour, yet he didn't treat it as a crazy whim. As long as I was involved in sports or medicine, we were safe and would always have something to talk about. In the thousands of hours we spent together, we never touched on anything psychological, emotional, reflective, or contemplative, but he was always at LaGuardia Airport to meet my flight at any hour, whether I was coming in from Casablanca, Morocco; Los Angeles, California; or Gainesville, Florida. I know that beneath his rough exterior was a very sensitive core. He could not stand the stress of confronting people on important issues, so he stuck to the superficial. He never said, "This woman thing is nuts!" But he would readily say, "You still can't hit those low balls!" And I would reply, "Yeah, I know, Dad. If I could hit the low ones, I could win the U.S. Open."

"Well, remember to bend your knees," he would add brusquely.

Like all of us, Dad had his peculiarities and his limitations. He did the best he could with the tools he was given. It would have been wonderful if he had hugged me and said something like, "I don't understand why you did this, Son, but I will always love you." However, he was incapable of such a gesture, and I learned not to expect it, but he would occasionally surprise me.

After we had breakfast following my third win at the Orange tournament, I had to leave to do interviews. I said good-bye to my father and got into my mother's old car to drive to Manhattan. I was several blocks from the house, driving down an inside lane on crowded Queens Boulevard, when all of a sudden, I heard *beep, beep, beep!* behind me. I looked in the rearview mirror and there was a Cadillac coming up on my rear bumper with its horn blaring. I quickly realized that it was Dad with his hand out of the window waving something at me. I edged my way over to the curb, and he pulled up right behind me, still waving whatever it was. I got out of the car and walked back to the Cadillac. Dad was holding out my purse, which I had forgotten when I left the house.

That gesture came as close to an acceptance of my choice as any my father ever made. It would have been so easy for him to despise that purse, a powerful symbol of his only son's embarrassing condition. He could have thrown it in a drawer or maybe in the trash. But he had been willing to chase after me in a very public fashion, waving it out the window. That was Dad in a nutshell.

My sister is in many ways the hardest of my immediate family to discuss. To this day, I am still angry about many of the things she initiated, but I think Jo has always loved me, at least on a conscious level. By contrast, in the last sixty years, I have gone through several phases in my feelings for her, with love predominating at some times and anger at others. I have found it very hard to accept that she, too, was a victim of circumstance.

Josephine was named for our grandfather, Joseph Baron,

who died on the operating table. This naming has always seemed to me an obvious reflection of my mother's desire to have a son, and Jo did her best to oblige. She grew into a tomboy of the first order and was well on the way to satisfying all the requirements of the family son by the time she was five. She was encouraged by my mother, who seemed quite comfortable with a boyish daughter as long as Jo would consent to put on a frilly dress and behave like a lady when protocol demanded. This was a mixed message that Jo never fully understood and resisted with all her childish resources, most notably a stubborn disposition and a capacity to scream. Of course, in the area of stubbornness, she was overmatched by our mother. If Jo could have played the boy's part consistently, she would probably have been more secure.

When I came along, Jo's insecurity surely deepened. I was the natural male, and much of the sense of importance that Jo had enjoyed before my birth was shifted to me. The often-noted indignation of an older child when replaced by a younger was increased because I not only usurped her privileged position as the family's only child, but I also took her position as the family boy. At some level she must have been outraged, yet she could not express it openly or perhaps even admit it to herself. She had to be the loving sister, and this was very likely the source of the so-called "games" that she played with me. When she put a pillow over my face and smothered me, I was supposed to accept it as a form of play. And even though I was in dire distress on some occasions and barely escaped blacking out, I still managed to think of the activity as a game of some sort. And after I had been let out from under the pillow and lay coughing and gasping, Jo would show me great concern and affection. Those were some of the warmest moments between us.

For many years, I assigned little importance to this game, but as a young adult on the psychiatrist's couch, I began to see it as an expression of Jo's deep anger. Even more obvious was her habit of hitting me when I wasn't expecting it. These attacks were usually aimed at my head, which she might have disliked because of my short hair, a masculine feature she was not allowed. These blows were sometimes no more than cuffs but could be openhanded smacks that hurt like hell. They usually came from the rear. Worse yet, Jo was unpredictable, so I never knew when she might go off, which made walking ahead of her a chancy activity. I learned to be on guard. However, in spite of the hitting and smothering, most of my youthful interactions with Jo were enjoyable. She was the person in my immediate family to whom I felt closest, and ironically she became my instructor in the manly virtues, assuming the role of an older brother. She taught me all the things that a brother passes along—how to ride a bike, fight bullies, and be fearless in the face of physical danger, all things, I might add, in which Jo was very accomplished.

Jo would have made a wonderful girl if she had just accepted her role. I certainly wanted her to do so. She was beautiful, with large eyes and a halo of light brown hair. My mother used to say she looked like Ingrid Bergman, and there really was some resemblance. She was not tall and slender, which was the ideal of the day, but her figure was good in a slightly stocky fashion, and when she got into the right dress, she looked great, a real *zoftig meydl*, a luscious Jewish princess. The boys in high school and college went for her, but she never made a conscious effort to attract them. Though she reluctantly agreed to wear dresses to school, she chose the frumpiest ones. I think she was afraid. She never realized how pretty she was or could be if she made an effort. Maybe she went the opposite way so as not to be accused of trying for something she didn't believe she could achieve.

In spite of her preferences, my mother supplied her with a huge feminine wardrobe, which I probably used as much or more than she did once I got started cross-dressing. Jo never became exactly feminine, though she was womanly in her way, a little like Katharine Hepburn, somewhat butch but not stereotypically so. She knew what my mother expected in a feminine affect, and as a teen she did try, but she could never bring herself to attend properly to her appearance. Makeup and jewelry were big things for girls of that era, but all Jo could manage was red lipstick—no powder, no eye makeup, no jewelry.

As strange as it may seem, the similarities between the problems of Dick and Jo took a long time to dawn on me, though as I grew into young adulthood, I was beginning to work them out. Years of analysis helped me see that we were struggling with the same issues. Dick's way of coping led him down a more bizarre trail, but Jo paid a regrettable price as well. For years I thought of her as a villain, but age and reflection have softened my attitude, though I don't know if my son will ever forgive her for the way she treated me as a child. He feels her abuse was the primary cause of my sex-change surgery, an event that eventually shook his world and continues to affect him to this day. I hope at some point he will realize that the blood in his veins ties him to his aunt whether he likes it or not and that he will find the courage to let his outrage go. But he must live his own life. I can't forgive in his name.

The important thing is that I have resolved much of the anger I felt toward my sister—not all, mind you, but a great deal. Though we seldom see each other, when we do I feel a rush of affection for her. However, like so many brothers and sisters from more normal backgrounds, there are many things on which we do not see eye to eye. I am happy when she visits from Arizona, but I find her companionship fatiguing. Josephine Baron Raskind Foerster is very much like my mother, Sadie Muriel Baron Raskind, controlling and eternally right. Perhaps that is the most fatiguing thing of all.

JO VISITED ME RECENTLY. I had marked the date on my calendar: "J-Day." She had been in Boston for a memorial service for her father-in-law, a professor at an Eastern university. Grandfather Foerster died at 105, outlasting our father in what Jo called their "contest" to see who could live the longest into his second century. With Jo, everything is a contest, even life span, though I have to admit that Dad himself was competitive in this area, relishing the thought of outliving all of his Yale classmates, which he very nearly did. I don't know if he was aware of the contest between him and Grandfather Foerster.

Jo had budgeted two days to spend with me and my personal manager, Arleen Larzelere, in Carmel, New York, before heading home to Arizona. She drove over from Boston, and fearing she would get lost on the last leg, she stopped to call the house from a pay phone. She does not own a cell phone. They are too newfangled for her. Fortunately I had arrived home after a day of surgery and was able to give her the necessary instructions and then race out in my car to intercept her on the causeway over the reservoir and lead her home like a harbor pilot.

Josephine is seventy-five, but her demeanor, dress, energy level, and character have not changed in forty years. She wore khaki slacks and a man-tailored long-sleeved shirt. She had on a military-style web belt with a canteen attached to one side. She is the only person I know who would wear a canteen for a drive from Boston to Carmel, but maybe it came in handy. Her hair was tinted sort of brown with some gray streaks left visible. She must have colored it herself because she never goes to a beauty parlor. She looked, as ever, like my sister Jo.

We settled into the house, and I let her make her own drink: Canadian whiskey, orange juice, four packets of sugar, and ice. She has one of these every night before dinner. Arleen cooked up a wonderful steak dinner on the grill outside. Jo and I are compatible on the cooking of steaks. We both like them rare, though Jo likes hers rarer than I. However, the similarity in our preferences doesn't go much further than that. After dinner she started telling "stories," usually beginning with the phrase, "This is interesting." After that would come something mildly interesting at best: accounts of her grandchildren, expositions on her ultra-left political views, and explanations of her causes, such as universal medical care and universal government (in this she has not changed since her college days as a member of the United World Federalists). These declamations were made even less interesting by the fact that Arleen and I had heard them before, minus a few insignificant updates. These sessions might not have been so tiring if she would allow some discussion, but she thinks she's right about everything, and it's useless to disagree. I just tried to look interested while I thought about playing golf the next day, an activity I knew I would sorely need in order to stay sane during her visit. She rambled on in her still-strong voice, her inflection halfway between that of a man and a woman. By eleven I was exhausted. Finally she ran down, and we retired for the night.

In the morning Arleen went off to work, and I hung around until midmorning, when my sister finally woke up. Once I heard her stirring, I set out the lox, bagels, and cream cheese that Arleen had prepared before she left, but when Josephine entered the kitchen, she announced, "I don't eat bagels and lox. I know we had it at home every Sunday, but I never ate it." Ha! She ate it, or my mother's name was not Dr. Sadie Muriel Baron Raskind. Jo proceeded to make herself two eggs sunny-side up. As I watched this exacting operation, I remembered when Arleen had once mistakenly served Jo eggs over easy, and Jo had made her do them over. Following the cooking of the eggs, Jo and I searched the house for half an hour to find honey for her English muffin. None of the jams, jellies, or preserves in the refrigerator would do. She takes nothing but honey. We never found it, and I imagine the eggs were cold after the honey hunt, but she ate them anyway, and then she had a little of the bagel and lox after all.

Following the eggs, muffins, bagels, and lox, Jo started to get outfitted for her hike. It was a little cloudy out, so as a precautionary measure she wore rain pants. She put on the web belt, of course, with canteen and compass attached. It took a half an hour to find the compass, but she had to have it in case a pressing navigational problem arose. She also carried a tiny flashlight and a knife. Around her neck was a pair of binoculars, the better to identify the birds; she's an expert birder. When she was completely prepared, she asked if I was coming along, but I declined, having been on enough hikes with her to last a lifetime. Along with the birds, she identifies every lichen, plant, tree, and piece of bark. She is an inveterate outdoorswoman and works on conservation crews in Arizona every Monday. Off she went alone up into the rocky hills behind the house, still unafraid and completely sure of herself, even at age seventy-five.

After breathing a sigh of relief, I took the welcome opportunity to escape with my dog to the club, where I whacked golf balls to my heart's content. My dog must have felt relieved, too. He took off, and it was two hours before he came walking up the driveway to the clubhouse. Clarence, the golf pro, put him in my car to rest and wait for me. The dog and I got back just as Josephine was moseying along the road in front of the house. She pronounced her hike wonderful, and as usual was full of misinformation. She insisted that she saw an old cross-country ski trail leading up from the Friery house next door, except that there is no ski trail. The red ribbons on the ground and on the trees are surveyors' markings, but one cannot dispute Josephine's findings. She simply won't allow it.

Anyway, you get the sense of the visit, and I'll bet it sounds familiar. Like so many siblings, we have taken separate paths, and now we have little in common but a lot to bait each other about. To the outsider, our relationship looks more contentious than it is. Under the sarcasm and button pushing is a pleasurable sense of acceptance. I may sound judgmental in describing Jo's visit, but you can be sure she had similar comments about me when she got back to her home base. Of course, she is at a disadvantage because she thinks nobody in Arizona is aware of her connection to Renée Richards. This is a tribute to her powers of self-delusion. Her friends all know, but they have the good sense to pretend that they don't. She and her husband will soon be celebrating their fiftieth wedding anniversary. All the Foersters have been invited. Our uncle Albert Raskind has been invited. I have not been invited. At one point in my life, I would have found this hurtful, but now it is only irritating. Jo will never change. I've accepted that.

During the rest of her visit, Jo was Jo. She left the kitchen and bathroom a mess, she ignored Arleen, she dawdled so dreadfully in the restaurant that they nearly closed the place with us in it, and she bent our ear with the same complaints she has been making for years. At several junctures I thought I saw smoke coming out of Arleen's ears. I knew that after Jo left, Arleen would have some choice commentary. "How can you stand it? I never believed how you used to describe your sister, but now I do. Your family must have been something!" I've never denied that.

On the afternoon Jo left, I brought out a big basket of old photos that had been in Dad's possession until he died. Jo spent an hour picking out the ones she wanted. She took many of the pictures from our childhood, those of her wedding, some of me, and of our mother and father. She looked at photos of some of the important women in my life and began to reminisce.

"I always thought you should have married Gwen," she said. "Denise was too nice for you. Gwen was tougher. She would have stood up to you." And then she added, "When Mother was dying I told her I thought you and Gwen would get married, but she said, 'No. It won't happen.'"

Having in this way broached the subject of my history, she continued, "You know, I have a friend in Phoenix, a child psychoanalyst, who has cured transsexuals with analysis. Of course, you have to get them young, you know." Had she forgotten that I had been analyzed by the esteemed Dr. Bak for eight years, that I had been a woman for nearly thirty years, and that at age sixty-nine, I was in no need of instruction about "getting them young"? Was she suggesting that all the grief in my life could have been avoided if only I had "been gotten" early?

This was not her first mention of these miraculous cures. On previous occasions I had been hurt. But Jo had forgotten the incidents, or, if she remembered them, she still felt compelled to defend the medical discipline she practices, regardless of its obvious failures. This time I just let it roll off me, and I felt good about being able to do so.

At length, it grew unnervingly close to her departure time, and she still had not packed. So, we rushed about gathering her many belongings. Her clothes went into plastic bags, then into suitcase compartments zippered shut to keep everything separate. Then we gathered all the small things: the compass, the canteen, the knife, the binoculars. Her cash went into one pocket of her jacket, her wallet into another, and her credit cards into a third. Everything else was put in her knapsack, which was then attached to her suitcases by a strap. I thought we had done a pretty thorough job, but she insisted on looking everywhere for things that might have been forgotten, even under the bed. Finally, she was satisfied, and I got her to the car with just a little time to spare. Before she got in, we hugged. It was a good hug with a lot of affection in it. I made sure she had the map I had drawn for her and hustled her into the car. A few moments later, she disappeared into the distance. When I went back inside, I found she had left behind her bathing suit.

As I expected, Arleen let loose once Jo was gone. She looks at my relationship with Jo from the viewpoint of one who has not lived through the ups and downs that went into our personal history. Circumstances may drive us apart, but they bind us, too. It is easy for an outsider to say, "When I hear you complain, and I see all that you have to complain about, I wonder why you bother. Wouldn't it be easier just to forget about it?" You either understand the answer or you don't: It's family. Jo is the only survivor from among those with whom I shared the house in Forest Hills, the only living reminder of my childhood, however traumatic. She is unsettling, yes, but as I watched her drive away, I looked forward to seeing her again.

CHAPTER 3

Then and Now

O H, HOW DIFFERENT IT would have been for you if you had grown up today rather than in the unenlightened era of your youth." I have heard numerous variations on this theme in the past ten or fifteen years as gender issues have moved from the *National Inquirer* to the Health Channel, but I can't say that today's politically correct atmosphere would have had a big influence on my behavior or on my development as a human being. Yet I can't deny that the world has changed, though I am not a professional historian and make no claim to objectivity. My perspective has been shaped by the peculiar conditions of my life. The broader issues, I leave to others. I can only say what it was like to be me then and what it is like to be me now.

Dick Raskind was born into a nuthouse situated in a conservative society. On movie screens, Andy Hardy's family set

the standard for the perfect home life. Andy was a bit of a ras-
cal but would always be set right by his father's gentle and
above all rational man-to-man talks. Upstairs, the Hardy parents slept in twin beds, an arrangement that the Hollywood
Production Code enforced on the premise that the sight of a
man and a woman in the same bed, even if married, was too
salacious for the general public. On the radio, we listened to
the *Jack Benny Show, Fibber McGee and Molly, The Shadow.* It
was escapist fare. For counterpoint there was the news of the
world, full of the buildup to World War II and later the coverage of the war itself. But even there, the public was protected.
The war reports stressed the ebb and flow of battle rather than
the brutal scenes of death that horrified audiences later in the
Vietnam era. To a great extent, popular culture attempted to
avoid shocking its audience, to portray a kinder, more orderly,
and more sanitary world than ever existed in reality.

Needless to say, there was no room in this scheme for transsexuals. The nearest American mainstream entertainment came
to presenting anything of the sort were a few films of the actress
Marlene Dietrich, in which she scandalized audiences by wearing
pants, even a tuxedo. However, if a man ever dressed as a woman
in a movie, it was for comic effect, and the same went for men
with effeminate mannerisms, who were typically seen as officious
hotel managers, butlers, floor walkers, and so on. Perhaps they
were recognized by some of the audience as homosexual stereotypes, but for most people they were simply hilarious jerks.

Rather than being a contributor to my gender problem, the
straitlaced culture of my time frequently offered a refuge from
the craziness in my house. The athletic fields were a major fac-

tor in keeping me grounded. The rules of the games were clear and made sense to me. On the tennis courts, I could interact with my father away from the scrutiny of my mother, and on the sandlot baseball and football fields I could pursue success in relative freedom. Of huge importance to me as a child was camp, which in its way highlighted some of the best things about the society of my era.

Deer Lake Camp was heaven on earth to me. I started at this sleepaway camp when I was five years old and continued until I was twelve. For its time, Deer Lake was progressive, but by today's standards it might be considered dangerous and lax. At age six, I was carrying around a hunting knife; at age seven, a fellow camper and I were sleeping alone in a tent and cooking our own meals over a campfire. We caught fish and frogs, cleaned them with our knives, cooked and ate them with gusto. Shocking? But from my point of view, then and now, that was the beauty of Deer Lake. It taught me self-reliance, and the directors assumed that kids, even young ones, could take care of themselves.

We rose to the challenge. Each summer campers were given jobs to help promote responsibility. One year, several of us were assigned to feed the chickens. One of my campmates failed to do so one morning and received a stern talking-to. When he neglected his duty for a second time, he was put in the chicken coop in the afternoon and not let out until the following morning. Harsh, yes, but he never again forgot to feed the chickens.

In many ways, the world at that time was a much tougher place than it is now, even for children whose parents could afford camp. At the end of the summer we chopped the chickens' heads off, watched fascinated as they ran around headless, and then hung them from a tree limb and plucked their feathers. The culture of my time may have been prissy about sex and gender roles, but it was not squeamish about other facts of life. Deer Lake campers knew that fried chicken did not appear magically in a cheerful cardboard bucket. We were aware from personal experience of the hard realities behind the food we ate.

Blessedly, at Deer Lake I was out of the Raskind house with its confusion, intimidation, and clothing issues. My everyday attire was swim trunks, a cap, and only occasionally a T-shirt. Mostly I went barefoot. Camp kept me busy with what the times judged to be hardy, masculine pursuits, and I was almost constantly with other boys. For the most part, my impulses at camp were those of a normal young guy. I remember going to the movies in town, a special treat made even more notable by the fact that it required a four-mile walk into Madison, Connecticut. There was no such convenience as a camp bus. It was a rainy afternoon, and we saw *Great Expectations*. I immediately fell in love with the young Estella and was hugely disappointed when Jean Simmons was replaced by an older actress playing the grown-up character.

Only on rare occasions did I feel the tug of Renée's personality while I was at camp. One notable case was when I was twelve, in my final year at Deer Lake. We put on a play that required someone to play a girl's part, and I volunteered for it. The same opportunity had presented itself at my public school in Forest Hills, but I had not even considered volunteering. My mother would have seen the public school play, and I could not have endured that. However, at Deer Lake, where I had established an independent identity, I felt secure. The camp director's wife provided me with a dress from her daughter's closet. I wore a kerchief over my short hair, and I put on lipstick, which I did not wipe off at the end of the performance. In fact, I never wiped it off. After a week, it had faded away.

Deer Lake helped plant the seed of patriotism that later led me to join the Navy in spite of a psychiatric condition that I could easily have used as an excuse not to serve. The shadow of World War II was ever-present at Deer Lake. One day a week was set aside to save food. On this day, we ate a little cereal in the morning, without milk, and only a few biscuits during the rest of the day. We were told that the food we saved by fasting would be sent to feed the hungry in war-torn Europe. We felt good about depriving ourselves. A few times we were sent to a nearby farm where we worked picking corn and tomatoes. We were told that these vegetables were going overseas. At the end of each row, we got to drink from a big bucket of cherry-flavored water to quench our thirst. We called it "bellywash."

And then there was spy night. Four campers had supposedly defected, become spies, and disappeared from camp. We were warned that they would try to infiltrate the camp and that we loyal campers would form a ring of sentries around the main house in order to catch them. If the ring were penetrated, the spies would be declared victors. All of us took spy night very seriously because we knew there were real spies in America. A few had even been captured nearby on the Connecticut and Long Island shores. The older campers knew that spy night was a game, but the younger ones were not completely sure of that.

As a sentry, I concentrated all my energy on looking for spies. If it was not a game, I did not want to be the one who let the camp down. When a captured spy turned out to be a camper from the oldest group, I realized the spies were not Germans off a U-boat, but what if they had been? We considered the whole exercise a good tune-up for the real thing, and I was proud to be part of the army that caught the spies, real or not.

But camp was not by any means the only place where I was reminded of the conflict that had enveloped the world. My parents talked a great deal about Hitler and the Nazis, especially the atrocities against the Jews in Germany. From the movies I saw every Saturday at the RKO Midway Theater, I had a clear picture of German and Japanese soldiers. I saw features like *The Purple Heart*, with Dana Andrews, and weekly serials that portrayed the enemy and the Allies, the evil and the good. In school we had air raid drills during which we were herded into the hallway, so as to be out of the range of flying glass. There were drills at home, too, at night, when the lights were turned off and a neighbor wearing a tin helmet of World War I design came by to make sure we were blacked out.

I first learned of the war's end while I was at Deer Lake. In August 1945, our counselor got us all together in the cabin and told us some news: a B-29 bomber called the *Enola Gay* had dropped a bomb with the power of 20,000 tons of TNT on the Japanese city of Hiroshima. Thousands of people had been killed. We were wide-eyed. It was hard to comprehend the scope of what he said, but we sensed his seriousness. A few days later, after another bomb was dropped on Nagasaki, we were told that the war would soon be over. My uncle Albert, by then a chief warrant officer of the 62nd Fighter Squadron, 56th Battle Group, would be coming home. And my gentle uncle Ben, who had marched with General Patton's Third Army through Belgium, France, and Germany, would be coming back to Far Rockaway, Queens. And there would be no need for any more spy nights.

That was my last summer at Deer Lake. I was one of the oldest kids, having hung on as long as possible. The friends I had made in previous summers were gone. Maybe they thought they were too old for camp. Alone, I would hike and ride my bike. I was not melancholy. I was growing up, and I had important things on my mind. I knew that I could not escape my family or myself at camp for the rest of my life, but at Deer Lake I had learned a great deal about how a young man should act in America and what values he should hold dear.

As for my personality split, well, American culture in that era didn't allow for a lot of soul-searching in disenfranchised minorities. That would come after the war, when people weren't dying by the thousands in air raids, or being herded off into concentration camps, or blasted to pieces on the field of battle. Back in those days, one willingly acted his assigned part because there were bigger things on the line, and there was a sense that things should be clear-cut. So, if something seemed out of order, you got called on it, as I did one day when a girl in my class for the intellectually gifted wanted to know why I had chosen to read *Little Women*. After all, wasn't that a "girls' book"? I was terrified. Maybe she sensed something. And when, as I sometimes did, I got somewhat gushy or overly enthused, my pal Josh would warn me that I was acting a little strange, sort of girlish. He was kind about it and treated the episode as an honest mistake, assuming that I would welcome some friendly guidance. To his way of thinking, no boy wanted to be caught acting like a girl. Perish the thought.

Yet, to my dismay, I was sporadically going far beyond gushiness. I was dressing as a girl, thinking as one, and occasionally treading the streets of Forest Hills as one. And as far as I knew, there was no precedent for this behavior. Nothing in the culture of the time gave me a sense that anyone else did this peculiar thing or ever had done it. Later, I was to discover that there was an underground, but that was not for nice Jewish boys. Nobody made documentaries about it to show at the local theater, where the married couples in the movies slept in twin beds. If regular sex was taboo, how much more taboo was irregular sex, even something as pathetic as an eleven-year-old boy in his sister's dress?

There did come a time when I pierced my culture's veil of secrecy, and it came appropriately enough through my mother, who conducted her psychiatric sessions in an office at the front of the house, a room she called her "foxhole." Inside, there was space for only a couch, an armchair, and a small desk with chair. The walls were pine-paneled except for the one behind the desk, which was covered with shelves full of textbooks and journals. The ceiling was insulated with a special sound-baffling substance, which together with a three-inch-thick door assured that nothing said in the room could be heard outside.

In my early teens, I started going into the foxhole and browsing through the medical books. I was fascinated by the subject matter and especially enjoyed looking over the illustrations, some of which were shocking pictures of wounds and physical anomalies. On one of my forays, I spotted an older book with a reddish cover. I saw the title, *Psychopathia Sexualis*, and perhaps the "sexual" component jumped out at me. When I opened the book and began to read, I was stunned. It was filled with case histories of sexual aberrations, and some of the descriptions I read could have been descriptions of me. But that was not the worst part: The subjects of these studies were confined to hospitals for the "incurably insane."

The already close quarters of my mother's foxhole tightened, and I fought back a wave of nausea. With horror, I read of a man who had strangled a woman and disemboweled her, and in the next moment (it seemed to me), I read about a man who felt he was "trapped in the wrong body" and was convinced that, though born a man, he was mentally a woman. A few pages later, I came to the case of a person who had sex with a goat. To my young mind, the implication was clear: People like me were lumped in with the murderers and goat-fuckers. Panic-stricken, I put the book away, vowing to shun it and cleanse myself of the horrible pictures it had put in my mind. But I was repeatedly drawn back to it. Eventually, I became familiar with all the cases close to mine. To this day, I remember "the celebrated Lottie," who dressed in women's clothes permanently.

For several years, *Psychopathia Sexualis* was my only reference on the subject of my impulses. Later in life, I would discover that it is considered an important book, one that broke the silence on taboo subjects and assumed there were causes for deviant behavior rather than attributing it to some innate perversity. Though the prose was supposedly kept dry and factual to discourage sensation-seeking readers, a phrase like "the forearm of the child was found in his pocket, and the head and entrails, in a half-charred condition, were taken from the stove" is hardly dry. Though the sections on gender confusion were comparatively benign, I could not easily put aside the knowledge that people like me had been placed in the company of violent psychopaths.

Yet I am proud to say that I did succeed in dismissing the notion that I was like those people or ever could be like them, though I never completely lost my fear of being institutionalized. When I examined myself as objectively as I could, I saw too much that was normal. Even though my culture did not openly recognize my condition, it did recognize Dick Raskind. I was a prizewinning athlete, and I did almost equally well in academics. I had friends with whom I did normal masculine things, which I enjoyed immensely. And while I was doing these things, I was not longing to be a woman. I was a full participant in what my culture offered, for good and ill. The dressing as a girl seemed a thing apart, an aspect of my mindset that would later lead my psychotherapist, Dr. Bak, to tell me that I had "an extremely well-compartmentalized psychosis." That compartmentalization served me well in overcoming the impact of *Psychopathia Sexualis*.

Things were loosening up in postwar Manhattan, or maybe I was loosening up; whichever was the case, in my early teens I spotted news of an event that marked my first sense that there was an organized group whose behavior was similar to mine. In thumbing through the entertainment section of the newspaper, I saw a notice about a ball. There were many specialized balls in those days for groups like the "young Irish." However, this announcement was different. I think it said, "Come dressed as you like," or some similar bland wording, but its tone suggested cross-dressing.

This was news both exciting and frightening. I wondered how dangerous it would be for me to go and how I would react to what I saw. There was certainly no question of my going as Renée, but to go as a voyeur was quite within the realm of possibility. Though young, I went all over the city on the subway, and there was little in that era that was out of bounds to me. One difference between then and now was that Manhattan was considered "safe," and the ball was to be held at the Manhattan Center on Thirty-Fourth Street and Eighth Avenue, which was in a respectable business section, though in those days not much frequented at night. My presence there after dark would be a little unusual, but if I were spotted, I could always claim to be investigating what New York's weirdos were up to, which was an aspect of city life that everyone understood.

So, I took a chance. Even before I arrived at the center, I saw several individuals dressed in formal gowns. From a distance they looked liked normal women, and they held up pretty well as I drew closer. Their expertise in dress and makeup was a revelation to me. They were doing as I did, but for them it was no hurried, fearful affair in their sister's things. They were enjoying themselves without restraint. Inside, there was a carnival air, very like a Halloween ball. All the cross-dressers were males in women's clothes, but fully half the crowd was dressed normally.

My attention was drawn almost immediately to a boy of

about my age, who was dressed in high heels and a blue satin cocktail dress. He looked completely fresh and pretty in his makeup, clearly delighted with himself and with the evening's entertainment. He was accompanied by a group of friends dressed in conventional male attire, all of whom praised him and showed him the utmost respect. This was one of my daydreams, to be with my friends and have them support my behavior, but Josh would have punched me out for my own good. Another thing that impressed me about this pretty youngster was that he did not have a homosexual affect. There was something else driving his behavior. I believe to this day that the boy was very simply a transvestite, the majority of whom are straight. I envied him his openness and especially his ease with himself.

But as to role models, that evening showed me both ends of the spectrum. A movement on stage drew my attention away from the charming youngster. What I saw repelled me. It was a little old man, tastelessly dressed and garishly painted, dancing—"cavorting" is a better word—before the crowd. Somebody hit him with a spotlight, which magnified his horrible fakery. If the young boy represented a possible present, this grotesque figure represented a possible future. I threw my soda in the trash and left the ball.

As time went by, I saw more men in feminine attire as transvestite revues gained prominence, though they were generally relegated to the Bohemian sections of town. As I watched these entertainments, I had many of the same thoughts as the general public: They were acts performed by weird, gay men. I never saw anyone as charming as the boy at the ball. The revues had only one appeal—they featured men dressing as women—but I knew that I was essentially different from these performers in that I wanted to actually become a woman, not just dress as one. That was my fantasy as I watched. Once a man came up to me and said, "You look like a nice kid. You shouldn't be in a place like this." I immediately assumed he knew what I was thinking, though of course he couldn't. He probably thought I was slumming or toying with homosexuality, and he felt moved to give me the standard advice.

In certain ways, back then I wished I was a homosexual or a transvestite. Their lives were not easy, but at least some sort of existence was open to them. By contrast, there seemed no way for a naturally born man to become a woman. That fact helped Dick keep Renée in check. She might want to come through, but nature had decreed she could not. At least that was the opinion held by both Dick and Renée until one shocking day that threw everything into question.

Ironically, this event took place against a thoroughly masculine backdrop. I was playing in a tennis tournament at the U.S. Military Academy at West Point. One evening, I was browsing in the very proper hotel stationery shop. For the most part, that was the only type of place I frequented. Beyond some curious looks into naughty stores, I kept myself pure. It is hard in these times to realize how strongly the prohibitions of that era affected the behavior of respectable children. In modern America, television, movies, and the Internet are so racy that it would be almost impossible to cultivate a modern child as naïve as my peers and I were in the 1940s and '50s. The situation cannot be comprehended by anyone born in the last forty years, not just the scarcity of sexual material but the aura of nastiness associated with what little there was—and that nastiness was mild compared to the vile onus attached to anything considered deviant. I suppose many normal kids shrugged off the prudish atmosphere more easily than I, but my secret made me especially susceptible.

So, when I saw a paperback with the title *Man into Woman* on the stationery rack, it stood out as if in neon. How had this inflammatory concept made its way into this respectable store? Clearly a mistake had been made, but if Dick had any idea of ignoring this opportunity, Renée did not. With great nonchalance, I took the book off the rack and, along with a couple of other items for camouflage, I presented it to the cashier. I half-expected her to say, "What does a nice young man like you want with this piece of trash?" But she didn't.

In a safe place, I found that *Man into Woman* described the life of a Danish painter named Einar Wegener, who had experienced feelings very much like mine and in the early 1930s had been surgically changed from a man to a woman. One of the most fascinating things to me was Wegener's report that he felt right in women's clothes, more comfortable and relaxed than ever before. This was familiar territory, and I thought of the many restful afternoons I had spent in my room dressed in my sister's clothes, feeling somehow insulated from the tensions of the Raskind house. Unlike me, however, Wegener did more than dress up. He began to aggressively explore the possibility of becoming a woman in reality, and against all odds, he managed it.

Even in Wegener's era, sex-related operations were being

performed, especially in the case of so-called intersexed persons, most often infants, who have partially developed physical characteristics of both sexes. The usual solution was to make the child a girl, as taking something away is easier than building something up. I knew of such operations—they are still done today—but since I was fully male, I had dismissed them. But Wegener did not. He underwent four similar operations that effectively turned him into a woman, taking the name Lili Elbe after his transformation. This was exciting for Renée, but Dick was more concerned with the fact that Lili Elbe's health had deteriorated throughout the transformation. She died after her last surgery.

Prospects still looked bleak, but shortly after discovering *Man into Woman*, I got a look at what American culture had in store for a modern Lili Elbe. Christine Jorgensen burst on the scene in 1952, preceded by the famous headline "Ex-GI Becomes Blonde Beauty." Like Wegener before her, George Jorgensen suffered from the sensation of being a woman trapped in a man's body. Unwilling to endure such a state, he began to read about new developments in the field of hormone research, which led him to eventually engineer a way to make his dream come true. I could only applaud George Jorgensen's courage and congratulate him on not having a force like my mother restricting his efforts.

Unfortunately, Christine had little to fall back on but her notoriety, and she succumbed to the temptation to exploit her fame by eventually going onstage with a nightclub act in which she sang such standards as "I Enjoy Being a Girl." I used to cringe at seeing Christine Jorgensen in a bathing suit spread in a magazine, even though such pictures in those days were demure by today's standards. And the Christine jokes were horrible: "If Christine's sister had a baby, would Christine be an aunt, an uncle, or an ankle?" "Christine's theme song is 'My Johnnie Lies Over the Ocean.'" And so on. I thought about what my mother would say if our family were dragged into anything remotely like that, and I vowed to stifle Renée by whatever methods I could.

One method I tried was to confess my problem to my mother. My motivation was complex, but as the struggle deepened, I suppose I thought that I might as well engage the help of the one person whose opinion most counted. And I guess I was hoping for some sympathy. What I got was a referral to a psychiatrist. Thus began my ten-plus years on the couch, trying to fix myself. If I were young today, I would go on the Internet to a page like *Trans*topia*, which offers the following advice: "In choosing a therapist to work with on teen gender issues, I recommend that clients think of themselves as 'consumers.'" The site continues with tips on how to find "gender friendly" professionals who will respect their patients' "rights," see to their "comfort," minister to their "unique needs," and facilitate a "smooth transition."

Such terms had nothing to do with my therapy. Instead of "consumer," substitute the word "pawn." My mother picked my psychotherapists, and it probably would not have made any difference which ones she picked. At that time, few mainline psychiatrists knew much about transsexuality, and those who did considered the concept hogwash. My Freudian therapy was entirely devoted to finding the unfortunate cause of my condition and purging me of it so I could start to enjoy being a man. Any discomfort on my part, any complaint about the therapist's technique, any disagreement with the tack taken in therapy or the conclusions drawn by the therapist, and any carping about patient rights would all have been labeled "resistance" and seen as an impediment to an eventual cure. The more uncomfortable I was, the closer Dr. Bak thought I was to discovering the core of my problem and the happier he was.

In spite of my conflicts, I enjoyed many aspects of manhood. To be an athletic, well-educated, white American male in the 1950s was to be in an enviable position. There was little standing between me and the full realization of the American Dream: no color line and no glass ceiling. Being Jewish was slightly uncomfortable in an Ivy League world, but my other attributes more than compensated. If I had not been a couch case, life would have been pretty much perfect. As it was, the years of my youth were spent on a roller coaster, ranging from euphoric masculine achievement to desperate and sometimes dangerous forays into femininity.

While I carried on my long psychiatric struggle, the culture around me was slowly altering. Sex change was still the subject of sniggers for most people, but the American medical establishment was slowly beginning to experiment with the surgery, though the procedure for qualifying was rigorous, involving complicated psychological testing and at least a year of living as the sex to which you were switching. In the main, I saw these precautions as sensible, though my unique situation was to make me pay a steep price when I eventually broke off with Dr. Bak and sought surgery in America.

At that time there were relatively few postoperative trans-sexuals in the world, but there were thousands more like me who were struggling with their identity and contemplating a sex change. The only publication I can name that seriously tried to treat things from the sufferer's point of view was the magazine *Turnabout*, edited by Fred Shaw. It was primarily for cross-dressers and was a poor thing, on newsprint as I recall, but it was sympathetic. Even so, the content of *Turnabout* reflected the level of sophistication that the publisher attributed to the average transvestite. Shaw presented smudgy before-and-after pictures of transsexuals and cross-dressers and poems and stories highlighting those themes. The quality of the photography and of the literature was generally low, though poignant in its naïveté. I read many poems like the following.

> *Danny or Danni?*
> *He or she?*
> *Neither? Both?*
> *Just me.*

Embarrassing, but I secretly read the magazine many times, along with others of similar quality. To be fair, Shaw also included essays that tried to explore gender confusion from a more analytic perspective.

Shaw published *Turnabout* in his basement. Upstairs, he hosted a support group for would-be transsexuals. As far as I know, it was the only such group going at the time. I was sent there by Dr. Benjamin, who by this time was overseeing my hormone therapy and helping me prepare for surgery. The group I attended offered as much discouragement as support. I had little in common with the grim group of misfits who met in Fred Shaw's house. It was a motley collection of people, many of whom, I soon deduced, suffered not merely from gender confusion but also a wide range of other psychiatric disorders. One of them went to Casablanca against the advice of his physician and the support group, had the operation, and subsequently committed suicide. Dr. Benjamin may well have sent me to these people as a form of reality therapy. If I had secret second thoughts, meeting with my supposed transsexual peers would have brought them out.

It is a revealing comment on those times that my accomplishments ultimately proved to be a major impediment to my surgery. Everything was going along well until one day I walked in for my hormone shot and was told that I should step back and review my decision. I, who had been reviewing my life on a psychiatrist's couch for the previous ten years, should think some more. The spoken reason boiled down to this: No person in his right mind would want to imperil what I had achieved in order to enter the questionable world of transsexuals. The unspoken reason was that their recently developed program might be harmed if a brilliant young doctor were allowed to change his sex and destroy his life. As long as Dr. Benjamin's program altered a bunch of misfits and nonentities, nobody would care, but the consequences of a foul-up with me were too alarming.

That rebuff marked a point of deep despair for me with regard to my culture. I had done all within my power to follow its dictates. Like my immigrant relatives before me, I had embraced the American Dream. I had used the nation's educational system to improve my mind, and I had developed my body and my competitive skills on its athletic fields. I had pursued a useful career in medicine. I had served in my nation's military. And I had done all this while battling a crippling mental condition. When I turned to the establishment for its help, I discovered that my excellence had become my enemy.

In 1965, an era of civil unrest and protest, this affront would have been enough to turn many young people sour. I could have seen it as just another example of an encrusted older generation denying the young their say. I could have turned into a counterculture commando, but I didn't. I was devastated, but maybe the lessons of Deer Lake Camp had sunk in too well. If they put you in the chicken coop, you took your medicine and tried to learn from the experience. Deer Lakers didn't whine. In the next few years, I engaged in some wild behavior, but I turned the knife toward myself, not my culture, often driving too fast and flying too recklessly. But all the while I continued to advance my career and to plan for how I could realize my desires through my own efforts. It was the way I had always lived my life.

In the end, I waited my culture out. When I went back to Harry Benjamin's office for another try, I found that the grand old man of American transsexualism had retired and been succeeded by his younger associate. We came to a speedy agreement, and within months, I was physically as much a woman as I would ever be. Dr. Robert Granato had done 157 sex changes by the time he got to me. It was still, as he put it, a "hell of an operation." The public attitude toward transsexualism had improved and "gender dysphoria," as it was then being called, was increasingly seen as a legitimate field of medicine, though it would not be until 1980 that "transsexualism" would find its way into the American Psychiatric Association's *Diagnostic and Statistical Manual* as a gender identity disorder.

All this had happened without my help. During the ten years between 1965 and 1975 I had pursued my goals as a private person. I had joined no groups, and I had written no congressman. After I got my operation, I wanted nothing more than to melt into American society and live happily ever after. I didn't hate Dr. Benjamin, who had blocked my surgery, and I didn't hate the citizens who had sniggered for so many years at transsexuals, sometimes without knowing they were in the presence of one. I didn't hate the medical establishment, or the government, or the preacher in his church. I'm not perfect, why should they be? The people I had the most trouble forgiving were those closest to me, particularly my sister and mother. That is where the real work had to be done. To the rest, I was willing to say, *"La guerre est finie."*

But there was one more battle to fight after I was outed. The word "outed" had not yet been invented, but that was what happened to me. I detested it then, and I detest it now. I believe in the American right to privacy. If somebody is harmlessly deviant and wants to keep it secret for whatever reason, leave him or her the hell alone! That is one way that the American culture of my youth was better than American culture now. At least when everybody was embarrassed by a topic, you could depend on the respectable press and your fellow sufferers to shut up and allow you to handle it in your own way.

I make this point because I want to be completely candid

about what I've done. I am proud of the stand I took, and I fully believe that my actions and the publicity surrounding them set the stage for today's more tolerant climate. However, I have never wanted to be pigeonholed as a transsexual, and I don't want to be remembered solely as one who took on the world in behalf of her kind and won an important battle. I am first and last an individual. When I think of myself, I don't think "transsexual." First, I am a doctor. If I have to characterize myself further, I am likely to say, "I am an old Blue." A Yale graduate. Why? Because transsexuality is something that happened to me; whereas, graduating from Yale and from the University of Rochester Medical School are things I made happen.

Interestingly, an event associated with Yale has recently brought home to me how much the world has changed. In April of 2004, Yale held its first "Trans Issues Week." Here is the description in the program:

Trans Issues Week is a series of events devoted to increasing awareness of transsexuality and its relationship with feminism and queer issues. The series will incorporate themes of transsexuality, transgenderedness, genderqueerness, butch, femme, and drag. The ways in which gender is defined, which include but extend beyond physiology, will be explored.

This agenda is enough to take the breath out of an old-timer like me. There are several topics that I don't even understand and am not sure I want to. The very term "genderqueerness" is enough to make me uncomfortable. I still think of "queer" as an insult, right in there with the infamous "n word," yet there are people who have embraced "queer" as a term of honor, and it seems to have made its way into the academic world as well. There's a web page devoted to "Deaf Queer Youth." In my day, such a phrase would not have been uttered in polite society.

It seems that in today's society, everybody is served, and even though I played a large part in opening this Pandora's box, I have my reservations about some of these changes. In particular, I am suspicious of people who make being "genderqueer" a way of life rather than an aspect of life. I am far more impressed by seeing the occasional genderqueer professional on television, who cooks, landscapes, performs surgery, or entertains an audience without making an issue of sexual orientation than I am by the "Queer Eye" guys, who I suppose are making a contribution, but who are nonetheless trading on something that has nothing to do with their expertise as lifestyle consultants. I am even more suspicious of groups with "attitude." Organizations who choose to name themselves things like Transsexual Menace are, I realize, announcing that they are brave and will stand up for themselves, but I can't help thinking that every time I fix the eyes of a child, I do far more for transsexual rights than any threat or in-your-face remark could accomplish.

In spite of my history, I am in many ways an old-fashioned American. I took my civics lessons to heart. I have never chosen my friends on the basis of their sexual orientation, religion, or ethnic background. I don't believe that American society should be a bunch of enclaves, especially enclaves centered on sexuality. I choose my friends based on personality and mutual interests, and I'm nostalgic for the days when there was less pride in what makes Americans different and more pride in what we have in common. Sounds like the melting pot. Well, I've admitted to being old-fashioned. My friend Larry Levine once remarked, "Renée, I have the most unconventional views but have led the most conventional of lives. You have led the most unconventional of lives but have the most conventional views."

In outlining its schedule of "queer issues," the agenda for Trans Issues Week at Yale mentions master's teas. This is an old Yale tradition in which I recently took part. Sari Siegel, a young woman who has been my patient since infancy, recently asked me to do a master's tea in her college at Yale, Saybrook, which is also my old college. Now, the mere fact that she is a woman premed at Yale reflects a big change at the school. A few years ago a male patient told me he had been a swimmer at Yale in the forties. I casually remarked that I had played college tennis only a few years later.

"Where?"

"Yale," I replied, smiling sweetly.

"Impossible," he barked. "Yale didn't admit women until the seventies!"

"I was a special case."

He thought for a moment and then said, "Oh, I get it."

Yale, as traditional as it is, has changed with the times, and was willing, even anxious, to have the notorious Renée Richards back for a tea. I wondered what my master, Basil Duke Henning, would have said about such a thing. The Duke, as we called him (out of his hearing at least), was a distant figure. Most of us never saw him or his wife, known as the Duchess, let alone set foot in their quarters.

But that was long ago, in Dick Raskind's time. This is the

time of Renée Richards, and the master of Saybrook who would preside over my tea would not be a man but a woman, Dr. Mary Miller, who currently lives in what I had always thought of as Basil Duke's lair. For company, she has her husband, their twelve-year-old daughter, a dog, and a cat. As I shook hands with Mary, noting her firm grip and close-cut salt-and-pepper hair, I thought Basil Duke would probably have approved of her: straightforward, confident, a trifle formal. On the door of the master's quarters I observed a flyer that had been posted announcing my appearance.

A Life in Tennis and Medicine:
A conversation with
Dr. Renée Richards,
Saybrook '55

On the left was the Saybrook coat of arms and on the right was a present-day picture of me and one of the cover of my autobiography, *Second Serve*. The date of the tea was May 2, the last day of the "reading period" before final exams. Mary had picked a Sunday so that she could be sure the tennis coaches could honor their special invitation to an event otherwise exclusively for Saybrook residents.

I MUST ADMIT THAT I didn't know quite how I would be received. I expected everyone to be polite, but I wondered if I would catch that uncomfortable look I sometimes see in people's eyes. I had been attentive to my appearance. The day before, I had gone to Hair Quarters in Mahopac, not far from my home, to get spruced up. They have two Lisas there. I call them "Lisa Nails" and "Lisa Hair," and the latter Lisa does just as good a cut, shampoo, and blow-dry as my city guy, Yona, at Filles et Garçons. I felt good when I left.

Arleen had put together my outfit as specified in my invitation: business casual. She chose a long crepe skirt slit up each side, a matching crepe short-sleeve top, and a patterned jacket of her own, with a little rust color in it to match my skirt and top. The yellow glass bead necklace I wore was also Arleen's. We both thought the outfit was perfect for an afternoon tea. As I stood in front of the little audience, mildly concerned with what the morning's wet weather had done to my hair, I was relieved to see nothing mean-spirited in the faces of the eighty or so residents who had taken a break from the reading period to rap with me. Here, I felt I was properly situated, part of a long line of academic and athletic effort, connected to a past that, as imperfect as it was, has so much to recommend it.

And that is how I began, with the past, describing how I came as a freshman to Vanderbilt Hall and how my father had said I could get from the hall to the tennis courts by taking the trolley the same way he did in 1916 when he played on the lacrosse team. Of course, the trolley tracks were long gone, even in 1951. At the time, I thought it quaint that my father would make that mistake, but now I see it as a passing of the torch, a sharing of history. And on my day as the Saybrook tea honoree, I did my best to continue in that tradition. I talked about what Yale was like in the '50s, about the gap between the preppies and the public high school kids, the alienation, and the drive to assimilate.

In those days, everyone wanted to be "shoe." The preppier you were, the more shoe you were, and you got that way by wearing the proper gear: khaki pants, narrow belt, button-down shirt open at the neck, and the ever-so-important white buck shoes, from which the adjective "shoe" derived. In the winter, you donned your houndstooth sport jacket and your skinny regimental tie, everyone the same, except a few like me, who might wear a wide flowered tie or something else mildly out of order as a gesture of individuality. But in spite of such gestures, the overpowering pressure was to conform, and I was frank in telling my audience that, for the most part, "conform" was exactly what I did. This prompted one student to ask a question that made my jaw drop.

"What was the gay community like, then?"

"Are you kidding?" I responded. "There was no gay community. The term gay had not yet been invented. Everyone on campus looked and acted the *same*. Nobody wanted to be seen as different. There were no homosexuals, even if there were. No Jews (except for a few diehard orthodox in Hillel). There were very few students who would even venture to say they were Catholic. From the outside, we were all preppy WASP super-athletes or literary geniuses from St. Marks or some other preppy school."

The looks on their young faces told me how great the difference is between then and now. Those faces were of all colors, of all backgrounds, a far more varied group of individuals than could have been assembled on the Yale campus of my era. Many of my listeners were shaking their heads in disbelief.

But our discussion also touched on happier subjects. I talked about records in sports and the rivalry between Chrissie and Martina, and their differences both socially and as tennis players. I described my experience coaching Martina, detailing my work with her game and in plotting strategy against her biggest rivals. I discussed the problems I faced in reestablishing my medical practice in New York and my brief return to coaching Martina in 1987. After an hour and a half of enjoyable chat, Mary ended the talk.

Afterward, Sari Siegel took me on a tour of Saybrook in its present form. The buildings have recently undergone much renovation, including a sandblasting that gave new life to their beautiful Gothic façades. The courtyard was likewise refurbished and was in bloom, full of spring flowers. Inside, the changes were more extreme. When Sari showed me her room, the difference between then and now was clearly evident. By contrast with her tiny quarters, the ones I enjoyed as a sophomore in the 1950s were positively genteel. My roommates and I had a nice living room with a fireplace and a windowseat overlooking the courtyard. There was enough room in the living area for a few armchairs and a sofa. The four of us slept in two small but still decent-sized bedrooms, one on each side of the living room.

Now such suites are a thing of the past and out of them have been created depressing little warrens containing four bedrooms that are more like closets. The students still sleep two to a room, but the space is so limited that they have almost no place to walk, like in a submarine. Their living room is a no-nonsense affair, half the size of the one that in my day used to serve four students. However, neither Sari nor her roommates seemed discontented. I met two of them, one a premed student from Montana and the other a documentary film student from Nigeria, both women, though the dormitory at large is coed. In spite of these changes in accommodations, changes in ethnicity, changes in backgrounds, and changes in sex, this was unmistakably still Yale, which has a power born in part of tradition. The students are changing Yale, but Yale is still changing the students.

We also toured the library, which was reassuringly familiar, as was the dining room, a big formal hall with casement windows and polished wooden tables. The only new thing was a soft drink machine at the end of the cafeteria line. Of course, the students were different, most studying with their laptops in easy reach and wearing informal attire, no less! In my day, a coat and tie were mandatory in the dining room. High above the ground level, I could see two formal pictures of the Duke and Duchess, honoring Basil Duke Henning's long tenure as master of Saybrook College: 1946 to 1975.

I dined in the early evening at the master's house with a group composed of specially selected teachers and students. A couple of the students were gay and keenly interested in gender issues. In this more intimate surrounding, I answered their questions as best I could. Normally, I try to avoid such conversations, but here in the Saybrook master's house, it seemed profitable and fitting to discuss transsexuality, though we used the currently fashionable term "transgendered." The students seemed more comfortable with it. Everything was friendly. We were just Yalies in a rap session, and the barriers came down. When we were done, Mary gave me a beautiful silk scarf that she had designed, featuring the bunches of grapes and the lion that are on the Saybrook shield. We hugged and said good night.

So, I came home. Not as a transsexual but as a distinguished alum, an old Blue. As always, I was honored to be invited back as one of Yale's own. Yes, the world has changed, but whenever I return to the campus, I am always relieved to see that some things have not: the architecture, the students going to and fro, the leaves swirling on a fall afternoon, the chimes. Here at Yale and places like it, then and now are balanced, and the future is mapped. Change is hard. No one knows that better than I. We try to keep the good and eliminate the bad, an uncertain and imperfect process. Still, we try.

CHAPTER 4

They Called Him Rastaman

WITHOUT QUESTION, LIFE FOR my son has been a challenge. Nick Raskind is now thirty-four and has experienced many triumphs and many reversals. The primary reversal was his father's sex change, but in a way this reversal may have inspired some of his triumphs because he certainly grew up thinking that anything is possible. It never occurred to him that he could not shape his own destiny. Though he never embraced academics and has waged an ongoing battle with authority (including mine), he has put together a varied string of achievements. Nick started a successful line of men's clothing, held a national sport karate championship, won large sums as a professional gambler, and developed systems for brokering commodities, eventually settling on a career in Manhattan real estate. He is smart like his father and headstrong like his father, and I'm proud of him.

Nick began to assert himself at an early age. When he was two and a half, his nanny, Mia, following my instructions, took Nicky across the street to enroll him at Temple Emanuel Nursery School. Mia was a Colombian woman, elderly and quiet, with her own way of speaking English. I had interviewed a parade of proper English nannies but ultimately chose Mia for her warmth and good rapport with Nicky. However, she was apparently not high-toned enough to impress the lady in charge. When Mia said, "I want to enroll this little boy at Temple Emanuel Nursery School," the lady kind of looked down her nose. Then, pointedly echoing Mia's slightly odd speech pattern, she responded, "Okay. What's this little boy's name?"

Nicky probably recognized the disparaging tone.

From just beyond the lip of her desk the lady heard a small voice saying, "My name is Nicky Raskind."

When she looked down, she saw Nicky, barely three feet tall, peering up at her. Turning her attention back to Mia, she asked, "Well, how old is this little boy?"

The voice from below said, "I'm three years old."

Still ignoring Nicky, she asked Mia, "What's this little boy's address?"

And Nicky answered, "Twenty-one East Sixty-sixth Street."

This time the lady looked at Nicky instead of Mia and asked, "What does your daddy do?"

"He's an eye doctor," Nicky replied.

Upon hearing this, the lady turned to Mia and said, "He can start on Monday."

So Nicky essentially enrolled himself in nursery school, thus starting his formal education, which went very well for a time. Every day at five o'clock Mia would bring him to my office, only a block away from our apartment across from Temple Emanuel, and we would often spend the rest of the day tooling around Central Park on my bike, Nicky taking in the view from his child seat on the back. Two of our favorite destinations were the carousel and the Central Park Zoo, where we would sit and watch the Delacorte chimes go around to count the time every fifteen minutes.

Before he went to bed, we would have a story time. Usually there were two stories, one "within a book" and one "without in a book," as Nicky would put it. The within-a-book stories were ones like *The Little Engine That Could* and *Pierre, the Boy Who Didn't Care.* But Nicky liked the without-in-a-book stories best, because they were always ones that Daddy made up about a little boy named Nicky who did heroic things. When I would start with the phrase "There was once a little boy named Nicky," his face would light up. And I would go on to spin a tale about how Nicky got lost in the woods in Central Park but found his own way out, or how Nicky found a man's wallet and returned it to him, or how Nicky rode fearlessly in his child seat when his daddy had to pedal like mad right through a bunch of tough guys who wanted to hold them up in the park. This latter story was based on fact. We were actually menaced by a gang who tried to ambush us at the bottom of a hill. By the time I realized their intent, there was nothing to do but ride through them. Luckily, I won that game of chicken. Life in New York is generally great, but it's not perfect by any means.

If being a father to four-year-old Nicky had been the only thing in his life, Dick Raskind would have been a happy man.

When my marriage collapsed, Renée started emerging with a new sense of urgency. I was approaching the upper age limit for surgery, and Renée knew that her chance for life was growing slimmer. Many evenings I would return to my apartment after a happy afternoon with Nicky and feel Renée's iron grip closing on me. No matter how I attempted to distract myself, she would still come out. In desperation, I tried another psychiatrist, which I had vowed never to do again. He actually said that I should "get laid." My God, what moronic therapy! It hadn't changed in twenty years.

A hundred times I looked at the many lethal substances I had in my office and thought how easy it would be to kill myself. The only reason I didn't was Nicky. But Dick had less and less control over what the despairing Renée might do. I was in a catch-22 situation. It seemed I could commit suicide and deprive Nicky of any sort of father; or stand pat and saddle him with an increasingly neurotic father; or have the surgery and present him with a transsexual father. They were three bad choices, but I think I chose the best of them.

I went back on hormones and began to feel better almost immediately. The changes in my body began again, but Nicky didn't seem to notice. Our time together was as fulfilling as before. I wore baggy athletic outfits that covered me pretty well, and though I was an object of scrutiny when I was alone, people were usually polite when I was with Nicky. After the operation, I realized that Renée Richards could not abruptly take on Dick Raskind's life without a gigantic upset for everyone involved: me, my patients, my ex-wife, and, most important, my son.

Reluctantly, I headed to California. Nicky was four and a

half. I phoned him on most days and visited as often as I could. On minor occasions that called for a father substitute, such as Halloween, my pal Herb FitzGibbon filled in. I tried to make it to town for anything big, and kept an apartment on the Upper West Side, where Nicky and I could spend the weekend during my visits. Being with my son was a joy, but putting on the short wig and man's suit I wore to disguise my new femininity was galling. Luckily, Nicky didn't seem to notice. At every stage of his life, my appearance had been outside the norm, so the wig and ill-fitting suit made little or no impression on him.

Nonetheless, I knew that he would have to find out about me someday. With that in mind, I decided to take him to a child psychiatrist. I chose Dr. Peter Neubauer, the preeminent child psychiatrist of the time. I was pleased when it became obvious that Nicky really liked Dr. Neubauer, whom he called "Dr. Newbarrow." I figured this distinguished man must be working magical therapy on my son, so I asked Nicky, "Why do you like Dr. Newbarrow?" Nicky replied, "Because he gives candy." This was the level of Nicky's response to therapy at this point.

When Nicky entered the first grade, Meriam enrolled him in a new school, the Episcopal School, popular with Upper East Side families. I remember asking, "Nicky, what did you learn on your first day at Episcopal School?" In response, he put his hands over his head and said, "Heaven above." Then he put his hands down by his sides and said, "Hell below." And then he shouted, "Joshua fit the Battle of Jericho!" This sort of Bible instruction was a far cry from the low-key approach taken at Temple Emanuel, which was run by reformed Jews who did not go in for histrionics.

During my final year on the women's tour, Meriam told Nicky, then nine years old, about my surgery. This was done while I was out of town, so as not to complicate the explanation with my presence. According to Meriam, he calmly commented, "Well, I can see why you and Daddy had to get a divorce. Two women can't be married." A couple of days later, she took him to Dr. Neubauer just in case. The psychiatrist asked, "How's your daddy?" Nicky replied, "Mommy told me my daddy is a lady now." He paused for a long moment, and then added, "But that's crazy."

During our frequent phone calls, the subject of my physical form came up but in no depth. Nicky and I would be chatting about typical stuff and out of the blue he would ask something like, "Daddy, do you have breasts?" I would try to answer as casually as possible, "Yes, I do." There was never a follow-up question. He would simply move on to another subject. I never pressed the issue, thinking it best for him to gather information at his own pace.

I had been gone for five years when I moved back to New York City permanently. A great deal had happened since my departure. Nicky was nine and had been pretty well sheltered from the turmoil surrounding me. He knew that I was a celebrity of sorts, but he tended to associate that with my medical career. Once while we were rowing in Central Park, he called to some people in another boat, "This is the famous eye doctor, Dr. Richard Raskind." They nodded appreciatively, and Nicky was pleased.

Except for my physiology, we were a pretty normal father and son. Nearly every weekend, like so many other divorced dads, I would pull up in front of my ex-wife's apartment house, and out would run my son. Truthfully, I feel worse about the impact of my divorce on Nicky than that of my sex change.

Nicky's grades were good through the fourth and fifth grades, but by the time he was in the sixth grade, he was beginning to fail, unable to concentrate in class on anything that required doing homework. He was certainly plenty smart, especially street smart, and he could think on his feet. When he was about ten, he and Arleen were standing in the pouring rain looking for a taxi. Finally they saw one inching along in the traffic, but it was displaying its On-Radio-Call signal. Undeterred, Nicky knocked on the window. When the driver said, "No, I'm on a radio call," Nicky opened the door, hopped in, and said, "Yeah, that was us." Getting cabs in Manhattan is a cutthroat game that Nicky mastered at a very early age.

The classroom was another story. His academic performance got worse and worse, until finally I was required to go for a meeting with the headmaster of St. Bernard's, the school where he had been enrolled since the third grade. By this time Nick was a seventh grader. The headmaster was very stern and incidentally an albino. Our conference was an intriguing matchup: Jewish transsexual father meets Episcopalian albino minister. As I left his office, I felt that he was leaning in our direction. Then it was Nicky's turn to go in. Five minutes later he emerged.

"What did you say to him?"

"Well," Nicky replied, "he asked me what I wanted to be when I grew up, and I told him a drug dealer in Thailand."

That was the end of his career at St. Bernard's. He was

kicked out of so many other schools in the next few years that I lost count. But the picture was not entirely bleak. In the summers, he went to Camp Robin Hood and did very well. The more self-directed the activity, the better he did. When I visited him, he and I would traipse around on our own through the woods away from the others. Nicky was proud of me in many ways, but you can imagine the problem of explaining my condition to an endless stream of new kids. One especially galling issue was the question of whether I was Nicky's mother or father. When a friend told her daughter, Eden, that Nicky's daddy was now a woman, Eden said, "Oh. Now Nicky has two mommies." That seemed sensible to Eden, but not to Nicky. I am still his daddy, albeit in a different form.

And children are not the only ones who cannot understand this. Adults often assume that because I have changed sexes, I must now be his mother. When someone mistakes me for his mother, Nick often says, "No, that's my father. One mother is quite enough." Nick has clashed far more often with his mother than he has with me, so severely in fact that they are frequently not on speaking terms.

When he was thirteen, we sent him away for the eighth grade to a boarding school in Massachusetts. The Fay School was a very nice coed institution in a small town, not too threatening and not too competitive, in which I hoped Nicky would settle down. Shortly after sending up a load of hockey equipment, a stereo system, and all kinds of wonderful furniture for his room, I was called by the headmaster. "You'd better pick Nicky up because he's threatening to tear the place apart."

Apparently Nicky had taken exception to the Fay School dress code, which involved wearing a tie and otherwise dressing conservatively, or as Nicky puts it even now, "Your socks had to be dark, for Christ's sake." I still don't see the problem, but for Nicky it was an issue. As I understand it, he and the administration had already clashed on the school's earring policy, which was that male students should not have them. Nicky thought he could not get along with fewer than two in one ear. But the terminal crisis arose when Nicky appeared at the school with a Mohawk haircut. The headmaster gave him the choice of either shaving his head altogether or being put on suspension until his hair grew out, to which Nicky replied, "I have a better idea. How about I burn down a few dorms and keep my fucking haircut?"

I told the headmaster to put him on an airplane, and Meriam and I went to pick him up at LaGuardia. I had paid for a full year at the Fay School, and that was a lot of money down the drain, not to mention the cost of the incidentals, but the worst thing was the disappointment. I knew a thing or two about dress problems, but I had put together a good academic record in spite of them. You have to make a living in this world. Where was his practicality? When Nicky arrived, he knew he was in trouble, because both Meriam and I were waiting for him, a sure sign that things had gotten serious. We took him to his Grandfather Raskind's house in Forest Hills to be registered at a public school.

It was during this time that our most unusual adventure together occurred. One day Grandpa found a scribbled note on the table in the front room.

Grandpaw,

Went to the city. Be back later

Love,

Nicky

Nicky was allowed to go into Manhattan on the subway like thousands of other New York kids, so when my father read me the note over the phone, I wasn't especially concerned. But as the day wore on I got worried. By 10:00 P.M. I was pacing and by midnight I was fit to be tied. I might have called the police then and there except that the timing of Nicky's disappearance was suspicious. It came just as I was trying to exert more control over him, having decided that my overindulgence had been partly responsible for his bad behavior. Just days before his disappearance, he had been caught smoking pot with his cronies in his room, and this had not been the first time. On the previous occasion, I had threatened to send him to live for a year with Jo in Arizona, and this time I was preparing to follow through. On the day he disappeared, he was supposed to be waiting around for a call from his aunt so she could explain the arrangements for the move, but Nicky was into the New York scene with all its diversity and grimy urban chic. He wanted to hang around with his best friend, Alex, from whom he had gained an intense interest in all things Jamaican. Alex's grandmother, Lady Sarah Churchill, lived in Jamaica, and Alex had often stayed with her, bringing back stories of island life that fired Nick's imagination. Disappearing was very likely Nick's way of punishing me for trying to move him away from the things he valued most, so even at midnight I tried to tell myself that his absence was not necessarily serious. He had innumerable contacts around town and frequently stayed overnight with friends, though never before without telling his family. I decided to wait until morning; when he still didn't show, I hired a private investigator with experience in missing children and notified the police.

An NYPD detective showed up at my office in the afternoon and listened to my description of Nicky: five foot five, 130 pounds, hair short on the sides and longer on the top, a cross-shaped earring, torn baggy black pants, a ragged pair of sneakers, a T-shirt with a rock group emblazoned on the front, and a skateboard under his arm. I thought it was a pretty distinctive description, but it probably fit 100,000 thirteen-year-old boys in the city. I told him about Nicky's interest in reggae music and Rastafarian beliefs, and I described his room, decorated with a Bob Marley poster and a Jamaican flag on the wall. I provided pictures of Nicky and went on about how handsome he was and what a good kid. The detective listened patiently and when I finished gave me a lesson on the distinction between a "missing" youngster and a "runaway." A child was "missing" if foul play were suspected, and a "runaway" if he had taken off on his own. In Nicky's case, the detective thought "runaway" most likely, but when he asked why Nicky might have left, I just answered, "He didn't want to go to school."

Later in the day I did it all over again with an operative from the team of private investigators. Nicky's mother answered the same questions. We were to be kept posted, but after work I couldn't sit in my apartment and wait. At the time of this incident, I had a father I loved dearly; a sister with whom I was slowly mending fences; a companion in Arleen, who had been a friend and rock of support for years; three marvelous buddies who had fought for me and protected me since childhood; a legion of grateful patients and professional colleagues; and a worldwide network of tennis chums. But when my son disappeared, my only thought was, "Nicky is all I have."

I collected my goofy Airedale, J.P. and drove down to Greenwich Village, where Nicky had dragged me many times to buy him clothes in funky little shops. We walked all over Washington Square Park, an unbelievable scene, what with the drug dealers, the Rastafarians, and me, the six-foot-one inch woman, shoulders like a halfback, with her Airedale on a string. It's a wonder I didn't get arrested, but I tailed every kid who looked remotely like Nicky until I got close enough to see that it was not my son. When it got dark, we went home. I called Grandpa, who said tersely, "No word." I called Nicky's mother: "No word." I called every person who could possibly have information: Nothing. On Tuesday morning, after seeing my patients, I went to the Sheep Meadow in Central Park with J.P. and showed Nicky's picture around. No luck. In the afternoon, we tried Washington Square Park again and stayed until dusk. That evening, leads finally began to develop, but they conflicted. One informant, the friend-of-a-friend type, swore he had seen Nicky riding a bike on Park Avenue. Another person closer to Nicky reported that she had lunched with him on Saturday, and he had claimed he was going to run away to Jamaica. I couldn't believe that she hadn't reported this to me immediately, but she hadn't known he was missing until Tuesday and added, "Nicky says a lot of things. I didn't believe him."

The Jamaica scenario made sense. It tied in with his taste in music, his posters, and the flag on his wall. And on a prep school application, he had been asked, "Who do you admire the most?" Answer: Bob Marley. But then, if he had gone to Jamaica, how could he have been seen on Park Avenue on a bike? I went to the skateboard/bike shop where he sometimes hung out. I showed the owner his picture. "He looks familiar," the young man said, "but I think he's into skateboards, not bikes." This seemed a minor point, so I said, "I know he's into skateboards, but he might have bought a bike, and if he did, it would have been here." He wrinkled his brow, looked once more at Nicky's picture, and said he thought Nicky had been there on Sunday morning, but he hadn't seen him since, and he hadn't bought a bike. "He's not into bikes," the kid repeated. "He's into skateboards. There's a difference."

I walked away mulling over this lesson in the fine distinctions of youth culture. Before that moment, I would have thought, "What difference, bike or skateboard?" But the shop owner made it sound as if Nicky would not be caught dead on a bike, yet I wanted very much to believe that he had been sighted on Park Avenue. I took J.P. and went through the questioning routine again: Central Park, Washington Square, back and forth. No result. I called a teacher at his old boarding school and asked him to quiz Nicky's best friend there, Tom. Under threat of being expelled, Tom admitted that Nicky had once said that if he ever ran away, it would be to Negril Beach in Jamaica. That was enough. I told Arleen to book me on a flight to Jamaica. She was stupefied. "You could get into serious trouble wandering around down there. You have no idea where to look." Usually,

I follow Arleen's suggestions to the letter. Her sense of what is good for me is nearly infallible, but after ten minutes of arguing, I cut her off. She was angry, but she recognized my stubborn look and gave up. My friend Dick Savitt, who visited Jamaica every winter, confirmed that Negril was where the kids went and added, "Be careful. Some of the people are very unfriendly, and sometimes there are murders."

The next day after surgery, I was on my way to Montego Bay, Jamaica, touching down just before nine in the evening. When I got to the immigration desk, I was handed a form on which I had to state my destination in Jamaica. I hedged and said my plans were open ended. The official grumpily accepted this but was adamant on one point: unless I had hotel reservations, I would not be allowed to land. He handed me a list of hotels. You can gauge my state of mind from the one I chose, the Doctor's Cave Hotel.

At the hotel, a young Jamaican named Jump took my suitcase to my room. "How are you doing?" he asked with a classic island rhythm. He was so reassuringly friendly that I confessed I wasn't doing very well. I told Jump that I was in Jamaica to look for a missing boy and asked him about the haunts of teenagers in Montego Bay. He described a thriving disco scene and didn't seem averse to doing some checking at the discos after he got off work. In fact, his toothy grin suggested he liked the idea. I showed him a picture of Nicky, and he left the room whistling.

Before going to bed, I called Lady Sara Churchill, who knows everybody of significance on the island. She said she would ask the head of immigration in Montego Bay to personally check the entry records and soon called back to say that no "Nick Raskind" had entered Jamaica the previous week. I went to bed but couldn't sleep and finally got out of bed at six in the morning and took a cab to the airport, nearly empty at that hour. I found two officers sitting at a desk guarding the entrance to the office of immigration. In spite of Lady Sarah's report, I was determined to check the flight records personally. I explained my mission, but the officers said that the flight lists were still mixed together, and it would be impossible to go through thousands of unsorted entry forms. However, they soon realized that I was not going to leave, so they heaved a sigh and took a look, but again nothing turned up. I simply sat in the office, staring ahead. Eventually, I realized the officers were speaking to me, saying for the fourth time, "Go home, your son is not in Jamaica."

Back at the hotel I reconnected with Jump, who reported that he had found nothing on his round of discos, but his energetic attitude made me feel brighter.

"Jump," I said, "we have to go to Negril. Have you got a car?"

He didn't have one himself, but he thought he could procure one. Within the hour, I was riding down the Jamaican coast in a minivan with Jump and his friend Johnson, the van's owner and a driver par excellence. We sailed down the road through Hopewell, Lucea, and Grand Island, stopping several times on the fifty-mile trip to show Nicky's picture in hotels, but no one had seen him. When we were near our destination, I checked into the Sundowner Hotel and left my bag there before continuing into Negril, which Jump and Johnson called "a pot smoker's paradise" where "anything" could happen.

Meriam had given me the name of a contact with a nearby estate called Seagrate, so I thought I might as well start my search there. Jump and Johnson found the address easily, and we rang a little bell next to a "Bad Dog" sign. Shortly, the Jamaican caretaker appeared and reported that the owners of the house were out of town. Like Jump and Johnson, the caretaker, Elijah, was sympathetic and gentle. I poured out the story of Nicky's disappearance, and he said simply, "If he's in Negril, we'll find him."

Leaving Elijah at Seagrate, we drove back to the beach, passing slowly by the young people. Occasionally my heart would skip a beat, but it was never Nicky. Eventually, Jump spotted a little Jeep with POLICE written on it, which we flagged down. The officer, who introduced himself as Constable Francis, told us he had been given Nicky's name and a brief description by a New York detective but had seen no one who fit. I had been told stories of Americans in Jamaica disappearing into the hills where not even the police are courageous enough to search. I worried that the ever-confident Nicky might have walked into the countryside following his Rastafarian dream. Out there, anything could have befallen him.

As Jump, Johnson, and I continued our circuit of Negril, the dread in me began to build. I became more feverishly attentive with every passing moment. And then I received a gift, perhaps the greatest gift of my life. No more than two minutes after we left the constable, I saw Nicky. He was barefooted, coming toward me wearing shorts and a T-shirt, walking with a Jamaican youth whose dreadlocks came down to his shoulders. The two were conversing in a familiar way.

I yelled, "There he is!" and pointed at Nicky.

Jump and Johnson looked intently ahead.

"I see him, too!"

"Slow down! Slow down!"

"Let's be cool."

Everyone was talking at once.

Johnson slowed the car and Nicky continued unawares toward the van. I put my head out the window as he came alongside and yelled, "Nicky! It's me! Get in the van!" He was shocked.

"What are you doing here? I'm not coming with you!"

I grabbed his arm through the window, but he wrenched free.

"Get him!"

That was all Jump and Johnson needed. Nicky had a good start, but they caught him and brought him under control. The Jamaican youth with Nicky was frozen in his tracks, staring with big eyes. I was shaking with emotion but managed to say, "Get him in the van." When they tried, Nicky began to struggle and throw serious punches. The scene was growing uglier by the second. The Jamaican youth fled.

"Nicky," I yelled, "you come with me or you come with the police."

At this, he became more manageable, and we got him into the back of the van, but the unpleasantness did not stop. Nicky was crying and screaming that this was his place, that he didn't want me there, and that he never wanted to see me again. And then he hit me. It was just on the arm, but it hurt. It hurt in many ways.

Jump and Johnson were marvelous, saying in their laid-back Jamaican way, "Take it easy, man. Take it easy." They got the situation stabilized enough for us to get going. We drove back to tell Elijah not to continue his search, and as I got out of the car at Seagrate, I heard Nicky yelling at Jump and Johnson, "Do you know who that is? That's my father! That person is my father!" Over and over, he shouted, "That's my father!" Each time I heard it I winced. Meanwhile, Jump and Johnson remained calm in the face of Nicky's onslaught. They gave the impression that there was nothing odd about a woman who was looking for her son turning out to be the boy's father.

Years later, Nicky explained that he had been attempting to play on the Jamaican paranoia over homosexuality. In his street-hustler way, he was using any tactic he thought would give him leverage, just trying to distract his captors so he could get away into the countryside. He also started to speak in Jamaican patois, which he had been practicing with Alex back in New York. He claims that Jump and Johnson were shocked by his knowledge of this idiom, but nothing he did caused them to loosen their hold.

Elijah came to the car to say hello to Nicky, and upon receiving a stony silence, turned to me and asked pleasantly if I would need help getting to the airport. I peered at Nicky, looking ready to bolt at any moment, and replied, "Yes. I think I will." Elijah promised to round up Constable Francis and meet us at the edge of town to escort us back to the Montego Bay airport. A wave of relief spread over me. I was going to get my son home. A few minutes later, Jump, Johnson, Nicky, and I were sitting on the terrace at a restaurant overlooking the beach. I asked Nicky if he was hungry, and he said that he didn't eat during the day, only at night, the Rastafarian way. He looked at me with a defiant sneer and said, "But I'll have rum." I glanced over at Jump and Johnson, both of whom looked discreetly into the distance, the corners of their mouths twitching slightly. To say the least, rum was not my idea of a proper lunch for a thirteen-year-old, but Nicky might be looking for a pretext to start another awful scene, so I didn't argue. Besides, I thought rum might have a sedative effect, which at this point was much to be desired. I needed some sedation myself. I ordered lunch and three beers for the adults and rum for the kid.

And the atmosphere did loosen up, with me swigging my Red Stripe beer, and Nicky working on a serving of 126-proof Wray & Nephew Rum with a chaser of Ting, a Jamaican grapefruit soda. We began to talk a little bit. Nicky kept repeating that I had ruined his life in New York and that Jamaica was his home now. By following him to Jamaica, I had ruined his life again. But at least we were communicating. Quietly, Jump and Johnson got up from the table and walked away. They were two of the best psychologists I ever met, and with no cue from me they saw that Nicky and I were at the point where we needed privacy.

Half an hour later, Elijah showed up with Constable Francis, but I canceled the police escort. I knew that it was no good to simply drag Nicky home by force. He would just take off again. Eventually, I got him to agree to come home if I arranged for him to live on neutral ground, not with me, or his mother, or his grandpa, or his aunt. This could be arranged by moving him in with his friend Alex, whose parents were people of means who liked Nicky and would welcome him into their home. To sweeten the offer, I said he could choose his next school without any interference. And those were the terms to which he reluctantly agreed.

Before leaving Negril, we stopped at Ozzie's Shack, where Nicky had been staying. He wanted to pick up his things and say good-bye to some of his Jamaican friends. Popular with the backpacking set, Ozzie's consisted of a series of small clapboard cabins, each with one room and no plumbing. Nicky disappeared into his cabin, while Jump and Johnson guarded the door and windows. I stayed in the van trying to keep a low profile, but I could hear them saying, "We ain't got all the time in the world, man. Your father wants to get goin'." As I sat waiting, a jovial Jamaican walked over and addressed me, waving his hand in the direction of Nicky's cabin.

"I'm Sonny, the caretaker here. I told your boy to go home, but he wouldn't listen. We call him Rastaman. We couldn't tell him nothing, but Rastaman's a good boy."

I thanked him and inwardly thanked the fates that Nicky had fallen in with this kindly character rather than some machete-wielding fanatic. While Sonny and I were talking, Nicky came up, said a warm farewell to Sonny, and got in the van. Things were under control but still very tense. Nicky and I were both simmering, each feeling self-righteous. Jump and Johnson did their best to lighten the mood, but it was a tough sell.

In the town of Reading, just outside of Montego Bay, we stopped at the estate of Lady Sarah Churchill. I wanted to let her know that we had found Nicky and to thank her for her efforts. As we pulled in, the car was surrounded by a mass of Jack Russell terriers, at least twelve of them, seemingly intent on attacking the car. The dogs were a part of Lady Sarah's security precautions. She was a remnant of colonial Jamaica and had once been brutally assaulted by members of an opposition political movement.

Lady Sarah appeared, and having shooed the dogs away, peered at me through the window of the van, saying, "Any luck?"

"There he is," I said, pointing over my shoulder.

She invited us inside, and after a few minutes of watching him sulk on the divan, she said, "Nicky must have been very unhappy in New York. Maybe he should stay here with me for a few days to cool off."

"That is a very good idea," Nicky chimed in, suddenly communicative.

"Thank you, but no," I said firmly. "He's coming home with me."

Then, in quite a natural way, she asked Nicky, "Well then, would you like to stay with Alex when you get back? My daughter has offered to let you stay in her home."

Nicky looked over at me, perhaps for the first time beginning to believe that my earlier offer had not been a con.

"Yes," he said. "That is the only way I will go."

Before we arrived at the Montego Bay airport, Nicky wanted to make just one more stop. He directed Johnson to pull over to a roadside stand, and he proceeded to buy souvenir T-shirts. Suddenly he was acting as if we were on vacation buying T-shirts! I was stunned by his lack of remorse over all the trouble he had caused, but I decided that this typical tourist activity might be a signal that the tide had turned. We spent some of my money and then moved on to the airport, where we were lucky to find spots on a flight leaving almost immediately. After thanking Jump and Johnson for their help, we approached the immigration post, which was manned by the same two officers who had advised me to go home earlier in the day. I was afraid there would be trouble, but one of the officers merely looked at me and then at Nicky, saying nothing of his having sneaked into Montego Bay under a phony name.

"I see you found your son," she said evenly, and then turned to Nicky. "Why do you give your mother such a hard time?"

Nicky looked at her for a couple of very long seconds, while I was thinking, "Here we go again with the mother thing."

But Nicky just as evenly replied, "Because she gives me such a hard time."

We boarded the nearly empty plane and settled into a bank of three seats, leaving the middle one vacant for a little space between us. We were both overwrought. I had been stirred up for a week, had hardly slept that whole time, and was emotionally exhausted, but now I could see light at the end of the tunnel. I began to relax. Nicky also showed signs of calming down. We both knew it was time to start mending fences, a process that has never come easily in the Raskind family.

At first, we chatted only about the details of the chase. Nicky told me that I had been incredibly lucky to spot him since he rarely used that road. Had I checked it the day before, the day after, or even ten minutes before or ten minutes after, he would not have been there.

"Nicky," I replied, "it wouldn't have made any difference if I'd found you at that moment or not. I wouldn't have left Jamaica without finding you."

He mulled this over and nodded slowly. I think that statement pointed up how important he was to me, in spite of the things I had done that had angered him. Seemingly none of the toys I had given him, or the stories I had read to him, or advice, or lectures, or praise, or hugs had the power of that statement. I know this is true, because Nick himself has said that our talk on the plane was one of the high-water marks of our relationship. It seemed to him that we were finally conversing as adults. I went on to say, perhaps for the first time, "I know I've been far from the perfect father. I've made many mistakes. You've had to endure a great deal from both your parents. It's been confusing and hard, but we have to keep trying." That admission made an impression on Nick that has lasted until this day.

It was a fine talk, but at the very moment father and son were connecting, a vial of hash oil was cracking open in Nick's sneaker. He had managed to conceal this potent marijuana distillation right under the noses of Jump and Johnson. According to Nick, when the vial broke, the whole plane began to smell like a skunk, but to his disbelief I didn't notice. "Oblivious," he says, shaking his head. Pardon me for concentrating on my son's emotional state rather than on the smell of his sneakers. So, at the airport in Atlanta, as we made a mad dash to catch an early flight to LaGuardia, Nick was squishing along, stinking up the airport and keeping an eye out for the police. When he got home, he squeezed that stuff out of his sneakers and smoked it or sold it; I don't know which. But I didn't know about that then. Thank goodness I didn't. For me it was enough to know that I had my boy again.

I took Nick to Forest Hills and presented him to his grandfather. On the plane, I had asked Nicky how he could have done this to everyone who loved him so much, and he had replied that the only pain he regretted was to his little half-brother and his grandfather. He was still too resentful to include me or his mother on the list. Grandpa and grandson went up to his room, almost as if Nick had just come from an uneventful evening in the city. I poured myself a healthy vodka and orange juice and sat in the kitchen. A few minutes later, Grandpa joined me, and I told him all that had happened. Eventually, I went upstairs and climbed into bed in my sister's room. Nicky was just next door in my old room. In thirty seconds I was asleep and had my first decent rest in a week.

I kept my bargain with Nick. He stayed for quite some time at his friend Alex's house. Alex's mother loved him. Nick can be charming and cooperative if it suits his purposes, or he can threaten to burn down your school. He is a player and, I must sorrowfully admit, a skilled manipulator who enjoys the sensation of putting one over. He is as difficult for me to understand as I must have been for my parents, and he is just as hard on me as I was on them. When I told him that I had been so upset over his disappearance that I had suffered three separate tachycardia attacks, and that I could have died from any one of them, he replied, "Don't do what you did to me again, and you won't get any tachycardia attacks." That's a tough answer.

In one way, our Jamaican adventure restored my son to me, but in another, it took him away. Afterward, I had to face the fact that without using brute force I could no longer control my child. I had used force in Jamaica, but I would not use it again. Nick had made his stand. Psychiatry, Outward Bound, strict schools, lenient schools, progressive schools, public schools—nothing worked. Jamaica had shown me what he was capable of, if pushed too hard. For weeks after, I had a recurring dream in which my son was lost, and I was endlessly searching for him, repeatedly calling out, "Nicky, where are you, Rastaman?"

After stints at local schools, one for the gifted, one for the troubled, one with individual tutoring, Nick finally ended up at another very good prep school in Massachusetts, the Williston Northampton School. I was feeling good about his chances there, having visited him and observed that he seemed to be doing well. And he might have continued to do so if I had not made a crucial mistake: I let him have a car for off-campus use. Technically, he was not supposed to have a car while at the school, but he had a driver's license and had made arrangements to have one of my cars, a Nissan Pathfinder, garaged off-campus so that he could use it on weekends. It was a typical Nick Raskind plan, somewhere in the shadows between legitimate and illegitimate. Yes, I was still indulging him, perhaps fearful that he would run off again if not indulged.

Things were going very well until I received a fateful phone call. I was in Miami, Florida, coaching Patty Murren in the Rolex Junior Championships. It was work, but it was the first time I had been out of the office for a year, so it felt like a vacation. On the evening of our first night in Miami I was having dinner with Patty and Arleen at the Doral Hotel. There must have been 500 junior players with their coaches and families in the restaurant. They all heard the announcement over the loudspeaker system: "Dr. Richards. Please report to the telephone." The operator told me that I had a phone call from Easthampton, Massachusetts. A teacher on the other end of the line said, "Dr. Richards. There has been an incident at school and your son has been arrested."

"What happened?"

"He was driving his car on the school campus."

"What?"

"Yes, he was driving his car on campus."

"Well," I said, "that's unfortunate, but it can't be too terrible an infraction. Deal with it as you normally would. Nick has to take responsibility for his actions."

I hung up and went back to have my dinner. Five minutes later, I got another phone call, this one from a policeman.

"Your son is in the jail. He was arrested for driving on campus while intoxicated."

Evidently, Nick and some friends had made a beer run to town and were drinking most of it on the way back. When a policeman started to follow them, Nick tried to outrun him and reach the safety of the campus, compounding his crime. I made a quick call to a friend in Easthampton, who referred me to a local lawyer, who got Nick out of jail, but that was the end of his career at Williston Northampton School. He was summarily dismissed. I paid the fine and we retrieved the car. As my thank-you gift for handling the situation, Nick managed to get a speeding ticket on his way back to Easthampton to be sentenced for drunken driving.

The Williston Northampton debacle marked the end of Nick's formal education at age seventeen, though I use the word "formal" in the loosest sense. Shortly afterward, he took off for California claiming that a friend of his had lined up a job for him parking cars at the famous Hotel del Coronado in San Diego and had offered him a place to stay. Like any good con man, Nick knew that specifics make a story sound good.

"I think this is a bad idea," I said, "but I can't do much to stop you. Keep in touch."

When I heard from him a week later, he announced that he was calling me from a phone booth on the beach in San Diego.

He had no job, no place to stay, no money. And then, when I ventured something in the nature of an I-told-you-so, with typical chutzpah Nick wanted to know how I could be so heartless as to leave him in that situation. As always, he had an angle. I reminded him that he had put himself in this predicament. I felt neither guilty nor responsible.

But he was right. I couldn't leave him in that situation. I pulled some strings and made arrangements for him to stay with my friends, the Gellers, in La Jolla. Years before, they had sheltered me during the media storm over my unmasking, and now they were willing to shelter my son. He seemed to settle down for a short while and even got a job in a boutique. But then the familiar reports began to come in: Nick was in trouble. He was promoting rave parties, he was involved with drugs, he was in danger of being attacked by unsavory associates, he was part of a gambling operation, the police were after his partner, the police were after him, he had to get out of La Jolla. I listened to these reports, unable to comprehend the details and unable to distinguish truth from fiction. I was growing numb.

He did get out of town, moving to Venice, California. I visited him there and found him living in an apartment in a nice garden complex. I began to think he was stabilizing, just enjoying his youth. I wished he were in school, but that battle had been fought and apparently lost. However, as always with Nick, turmoil was just around the corner.

One day, I got a call at the office from a doctor in Los Angeles reporting that Nick had experienced a convulsion. He might have a brain tumor, and he needed an MRI, which I okayed immediately. I continued with my patients and got a report later in the day that the MRI was normal and Nick was being discharged from the hospital. The attending physician tactfully suggested that the convulsion might have been drug-induced. On a personal level, I found this disturbing. On a professional level, I had to agree that it was likely. Shortly after this incident, Nick came home to New York. If we had made any progress since Nick had run off to Jamaica, it was that afterward he always kept in touch, and he always felt that he could come home. It might not seem like much of a triumph, but it was something.

I was encouraged when Nick agreed to go back to school for his high school diploma, but shortly afterward he started missing class. When he returned from a mysterious trip to Miami with a horribly fractured hand, something that could not have been a normal accident but must have come from punching someone, I blew sky high, and we stopped speaking. However, Nick continued to plug away at his schooling, while at the same time starting an edgy clothing business called Head Hunters, which eventually turned into a million-dollar enterprise. Nick says that he would have stopped school altogether and concentrated exclusively on business, but he wanted to finish high school for me. He did, and I still have his diploma on display in my office.

In the years since he got that diploma, Nick has been up and down. Head Hunters flourished with huge sales in Japan, but the business eventually went under when the Japanese economy tanked. He gambled professionally for a while and became an expert at many games, especially blackjack. He was the type of high roller that casinos fly out to Vegas and provide with a complimentary luxury suite and a private room in which to gamble. He bought a Ferrari and then a Ducati racing motorcycle. He rented an apartment with a view of the front door to my office. I said, "You run three thousand miles to get away from me, and now you come back here so you can check on my comings and goings?" He just said it was a good location.

During this time, Nick began to seriously study karate. He had been involved with martial arts from childhood, but he was finally stable enough to get serious about it. He trained from the ages of twenty to twenty-five and ultimately got his black belt in Chinese Kenpo, a very rigorous form of karate considered by many to be the most deadly of the martial arts. At twenty-four, he was a North American Sport Karate Association national champion in two divisions.

Then things changed again. Somehow, his income dried up. Maybe his gambling luck went bad. Anyway, Nick moved back in with my father, which was a great thing for both my father and for me. By this time, Grandpa Raskind was in his late nineties, and though his health remained fairly good, he was getting addled. When Nick and his beautiful girlfriend, Oxana, took up residence in the house, I was relieved to have a close relative there in addition to the full-time nurse. Grandpa loved having Nick around, and he also loved Oxana. When she would come in with her midriff on display, he would say delightedly, "Oh. I can see your navel."

But Nick was the key thing. He loved spending time with Grandpa. Grandpa would ask him, "Where's Dick? Where's Dick?" and Nick would say, "He's in the city seeing patients." And Grandpa would say, "That's good. How are you doing?"

And Nick would say, "I'm doing okay." And Grandpa would ask, "Why are you here?" And Nick would say, "I'm living here."

Nick and the nurse did not get along well. My father was still a strong man, and she tried to keep him immobile a lot of the time, afraid he would escape her control and hurt himself. She was dictatorial, and that rubbed Nick the wrong way. He often defied her and took Grandpa for walks outside, which Grandpa loved. One night, when Grandpa was ninety-nine, Nick gave the nurse a night off so Grandpa could be out from under her thumb. He and Oxana called me and said, "He keeps asking for a drink. Can we give him a little one?" It was the holidays, so I said, "Sure, you can give him a little drink. At this stage, what could it hurt?" The three of them were full of good cheer and Grandpa apparently downed his vodka and tomato juice with great gusto. Nick reported later, "It threw him for a loop. He couldn't even move, but he was happy."

At one hundred years of age, Grandpa's health failed seriously, and he was hospitalized for good. Nick visited him every day and showed great patience and tenderness. I saw my son's best side under those trying circumstances. During Grandpa's last hours, Nick went over to his bedside. Grandpa was in a fog, but he recognized Nick and grabbed his arm. Nick said, "What is it, Grandpa?" Grandpa pulled him closer and said, "Get me out of here!"

I trust that in similar circumstances, Nick will be as kind to me as he was to Grandpa, and if I say, "Get me out of here," I hope he will give me the same fond answer he gave Grandpa: "I wish I could. I really wish I could."

CHAPTER 5

An Adolescence for Renée

MY CASE WAS MUCH different from those of the so-called "transsexual teens" who are profiled on the Health Channel these days. I started my life as a woman on the verge of middle age. As Dr. Renée Richards, I settled into a routine very much like the one Dr. Richard Raskind had pursued: medical duties, tennis at the club, dinner out, a little romance. It was very nice but in a safe way. If the blow-up over my unmasking in California had not occurred, I might have gone on like that indefinitely, but the vilification that came afterward struck me as a challenge to my right to a life as Renée and, like a rebellious teenager, I insisted that Renée be accepted on her own terms. My fight for recognition and much of Renée's tennis career can be seen as her adolescence, full of the risk taking and extravagant behavior that youngsters often exhibit.

I risked a great deal, even if you discount the death threats.

As an eye surgeon, I had been making more than a hundred thousand dollars a year, more than most top tennis professionals made in those days. Though I was accused of having a sex change to make a killing in tennis, I actually cut my income to a pittance, and I came out of the experience deeply in debt. Furthermore, medicine, especially in a highly technical area like eye surgery, requires never-ending study, and to neglect it is to risk falling so far behind that it is impossible to catch up. Renée took that risk. In spite of dire warnings by friends, family, and colleagues, I decided to let Renée have her adolescence.

The early days of my tennis career hardly count as part of my adolescence. They were too surreal to fit into any category, but eventually the media pressure and mob scenes settled down enough to allow me to concentrate on living rather than just surviving. Once I gained permission to play on the women's tour, I had to go on the satellite circuit to build a ranking that would allow me to play in major tournaments. I was thrown in with juniors on the rise and veterans winding down. Once again I was an unclassifiable creature. I was old, but rather than winding down, I was just beginning, so on that basis alone I was an oddball, never mind my gender history.

Like a kid at a new school, I had to prove myself, and I did gradually gain acceptance and some popularity with most of the players, partly because of my sincere effort to be friendly but mostly because it soon got around that I was an avid student of tennis and had the genius to analyze the play of others. I tried to help those who came to me, not only with their strokes but also with tactics, which is the toughest challenge for gifted young players. There was not exactly a constant parade of youngsters seeking my tutelage, but I gave a good deal of instruction, especially to the kids from Eastern Europe and the Far East.

In spite of my age and tennis wisdom, I lived hand to mouth just like the other players on the satellite circuit. My pocketbook was close to empty when I arrived in Pensacola, one more stop on a tour that had so far produced mediocre results. Satellite players are provided housing, usually with volunteers from the host club. I was assigned to a pleasant family with several children. My hosts, Paul and Sheila, were around forty, which made my surrogate parents younger than me. When they first volunteered their spare room, they may have expected to receive a teenager with braces, but the couple showed me the same consideration they would have lavished on a vulnerable adolescent, which in a way I was.

Like everyone else who adopted me at that time of my life, my Pensacola family got more than they signed up for. The paparazzi had no respect for their privacy and would often knock on the door or poke around the yard peeking in the windows. Rather than blaming me, my hosts closed ranks, not only providing food and shelter but also protecting me in any way they could, sneaking me in and out of the house, chauffeuring me about, cheering for me at my matches, and even confronting the boorish reporters. I'll never forget how Paul stood on the front porch of his house, leaning over the railing and gesturing as he shouted, "She don't want to talk to you. Get outta here!"

Maybe the support I received from Paul and his family made a difference, because I finally won a tournament championship in Pensacola. In the finals, I beat Chris Evert's younger sister, Jeanne. She was a very good player, not quite as good as Chrissie, but with the same strokes. On the one hand, I was happy, but I felt a bit of dread as I accepted the championship trophy. I knew my win might bring some cutting comments from players I had not managed to befriend. I was right, but one thing that made me feel better was the attitude taken by Jeanne Evert's mother. I had never met Mrs. Evert before, but she was in a unique position to dislike me.

In those days many articles were published contrasting Renée Richards to the ultrafeminine Chrissie Evert. In the popular mind, Chrissie was the embodiment of what a woman tennis professional should be: pretty, blonde, soft-spoken, light on her feet. So, whenever anybody wanted to throw a scare into the public about the transsexual threat, my dimensions and characteristics were invariably compared to Chrissie's, making it seem that she was a tender flower about to be squashed by a surgically enhanced steamroller. I don't know how many of these articles Mrs. Evert had read, but she couldn't have been nicer in Pensacola, wishing me well just as she did all the players who had competed against her daughter.

After Pensacola, I immediately experienced another set of highs and lows in a Tampa tournament. It was hot and muggy, and I had to make my way through the qualifying rounds to get into the main draw. I managed to do so, winning three matches on clay in two days, really tough for a forty-two-year-old, especially when two of the matches are played back to back, as usually happens in the qualies. But I had trained like a demon to keep up with the youngsters. At one point, my body fat was measured at 11 percent, so it was not a fluke that I could bear up under the brutal schedule.

Then I learned that I had drawn the top seed, Rosie Casals, as my first-round opponent in the main event. In spite of having run myself ragged in qualifying, I managed to beat Rosie in straight sets 6–4, 6–2. I moved well, chased down every ball, and made very few errors. This showed that I did not have to rely on overpowering a diminutive opponent, so I felt good about the way I had won. I eventually lost in the final to Laura DuPont, but the focus remained on Rosie, who was a much bigger name than anyone I had ever beaten in singles. Predictably the complaints started again, led by Glynis Coles and her friend Lesley Charles, mid-level players from England making good money playing on the U.S. tour. These were not well-educated players of foreign extraction, like Virginia Wade and Wendy Turnbull, who never complained about me. Frankly, I doubt Glynis knew what a transsexual was. She probably thought I was still a man. As always, they complained that I was too overpowering to play with the women. Never mind that up to that point I had lost many times and that I eventually lost in the finals of this tournament. By the way, Glynis never played me in singles, but we met in doubles. She didn't have enough conviction to refuse to play a match against me, which would have meant losing her prize money. Complaining to the press and not shaking my hand at the end of a match were more her style. My other memory from that Tampa tournament is of being knocked cold by my doubles partner, Billie Jean King. I turned back from the net, and she crushed a volley right into my forehead from only ten feet away. I woke right up, more stunned than injured, and carried on. We won the tournament.

My results in Pensacola and Tampa improved my ranking

enough to allow me to compete in bigger events, which is how I wound up playing in São Paolo, Brazil. I began well by beating Paula Smith in the first round, but then Paula complained about my participating in the tournament. I might have shrugged this off as sour grapes after a loss if it weren't for my long-standing friendship with Paula, dating back to when I was living anonymously in Newport Beach. Paula came from nearby San Diego, and I had practiced with her and helped her a little with her game. I even had a passing acquaintance with her parents. If a friend and countrywoman would use my background against me, I felt I might never be accepted. The more I thought about it, the more depressed I got.

I was rescued from my mood by Martina Navratilova. With my usual luck, I drew her in an early round, and even though her career was in its first stage, she was already one of the world's best players. The match was a good one, with Martina winning it in two tiebreaker sets: 7–6, 7–6. Even though I had lost, it was by a narrow margin to a top player, so I had reason to be proud. When we met at the net after the match, Martina gave me a warm hug and we headed for the dressing room. Most of the tournaments on the women's circuit are in pretty elegant places, and the showers are usually private, consisting of single, enclosed stalls. But the facility at this venue was far from elegant, just one big cement room with shower heads sticking out of the walls. Martina and I wound up in the shower at the same time, and she was completely friendly and completely unconcerned about being in such a revealing situation with a notorious transsexual. So, after some mutual compliments on the level of tennis in our match, we didn't just turn to the wall and ignore each other. We continued to chat, and I mentioned how upset I was at the bad feelings that had come out of my beating Paula Smith.

"Don't be discouraged," she said. "Keep it up. You're going to do just fine."

An hour before, I had nearly beaten Martina. The next time, I might succeed. From a strictly competitive point of view, she might have gained by undercutting me. Instead, she gave me a pep talk. On that occasion, Martina was the source of great encouragement, and in the future there would be many other moments of kindness and support between us.

The scene I have just described is very unusual for women's events. The São Paolo tournament was an invitational affair with good prize money, but not part of any series, which is one reason why the facilities were more like those in an old-time gymnasium. Generally speaking, high-class tournaments offer much more elaborate amenities. The players shower privately and put on their underwear before they come back to their lockers to finish dressing. I never saw an exhibitionist while I was on the tour, though there is little prudery, especially among the veterans. In general, the woman on tour are more like businesspeople on a job than they are like the members of a local tennis club, where gossiping in the dressing room is part of the fun. If you want to converse at a tournament, you are more likely to do it in the players' lounge. Professionals tend to get in and out of the locker room quickly without much gab. In fact, the primary sound I associate with the women's locker room is of blow-dryers, but I think the same can be said of the men's locker room in this era.

By the time I hit the women's tour, I was accustomed to the

women's locker room from having used the one at the John Wayne Tennis Club in Newport Beach. I quickly observed that one of the basic differences between male and female behavior is towel placement. Men tie it around their waists and women fasten it up under their armpits. I kept mine under my armpits. As far as I know, my presence in the locker room was an issue just once on the professional tour, and then only in a roundabout way.

The incident happened during one of the early big-time tournaments I entered after I returned from South America, and I was very much looking forward to competing again with Martina and other top players. The tournament did not start well for me. During my opening match, I repeatedly aced JoAnne Russell, who started shaking her fist at me and then progressed to giving me the finger. Next, I played Kerry Reid from Australia. She had won the Australian Open in 1977 and was highly ranked. Before we even started the match, she and her husband, Raz Reid, complained vigorously about me. Raz pretty much called the shots for Kerry, functioning as both her manager and coach. The first few games of our match were close, and I just managed to eke out wins, but when I got a service break to go ahead 4–1 in the first set, Raz left his seat in the stands and came down to the court.

"That's it," he announced. "She's not playing anymore."

Kerry picked up her racquets and left, which set off another firestorm of debate over me at every level of tennis and in the national press where headlines proclaimed: "Kerry Reid Walks Off Court in Match with Renée Richards." It was the only time that something so extreme happened because of my playing in a tournament. In retrospect, I think that Raz's attitude sprang in part from the fact that in his playing days, he had shared a locker room with Dick Raskind at the U.S. Open, and he could not make the adjustment to his wife's doing the same with Renée. I don't blame him.

Though many people assume that my presence in the locker room must have been a point of concern, I never seemed to cause much of a stir on the tour, where players can usually be as private as they want. In fact, at the French Open, the male masseur comes in and out of the locker room at will and nobody gives him a second thought. Private clubs are a little different, and when I was famous, there were a couple of complaints about my using the women's facilities. In those cases, it was easy to move to a different club. I never made a fuss.

In my dotage, I have become increasingly discreet in locker rooms. Strange in a way, because I am much less famous now than I used to be and somehow there seem to be more tall women nowadays, so I am not nearly the curiosity I used to be on that score. With age and anonymity have come a welcome freedom from scrutiny, but I don't hang around the women's area much. I use my own hot tub and my own masseuse.

But the locker room in all its aspects was not on my mind during that first trip to South America. In spite of the complaints from Paula Smith during the São Paolo tournament, Renée was beginning to enjoy her adolescence, and she was making friends. I was invited to play in Buenos Aires by Raquel Giscafre, who was the promoter of a big event held at the Buenos Aires Lawn Tennis Club. The winner of the tournament would be crowned Campione del Rio de la Plata. I agreed to come.

Buenos Aires in the late 1970s was a little scary. The city

was virtually under martial rule. Everywhere I went there were intense young men with rifles, some barely older than sixteen, standing guard around public buildings and even in certain restaurants. There is nothing like dining under armed guard. Some city streets contained stretches where drivers were not allowed to stop because the authorities feared that a public building would be the victim of a car bomb. The teenage soldiers had permission to shoot you on sight if you stopped. God forbid that anyone would have a flat tire while driving in those blocks.

We had the same kind of guards at the tennis club, but in spite of the implication that we might be attacked by guerrillas, the tournament went smoothly. I beat Ivana Madruga in the final and found that life for the Campione del Rio de la Plata could be a lot of fun, so pleasant in fact that I hung around Buenos Aires for an extra five weeks. There were many friendly young people there, and they were all curious about me. Having spent many months in a cauldron of controversy, I enjoyed the easy way that the people of Buenos Aires related to me. I was traveling by myself, which was rather lonely, and to have them invite me to their homes and to their social functions was wonderful. They saw me as a celebrity, of course, but I felt more the human being in Buenos Aires than I had in a long time. What forty-two-year-old adolescent could resist that feeling? In one of the friendly gestures that made Buenos Aires so appealing, Raquel Giscafre offered to let me stay in her apartment while she was out of town. It was an elegant place on a street of elegant places near the city's government center. Given the bomb situation, the close proximity of government buildings was not reassuring, but I accepted Raquel's invitation anyway.

The tennis club was my social center. Every day I played against some of the men among my new friends, many of them good players who made me cope with the tremendous topspin that South American men put on the ball. I also had a chilling experience when I attended a tournament at the club in which the son of an old friend was playing. I had known young Michael Fishbach since he was a baby. I should say that Dick Raskind knew Michael, but now Renée, having just played in a women's tournament, was watching this baby from Dick's past, a baby who was now sporting a beard. Michael was the son of Joe Fishbach the crusty old pro at the Great Neck Country Club on Long Island, an excellent player in his time and holder of the record for the obstacle course at Fort Dix during World War II. Michael was the pet of his family, unquestionably spoiled. He was a small player but highly competitive and full of Fishbach moxie. In 1977, the year I made my first appearance in the U.S. Open, Michael beat Stan Smith, a former Wimbledon and U.S. Open champion. He accomplished this feat by using a racquet strung so loosely that it was referred to as "spaghetti-strung." This innovation allowed a player to put such severe spin on the ball that it was torturous to return. After Michael's victory, the racquet was outlawed.

Unfortunately, things weren't going Michael's way in his Buenos Aires match. The worse it got, the more he cursed himself, gesticulated, and threw his racquet. To worsen matters, Michael had "rabbit ears," meaning he tended to hear every shuffle, cough, and mumble from the crowd. The audience had consumed more than a few *cervezas*, and though they were not exactly impolite, this was no hushed Wimbledon cathedral of tennis. Perhaps even more annoying, the shouts of the food vendors were an accepted part of the crowd atmosphere. One of them shouted, *"Helados!"* ("Ice creams!") a couple of times during Michael's serve, and Michael suspected it was intentional, so he started glaring at the vendor and screaming back sarcastically, *"Helados! Helados!"* The crowd began to mutter. And maybe the vendor began to yell *"Helados!"* on purpose during Michael's serve. It was not a pleasant scene, but the worst was yet to come.

Finally there was one *"Helados!"* too many, and Michael jumped a three-foot railing and made for the vendor, an act so bizarre that even the raucous Buenos Aires crowd was stunned. The vendor, who was in the lower rows of seats near the court, leaned back and put his ice cream carrying case between himself and the crazy Americano. Michael rushed up to him and started yelling *"Helados!"* in his ear. The minute Michael leaped the railing, I got up and started to run toward him. My move probably kept the crowd from doing something rash. I had become a popular local celebrity, and they were willing to let me deal with Michael if he was a friend of mine.

"Michael! Stop that!"

He turned to me.

"Look around," I said. "This is not Great Neck."

By this time some of the teenage guards had taken an interest in the proceedings and had their automatic weapons half-unslung. Michael glanced around. I was something of an authority figure to him, in spite of my new anatomy. He nodded and started down the aisle. When the crowd saw him heading back to the court, they relaxed and the match went forward. I think Michael lost the match, but the main thing is that he wasn't a casualty. He is now married with children and earns his living doing hiking tours in Vermont, still a free spirit.

BUENOS AIRES WAS FULL of action of various sorts. Many of my new friends were the sons and daughters of German expatriates. There may even have been some former Nazis among their parents, but the youngsters warmly accepted a transsexual Jew. Together we made the rounds of night spots like Zum Zum, a popular rathskeller. Renée stayed out late and partied like any adolescent on the loose. Once, after an evening at Zum Zum's, I was abruptly awakened at five in the morning. Why was the bed trembling? Why were the pictures falling off the walls? Had a bomb gone off? After the trembling ceased, I ventured to the window and looked into the street below, a sure sign of my concern because I detest heights. The people down below were milling about, though seemingly not in a panic-stricken way. I put on a warm-up suit and tried the elevator. It was out of order, but the lights in the stairwell were on, so I went down that way. Outside, I asked what was going on.

"Earthquake."

Nobody seemed overly concerned. The quake registered only about six on the Richter scale, hardly worth noting for the locals, except that it was always good to get out of the building in case the walls caved in. We stood around for a bit, and when the old hands judged it was safe, we went back in. I climbed back up to the apartment, swept up the broken dishes, and re-hung the pictures. I never heard another word about it.

In the next few weeks, I played in tournaments and exhibitions in Uruguay, Bolivia, and Peru. In Carrasco, Uruguay, Jeannie Evert avenged her earlier loss to me in Pensacola. The lighting wasn't so good and the court wasn't so good, but the fans were very friendly. Jeannie beat me in the final and everybody was happy for her, including me. When she came up to the net to shake hands, she was beaming.

"Renée, I've found my country," she said, giving me a hug. Jeannie had been in her sister's shadow for a long time, but at that moment in Uruguay, she was the Evert that everyone was cheering.

On that same trip, we were scheduled to play a nighttime exhibition match and four of us were walking from the hotel to the courts, a distance of about a quarter of a mile, on a narrow dirt path through an area where some construction work was going on. The lighting was poor, so we were picking our way carefully. Raquel Giscafre, who was in the lead, came to a big hole, turned to Mary Carillo and said, "Watch out for the hole." Mary turned to me and said, "Watch out for the hole." But I forgot to repeat the warning to Jane Stratton. There was a thump and a grunt behind me, and when I turned around, I discovered that Jane had disappeared.

"Down here," said a voice from the bowels of the earth.

I looked down and could see Jane's tennis racquet protruding from the hole.

"Renée, you idiot. Take this."

We fished her out unharmed and had a good laugh over it. This was the kind of acceptance I had been hoping for, and I loved being one of the girls on a South American adventure.

In fact, I was having such a good time that I planned a

little exhibition tour with Susanna Villeverde. Susanna's father, a charming man, drove us to the airport in his big yellow school bus. We were the only passengers, and I remember that bus as one of the most memorable courtesy vehicles I've ever been provided. After Papa saw us off, Susanna and I flew to La Paz, Bolivia, which is on a plateau three miles above sea level, so the plane doesn't really have to go down, it just has to sort of settle. The air is so thin that it seems impossible to breathe, and with oxygen deprivation comes the bonus of a brutal headache. The first night, there was no such thing as sleeping. I spent my time at the window of the hotel room gasping for air. If I didn't keep up my deep breathing, the headache would become intolerable. As most travelers do in Bolivia's high altitudes, we drank *mate coca*, which is tea with the coca leaf in it. And we put a coca leaf against our gums. These measures gave some relief, but we were not in La Paz long enough to get truly acclimated, so it was impossible to play well. We had to have oxygen at the umpire's stand so that when we changed sides, we could gulp enough to survive. The stadium was cold, dank, and once again poorly lit. Worse still, we couldn't control the ball in that thin air; it just sailed into the distance nearly every time we hit it. We played some ugly tennis in La Paz.

Peru was a different story. There, I met up with two old friends from my days on the men's tour, Enrique and Eduardo Buse. They welcomed me with open arms, and Susanna and I played some good matches in Buse Stadium, which is named for my friends. We also took a side trip to Lake Titicaca, which some say is the most spiritual lake in the world. I tended to agree as I sat on its banks watching the locals in their reed boats and smelling the smoke from the fire, where an Indian was cooking us a meal of the fish we had caught. The lake is an intense blue, and I marveled at the beauty of its setting among the snowcapped peaks. It seemed a long way from the turmoil and bad feelings I had experienced just weeks before. I left Lake Titicaca with regret.

During my stay in South America, I also played some exhibitions on my own, even going into the interior of Colombia, although I could speak just a few words of Spanish. I wound up in Baranquilla, so far out of the mainstream that the merchants did not accept credit cards, not even American Express. You know you've reached hell-and-gone when you outrun American Express. The court in Baranquilla was like a parking lot, and the lighting was worse than ever. My opponent was a young man. I guess they couldn't find a woman player. Anyway, I beat him, but at the close of the match I knew I was finished with bad courts and bad lighting. I canceled the rest of the tour and never experienced the pleasures of playing in Bucaramanga, Cartagena, and Cali.

It was lucky I canceled because, slipshod adolescent that I was, I had run two days over my visa limit, and the people at the customs office at the Bogotá airport were not amused. They wanted to know what I had been doing for two extra days, and I could barely make them understand that I was in Colombia to play exhibitions.

"*Soy* tennis professional. *Yo* . . . uh . . . play in Baranquilla."

After much eye squinting and a thorough rifling of my effects, they let me go. Thankfully, I had not taken the suggestion of a few friends, which had been to hollow out the handles of my tennis racquets and fill them with cocaine so that I could make a killing when I got back to the States. What would happen to Renée Richards if she were thrown into the Colombian prison population did not bear thinking about. That was not the kind of adventure I was seeking.

Another aspect of my second adolescence was playing World Team Tennis (WTT), a professional circuit started in 1974 and lasting through 1978. This league, in which Billie Jean King was a prime mover, gave me new life when my prospects for playing tennis as a woman were at their bleakest. Even though the WTA had not yet recognized me, the Cleveland Nets offered me a contract. Shortly after I joined the team, it moved to New Orleans and eventually became the Sunbelt Nets. This change was applauded by the players, since there were many more ways to get into mischief in New Orleans than there were in Cleveland.

I guess the adolescent Renée was at her most mischievous when playing for the Nets, where there was a much looser atmosphere than in the more traditional events. Once in San Diego, Vitas Gerulaitis pursued the San Diego Chicken into the stands. This famous character was employed to add entertainment to the WTT experience. However, when he insisted on cackling and flapping his wings during Vitas' serve, Vitas jumped into the stands and the Chicken ran for cover. That was the style on the WTT; I loved that type of thing—as long as no one with automatic weapons was standing by.

The WTT's unusual competitive format was likewise conducive to eccentric behavior. The matches were composed of one set each of men's singles, men's doubles, women's singles, women's doubles, and mixed doubles. Another interesting wrinkle was that World Team Tennis allowed substitutions. If a player was doing poorly, the coaches could substitute any time during the set. Frequently, Bjorn Borg, who played for the Nets and was the number-one player in the world at the time, would be ahead in his match, let's say 4–0, and he would tell Marty Riessen, our coach, "I am tired. I don't want to play anymore." Then he would sit down, and Marty would have to substitute either himself or Iron-Arm Pattison to play the rest of the match. Sometimes the substitute would win, sometimes not. Borg would never have endangered the outcome of a match on the ATP tour, but World Team Tennis seemed a place where you could indulge your whims.

Once, Borg invited the team to his apartment for a special meal of Swedish meatballs. They were quite good, and we were all enjoying them when we heard a strange *ping!* from the closet. Sometime later, we heard another *ping!*

"What is that, Bjorn?"

"Just the strings on my racquet popping."

The average male player in those days strung his racket at a tension of about sixty pounds per square inch, but Borg strung his at eighty, and the strings sometimes popped from the strain.

JOHN LUCAS AND I were usually the Nets' mixed doubles team. John was a great tennis player who also played professional basketball in the NBA. He and I bonded in spite of coming from very different backgrounds. We were known on tour as the Odd Couple. John was black, and I was white; he was six foot three, and I was six foot one; he was a man, and I used to be. We were also both left-handed, which affected our game strategy. In women's doubles, I always played the ad court (the court on the players' left) because I was left-handed and had a good reach, so I could use my forehand to handle an opponent's cross-court shot. My left-handedness was such an asset that I frequently played in the ad court with male partners, even great players like Ilie Nastase, who was right-handed. But with John, I never played the ad court, which made me feel quite feminine, along with the wonderful fact that with John, I was not taller than my male partner. But even more important, we played well together. In fact, we had the best mixed doubles record in World Team Tennis, except for Ilie Nastase and Chris Evert, who played for the Los Angeles Strings. They beat us the only time we played, and John and I were hoping for a chance to even the record, but the league folded before that chance came.

Everyone on the Nets had a nickname. Marty Riessen was known as "P.C." for Player Coach, and Wendy Turnbull was known as "The Rabbit" because she was so fast. Andrew Pattison was "Iron Arm." John Lucas was "Luke," and I was "No Way Renée" because I was always doing something that caused my teammates to shake their heads and say, "No way, Renée!" Like most adolescents, I was out for fun, and I didn't see why everything had to be deadly serious, an attitude that led to the banjo controversy.

I thought that New Orleans was a terrific place to take banjo lessons and learn to make one of the signature sounds of the Old South. Dick Raskind had studied the violin, and Renée didn't see any reason why she shouldn't indulge her musical tastes. My choice of the banjo, a happy, carefree instrument, says a lot about my state of mind. I thought it would be easy compared to the violin, but I soon realized how wrong I was. Learning the chords was quite difficult, and the more involved I got, the harder it became on me and on anybody who had to listen to me. But I finally got to the point where I could play a few tunes, among them "Sweet Georgia Brown," "When the Saints Go Marching In," and my showstopper, "Cripple Creek," which is a damned demanding piece, if I do say so myself.

My musical career was not encouraged by Marty Riessen, who was a real straight arrow and especially didn't like it when I brought my banjo on tour. He helped create that problem himself, because he insisted that we hand-carry our baggage so that the airline could never lose it. Especially in the taxicabs to and from the airport, the presence of a banjo irritated Marty because it had to be stretched across people's laps along with the tennis equipment. I never saw it as a big problem. After all, a banjo is about the same shape as a tennis racquet, and I only had three or four of those. Borg used to carry about twenty racquets, and I never saw Marty chastise him for having too much luggage. Obviously, being the number-one player in the world has its perks.

Another thing that irritated Marty was that I never found a racquet I really liked, so I tended to change frequently from one to another. One day I'd be playing with a graphite racquet made by one company, and the next day with an aluminum racquet made by another company, and the following day with something else. Marty thought my level of play would be better if I made a choice and stuck to it. One day he took a look at me using yet another racquet, strode over to the practice court, and, assuming his most authoritative tone, made this pronouncement.

"Renée, you can play with one racquet, and that will be the racquet you're using today. You're not allowed to change anymore."

"Sure, P.C.," I said agreeably.

Of course, by the next week I was interested in a different racquet, so I put the cover of the previous racquet on the new one and went on my merry way. It wasn't long before P.C. saw through my scam.

"That cover isn't fooling anybody. I know you've switched racquets again."

This was silly stuff, but it kept me and my teammates entertained. As long as I kept winning, P.C. let me get away with my little follies. He had to admit I was good for business, especially when teamed with John Lucas, and that was a pleasant surprise considering our fan base. As the Sunbelt Nets, we played all over the South, in places like Huntsville, Birmingham, Tuscaloosa, and Biloxi, right down to little old Thibodeau, Louisiana, and there was seldom any comment about John's race or my gender.

In South La Fourche, pronounced "Soot La Foosh" by the locals, they even auctioned off a Renée Richards racquet for charity. One guy, who looked fresh in from the swamp, came up to me with a big smile.

"What you name? Reeshard?" he asked.

"Richards, actually."

"That you back name. What you front name?"

"Renée."

His smile grew broader.

"Raynay Reeshard! Man, you got a good front name, and you got a good back name! Why you don't pass yousef by my house sometime?"

I was in many Louisiana homes on invitations like this, stuffing my face with Cajun-style shrimp and listening to a band with a big bass fiddle.

The team of Lucas and Richards provided Renée with a surrogate brother to care for her and to help her keep things in perspective. John was great at tennis and basketball, having been an All-American in both at the University of Maryland, but he was also very smart, valedictorian of his high school class and a successful student in college. You could speak intelligently to him and get an intelligent response, which is not always the case in the world of sports. But John was not just a good tennis partner and conversationalist, he was concerned about me on a personal level, and he looked out for me in many ways. In those days, I was still smoking cigarettes sometimes, and he would open up my purse, take out the pack, and throw them away.

"You're making your living with your body," he would say with much seriousness, "and you shouldn't destroy it with cigarettes."

Ironically, he later developed a drug and alcohol problem so severe that it threatened to destroy him. John eventually got treatment, and after retiring from the NBA in 1990, he set up The John Lucas Aftercare Treatment and Recovery Center to help other substance abusers.

John would not tolerate rude remarks about me if it was in his power to stop them. On one occasion, when the Nets were in Indianapolis for a match against the Indiana Loves, he was in a weight room working out, and some men nearby were making snickering remarks about Renée Richards. John let the first ones pass, but when the men kept going, he got up from his weight station and moved over to theirs, where he bent down and added a fifty-pound weight to each end of the bar they were using.

"I don't think you'd better say anything more about Renée," he said, easily lifting their weight plus a hundred more pounds straight over his head.

The men watched that weight rise nine feet in the air and winced as John let it clang to the deck in front of them. That was the end of their remarks about Renée.

However, on one memorable occasion, it was I who came to John's aid. The Nets were in Lakeland, Florida, to play a match. Our team's scheduling was sometimes hard to fathom. We wound up playing nearly anywhere the southern sun shone. Back in those days, the area surrounding Lakeland, which is midway between Orlando and Tampa, was dedicated primarily to orange groves and cattle ranches. Much of the population had what could be generously called a conservatively rural mind-set. The less generous would say "redneck," and not in that accepting "Soot La Foosh" way. We finished our match and left the arena around 11:30 p.m. John, his girlfriend, and I were on the way back to the motel in a rented car when John said he wanted to stop for a six-pack of beer. Now, in spite of all his intelligence, John was pretty naïve about some things. I glanced doubtfully at John's girlfriend, a pretty white girl named Frances.

"I don't know about that, John," I said warily.

"Only take a minute," he replied, entirely missing the reason for my hesitance.

We kept driving, but we couldn't find anything open. Eventually, the buildings thinned out, but before civilization disappeared altogether we saw a lighted place in the distance. It turned out to be a roadhouse with a neon sign out front saying "Bar and Grille." John pulled into the dirt parking lot and stopped among the pickup trucks. The roadhouse door was wide open, and I could see figures in cowboy hats moving about inside. The twang of country music vibrated in the air. It didn't take a genius to see that this was no place for a black basketball player, his white girlfriend, and his transsexual sidekick.

"John, you can't go in there. Let's just forget about the beer."

John brushed this off. He did not believe that any doors were closed to him, including the door to a roadhouse in rural Florida, and no amount of cautious argument from me was going to keep him from walking through it.

"All right. If you have to go in there, I'm going with you."

Frankly, I didn't know whether my presence would be a good or a bad thing. I just knew I had to go. We got out of the car, leaving Frances hunched down in the front seat. The music grew louder as we approached the door. It was Waylon Jennings singing "Tonight the Bottle Let Me Down." I listened to him often. While with the WTT, I had become a country music fanatic. New York transsexual Jew goes country. Just another reason they called me No Way Renée.

When John and I hit the interior of the roadhouse, everybody except Waylon went silent. The people playing pool stood with their cues hanging ominously at their sides. The gray-haired bartender was frozen with a liquor bottle in one hand. A few wiry men sat on stools opposite him, their heads craning in our direction.

No doubt John and I made a riveting sight standing in the doorway: a six-foot-three-inch black man and a six-foot-one-inch white woman, both incredibly fit, both wearing sweat suits.

The silence lasted for a few long moments before one of the men at the bar broke it.

"Holy Christ! A fuckin' nigger!"

At this, I saw John's jaw tighten. Mine did, too. He took a slow look around and then advanced to the bar.

"I would like a six pack of beer," he said.

Instead of complying with John's request, the bartender continued to stand frozen, his eyes darting around the room. He wanted to give John the beer and get us out of there, but with the patrons standing around like a pack of jackals, he didn't dare make a move.

"I'd like a six-pack of beer," John repeated, putting a strong emphasis on each word.

And nothing happened.

The atmosphere was terrifying. It was if they were waiting for someone to bring out a lynch rope, but John stood solid, waiting. I knew it would crack soon and when it did, the result might be ugly. I walked quickly to the bar.

"Please," I said, "I would like to have a six-pack of beer."

I saw a look of relief flood the bartender's face. He couldn't serve a black man, but he could serve a white woman. In a second, his hand darted under the counter and came back holding

a six-pack. In another second he had put it into a brown paper bag and pushed it across the bar to me. I fished some bills
out of my purse and gave them to the bartender. John was still
standing next to me staring ahead.

"Come on, Lucas," I said. "Let's get out of here."

He looked me in the eyes, glanced away for a moment, and
then nodded. We walked out side by side. The night air was
refreshing, but I could feel eyes on my back as we crossed the
parking lot to our car. Frances was still making herself small,
and I don't think she was ever seen. If she had been, the story
might be different. I felt safer as the "Bar and Grille" sign disappeared into the distance, but I wasn't completely comfortable until we were well out of the area.

John and I had an entirely trusting relationship, in spite of
all that might have stood between us, though often that trust
was reflected in banter that might have seemed insulting to
an outsider. He was very fond of fried chicken and collard
greens, and he ate the combination whenever he could get it,
which seemed to me every night of the week. Regardless of our
geographical location, he could find fried chicken and collard
greens. I used to kid him about it.

"Don't you have any self-respect? Will you have watermelon
for dessert?"

John was unflappable.

"It's what I like."

Frequently, as we waited in airports, we heard the announcement, "If you want to make a reservation, please use the white
courtesy phone." I would turn to John and say, "Remember,
that's not for you. You have to use the black courtesy phone."

But he gave as good as he got. Once he spotted a bald guy in a hotel elevator.

"Renée, look. It's Telly Savalas. I bet you won't go over and say hello to him."

"You sure it's him?"

"Yeah, yeah. I bet he'd like to meet you. Come on, as one famous person to another."

So, I went over to him, and of course it was not Telly Savalas, which I might have put down to a simple case of mistaken identity if not for the shit-eating grin on John's face.

The question of which of us was the bigger name caused a lot of kidding. He used to crow about how popular he was in Houston, and I would say, "How big you are in Houston is nothing to how big I am in New York." I'll never forget the expression on his face when we finally went to play in New York, and on the way in from the airport, the toll taker at the Queens Midtown Tunnel took a look into the car and said, "Hi, Doctor Renée. Welcome back."

"You *are* big in New York!" John said.

"That's nothing. Just wait."

Later at Madison Square Garden, when the Nets were introduced prior to playing Billie Jean King's New York Apples, I got such an ovation from all the New York tennis people that Billie Jean grabbed the microphone and said, "Hey! Let's hear it for the New York Apples!" John was duly impressed.

Fittingly, the last time I saw John was in New York, long after the WTT had disbanded and I had left professional tennis to return to medicine. He was playing for the Milwaukee Bucks and was in town to play the Knicks, so a couple of my friends made sure I was in a prominent seat in the first row, under the basket on the Eighth Avenue side. Word reached John that his old pal Renée Richards was there, and he went wild that night. Every time he handled the ball, he would yell, "No way! No way!" The fans might have thought it was just standard trash talking, but I knew it was in my honor.

That night the Bucks soundly beat the Knicks. At the final buzzer, John drew a foul and went to the line right in front of my seat. He looked straight at me and yelled, "No way!" Then he closed his eyes and drained the foul shot. The next second the buzzer sounded, and John ran off the court, disappearing under the stands. That night I went home full of the memories of all we had experienced together during Renée's adolescence. I haven't seen John since that memorable game, but when I read something about him in the paper or a friend brings me up to date on his doings, I always feel a rush of sisterly feeling for my old partner in mischief.

These are some of the earliest memories that belong to Renée alone. They are consequently very precious. Luckily, though players, friends, and family often muttered, "No way, Renée," or some equivalent, they stuck with me. Eventually I worked through my growing pains and became a responsible adult who can say with so many others, "I'm just happy to have survived adolescence!"

CHAPTER 6

Renée and Martina

M Y PROFESSIONAL COACHING CAREER was
certainly a part of Renée Richards' adolescence, but
Renée was beginning to mature, and this was one of the keys
to my relationship with Martina Navratilova. The general public has much too simple a view of Martina. They picture her
striding the court, muscles bulging, almost haughty, most often
triumphant, and they think that she was steely and confident
through and through. However, the Martina I knew was far
different from this popular image. Ted Tinling, fashion designer
and tennis insider, once observed, "Martina can go from arro-
gance to panic with no stops in between," and this was sometimes true, especially before I started to coach her. When things
were going well, she tended to strut, but if she ran into a bad
patch, her confidence would wither. The fans saw little of this,
because she hid it behind a stoic exterior, but if you knew what

to look for you could see the symptoms: her frustrated glances toward the friends' and coaches' box and her hurried attempts at outright winning shots when the situation was not right. As her career progressed, she grew much more stable, and I think I had something to do with that.

Martina is brash, outspoken, and fearless, but she wears her heart on her sleeve. She is always an advocate for the weak and disenfranchised, as is reflected in her devotion to animal rights. If there is a homeless two-legged dog in the area, Martina will find him. Okay, only one of her dogs had two legs. Another had three. He was K.D., the ever-present "killer dog," who guarded her tennis gear in the locker room. I believe all the rest had four, but if it wasn't a leg problem, there was always something else—a heart condition, a skin disorder. She cannot resist a pathetic animal, and under her care they thrive.

However, Martina's linking up with Renée Richards was not a matter of compassion for the disenfranchised. Her choice was influenced primarily by the hope that I could help her win against her archrival, Chris Evert. Most people misjudged the characters of these famous opponents. They thought of Martina as beating up on America's sweetheart. Poor Chris was fragile and was lofting balls back from the baseline in a panic. Ridiculous. In a crunch, Chrissie was as hard as nails. If you looked into those narrowing eyes and you observed the set of that little mouth, you could see that it was Evert who was solid. And those baseline shots had the weight of lead cannonballs.

Becoming Martina's coach was like so many other significant occurrences in my life: It just happened, almost on its own. However, when the opportunity arose, I was well prepared. As a tennis player, I had often been in positions of authority both formal and informal. I was the captain of numerous teams, including the Yale team, the U.S. Maccabiah team, and the U.S. Navy team, to mention just three. Being a captain encompasses some coaching, some strategizing, and sometimes enforcing of discipline, so from an early age, I got used to acting in those areas. And I probably did more than most captains because I was known not only as a skilled player but as an analytical one. A player can go a long way on physical talent, but when great talent is blended with solid fundamentals and a well-considered game plan, the effect is spectacular. Over the years, I have often been sought out by people who have a lot of physical talent, perhaps more than I, but who cannot see tactical issues that are clear to me.

While I was on the satellite circuit and later on the major tour, I often gave tips to young players who regarded me as a sage. Quite often I had beaten them, and they were a little confused about how I managed to do that at my relatively advanced age. To their minds, exuberant youth should always prevail. The shallower players thought they found their answer in my sexual history, but the sharper ones knew there was something else, and they were right. I outthought them. Sometimes I would get into a tutoring relationship through a casual observation on the practice court or in the players' lounge. Like most other players, I loved talking about tennis, but my comments often went beyond the usual generalities or competitive ragging. Players tended to remember my observations about court position or shot selection, especially if they took a tip and succeeded with it. It was this sort of observation that led to my coaching Martina, but the process took a couple of years from start to finish.

I think the foundation of our coaching relationship began in Baton Rouge, Louisiana, in 1978. She was playing for the Boston Lobsters in World Team Tennis, and I was playing for the Sunbelt Nets. She was about to go off to Wimbledon, and I suggested that this was the year for her to win the tournament. It was quite obvious to me that she was ready, but she didn't seem at all confident.

"Do you really think that I can win Wimbledon?" she asked.

"I'm quite sure that you are good enough," I replied.

"You do?" she repeated thoughtfully.

And she did win. It was the first of nine Wimbledon victories, an all-time record. Of course, I had nothing to do with that outcome, except that predictions like the one I made stick in a player's mind when they are not some pie-in-the-sky comment from a know-nothing or a hanger-on. I continued to observe Martina's game because she was a talented player who I felt was not using her talents to best advantage.

I saw this very clearly at the 1981 Amelia Island tournament, three years after Martina had won that first Wimbledon. She played Chris Evert, who is the patroness of the Amelia Island tournament and without question the greatest woman ever on clay. Martina had won Wimbledon two years before and had beaten Chris numerous times, yet in this match Chris beat her 6–0, 6–0. How could a player of Martina's talent win not one game against Chris, even if Chris was the admitted queen of clay courts? This loss was a disaster for Martina, who should have been riding high. Yet the reason she lost so badly was easy for me to see: She had no idea how to use her game as a weapon against Chris's weaknesses.

Worse yet, her tactics enhanced Chris's strengths. Martina was trying to serve and volley on clay, which is difficult to do against even a competent clay-court player and was nearly impossible against Chris. Over and over, Martina found herself watching a yellow comet streak by just out of her reach. When serving and volleying failed, Martina would try to outhit Chris from the baseline, which was also impossible because Chris hit with machine precision and with machine power. Martina could stay with her for a while, sometimes a good while, but in the end she would lose a hitting contest.

At this stage in her career, Martina was lost. She had no idea of how to run Chris around the court by hitting the ball deep down the line and then short cross-court, thus making her run on a diagonal, rather than allowing her to cruise the baseline. Though Chris moved well, speed and agility were not her greatest assets; Martina should have been stretching her. However, she could not figure a way to bring Chris in, let alone bring her in so as to force her to cover as much court as possible in the process. The thing that made me grind my teeth was that Martina had the shots to do it. She had the slice backhand that she could hit deep down the line or else short cross-court. She could also pull her forehand sharply cross-court with topspin if she wanted to, or hit it flat, deep down the line. If Martina could just put the shots she had already perfected to their proper use, she would prevail. And she had to give up the idea that serving and volleying could work routinely on clay against a top opponent.

There were many changes that could improve her game, but they were tactical ones that Martina didn't recognize because of her youth and inexperience. She had succeeded thus far on raw talent. As a student of the game, I saw what a marriage of Martina's physical gifts and proper tactics could mean. However, I didn't have much to do with Martina at that Amelia Island tournament. I just filed away my observations.

That same year, at age forty-seven, I found myself at a personal crossroad, fighting a losing battle with time. I was trained as tightly as anyone could be, but I was losing to players whom I had beaten the year before. I tried to keep up, but regardless of how many stairs I ran, drills I did, or practice balls I hit, I couldn't beat time. My stamina declined, my reflexes slowed, and my capacity to track the ball deteriorated.

Just a few months after making my mental notes on Martina's game at Amelia Island, I found myself scheduled to play Andrea Leand in the first round of the 1981 U.S. Open, which was a sharp reminder of the ticking clock: Andrea was the daughter of one of my Yale classmates. She was a very strong player, and like Martina had all the physical tools but only a rudimentary idea of how to manage her game. I played Andrea a close three-set match, but in the end my court savvy could not make up for my declining physical skills. I was out in the first round, and I knew in my heart that I was close to being out permanently. However, I resisted the impulse to cry in my pillow and instead asked myself, "What can I do to make this tournament memorable?" Then I thought of Martina, who was just starting the tournament herself. I had always liked her. I remembered the encouragement she had given me in São Paolo years ago when I was downhearted and thinking of quitting. I liked the idea of doing something for her, so I took her aside.

"Look," I said, "I'm out of the tournament now, and I have no responsibilities. I think I can help you. I see that if you get to the semis, you're going to play Chris Evert, and if you want, I will coach you on how to beat Chrissie."

"Do you think you can do that?" she asked.

"I think it's very doable," I replied.

Martina thought for a moment. Maybe she remembered that I had predicted her win at Wimbledon three years before. Maybe she knew of my reputation as a mentor for young players. Maybe she was just willing to try anything that might work. After a few moments she nodded.

"Okay, Coach."

At the time she made this decision, Martina had played Chris in forty matches and had lost twenty-six of them, and though she had been winning more frequently of late, she was fighting the memory of her recent humiliating loss at Amelia Island. It is true that by 1981 Martina had won three grand slam titles, but Chrissie had won twelve. She was a scary opponent for Martina.

So I began to coach her, and she won all her matches handily, right through the quarterfinals, which brought about the expected semifinal matchup with her nemesis. Secrecy was an essential part of my plan, and from the early rounds my New York connections had served us well in that regard. I knew many people on Long Island who had private courts, so with their help I kept Martina out of the public eye and moved her from one location to another nearly every day, which effectively foiled press snoops. During those sessions, I saw all the characteristics that I became so familiar with in the next few years as her coach.

First of all, Martina showed a keen intelligence. Martina is like most great people of action. She has little time for discussion or philosophizing; her intelligence manifests itself in other ways. She speaks several languages, not because she is a student of language, but because being able to do so helps her accomplish things. And, like many accomplished people, she does not appear at first to be a good listener. Many times I tried to talk to her, only to be upstaged by the television set or another person in the room. It used to make me angry, but the next day I would see that she had taken in every word because she would be following the advice I had given the evening before.

And this brings me to Martina's most endearing trait from a coaching point of view. She was able not only to comprehend what was needed but also to put it into action. With some athletes, you can talk a blue streak and they can seem to understand, but when they start to play, they do the same thing they have always done. They have one groove and they cannot jump to another. That's not Martina.

The day before the semifinal, I played the part of Chrissie, and I had Martina do all of the things that were necessary to win against her. The next day she triumphed in a wonderful match: 7–5, 4–6, 6–4. Her friends looked at me in wonder (friends who against my secret wishes had always been at the practice sessions), and one of them said, "Renée, it looks like déjà vu all over again," so closely did the match resemble our practice sessions.

The Navratilova camp was ecstatic at the prospect of the finals, where Martina would meet Tracy Austin, who in 1979 had become the youngest player to win a U.S. Open. She was a great player, but I expected Martina to prevail because Tracy had a game similar to Chrissie's, a two-handed backhand and a flat forehand with just a bit of topspin. Her serve and volley were adequate but not by any means overpowering. Her greatest strengths were her consistency—like Chris, she seldom committed unforced errors—and her heart—she was a deadly competitor. At first it appeared that Martina would waltz through it. She won the first set 6–1, but Tracy fought back in the second set and took it 7–6. The third set also went to a ticbreaker, and during that breaker, I sat helpless in the stands and watched something happen that neither Martina nor I had anticipated: Tracy, having not played to Martina's forehand the entire match, hit almost every ball in the tiebreaker to the forehand side. Prior to this event, Martina's forehand had been considered an effective weapon, so Tracy's attack surprised and flustered Martina. As I watched her try to deal with Tracy's shots, I saw a weakness in Martina's forehand that had previously escaped my notice. It was so flat that it had to be hit perfectly; if not, the result would be an error. This flaw had not been obvious because Martina was such a good athlete, and she could manage that forehand perfectly in most situations. However, in a tiebreaker in the U.S. Open, the pressure disturbed her concentration, making her forehand vulnerable. Martina lost.

But what had caused Tracy to adopt this strategy? I have a hunch it was her coach's idea. I knew Marty Riessen from our time together with the Sunbelt Nets, and he was an astute student of tennis. We had often clashed over training techniques, but I never questioned his guile as a player or coach. However, I never asked him if Tracy had acted under his instructions. I thought it better to simply correct the flaw in Martina's game, and I was given that opportunity, because despite losing in the finals Martina was pleased with our collaboration and invited me to become a member of "Team Navratilova," as her entourage was to become known. At the time, I had little idea of the sort of carnival I was joining or of the coaching problems it would create. In addition to coaching Martina, I frequently found myself functioning as bodyguard, traffic cop, and purveyor of common sense.

Probably no other player of the time accumulated more dependents and worshippers than Martina. She was usually surrounded by concentric circles of people on whom she lavished greater or lesser attention as their positions warranted. This circle expanded and contracted according to the situation. Sometimes, on a long expedition (as for a tournament in Tokyo), the number would be few, maybe Martina, her girlfriend, and a couple of family members or friends. At other times, the crowd would swell to ridiculous proportions. At Wimbledon, for example, she would rent two houses, one for her and her immediate staff and one for everyone else in her entourage, and that does not count the many young athletes and the celebrities of all descriptions who would drop by the houses and hang around.

At the center of the system were Martina and her girlfriend. When I signed on, it was Nancy Lieberman, who also served as her fitness coach. Later, Judy Nelson occupied this position of immense influence. When Martina makes an emotional commitment, she does so wholeheartedly, so she believes her current girlfriend is the planet's most wonderful human being.

In the next circle were Martina's family members. She was devoted to them on every level. Having come from the eastern bloc, she had a streak of wariness, perhaps from looking over her shoulder for the KGB. Martina's family had proven themselves trustworthy in a repressive communist environment, and they had her loyalty. She would sometimes choke up when she spoke of her grandmother.

In the third circle were close friends. This could be a rather fluid position, but while you were in that circle, you were given the royal treatment. Step out of line, however, and the door could close in your face.

In the fourth circle were people of professional importance, like me. I shared this circle with a variety of individuals, including "Doctor" Robert Haas, Martina's nutritionist, who was antagonistic to me because I never bought his glib routine and suspected that he was using Martina as a stepping-stone to personal fame. Though I found him paranoid about his credentials, he did go on to write a successful book on sports nutrition, and I will give him credit for prescribing a pretty fair diet for Martina.

The fifth circle was occupied by the dozens of peripheral hangers-on, who were there because they were famous or friends of somebody in one of the other circles. These people would blow in and out of Martina's sphere, sometimes receiving a bit of attention from her and sometimes passing through without notice, happy to tell their friends that they had been over at Martina's on a certain day, perhaps having shared space with celebrities such as Jack Nicholson, Lynda Carter, Sugar Ray Leonard, or Frank and Kathy Lee Gifford.

The fact that there was often a crowd around her does not mean that Martina was open to all. To say that she could be dismissive is an understatement. She was not like those expansive personalities who, however famous they get, never forget a name or a face. Far from it. I had friends whom she met probably twenty times, and she still could not remember them, let alone their names. If you did not rate with Martina, you were effectively a nonperson, and she was quite capable of turning away as if you did not exist.

Yet for those on whom she shone her attention, she was a loyal, generous, and entertaining companion, surprisingly playful and inclined to make all activities into a competition. She loved games and played incessantly in her free time, Scrabble, bridge, and her special favorite, Boggle, in which she used to beat the other players on tour—though to be truthful, word games were not the strong point of most of the players with whom she associated. Still, she was very adept. When the first cumbersome home Pacman games came out, she bought one, placed it on a heavy table and played all day with her friends. Nick joined the troupe a few times, and Martina was extremely friendly to him, taking him skiing and energetically engaging in snowball fights with him and Nancy.

But when Martina wanted to control the crowd, she was quite effective at doing it. For example, when the circus was at its most raucous, at Wimbledon, Martina was not to be bothered until after breakfast. In the morning, she got up and went to the dining room, where her breakfast was brought to her and all the London papers were laid within reach. Others might eat at the same table—Nancy, or me, or Martina's mother, perhaps one or two others—but we spoke not one word, not to Martina and not to each other. This was Martina's quiet time. We kept an absolute silence while she read the newspapers and ate her muesli.

This was the environment in which I found myself, certainly not the most eccentric I ever experienced but with its own fascinating aspects. I was soon being called "Moose," a nickname probably stemming from my size and physical aura. There was certainly a disparity in size between me and Martina and most everyone else on the team, though that does not account for the sum total of my impact. I get noticed, and that's just a fact. "Moose" was conceived as a term of endearment, though as is so often the case in jock circles, it was not the most tactful choice. But it stuck, and nearly two decades later, when I was inducted into the Eastern Tennis Hall of Fame in 2000, I received a congratulatory telegram from Martina. The salutation was "Moose."

I think the physical presence that brought about the nickname did make Martina and Nancy feel more secure, and I sometimes played the part of bodyguard, especially in crowds. However much Martina's political background might have made her wary of the government, she was remarkably naïve about plunging into crowds, especially in faraway places like Tokyo, Japan, where I bulldozed a way for Martina and the others through a throng of adoring fans. If nothing else, I was easy to follow, looming over the heads of the diminutive Japanese. But bodyguarding was not my chief function. I was hired to coach, and that was always where I put my greatest attention, or tried to.

Any good coach must deal with two elementary categories, physical and mental. The easiest category for me to address was the physical. Martina was blessed with as much natural ability as any player in history: strong, fast, flexible, and athletic.

But not everything was in order. My first project was to correct the forehand that had cost her the U.S. Open. Martina hit her forehand flat and hard, but it was a shot that gave her no safety margin. In order to put the percentages on her side, especially on a slow surface like clay, she would have to learn to drive the shot as hard as she could but in doing so come over the ball, imparting topspin so that it would drop down and land inside the court. Without that spin she had no leeway, and if her stroke was a little off, she was in trouble, especially when she needed a passing shot. As soon as this reasoning was made clear to Martina, she added the topspin forehand to her arsenal, and it became a very effective shot for her. While we were dealing with the forehand side, we adjusted her forehand volley, which was shaky because she held her elbow out and took too big a backswing, which made for poor stability. I suggested that she keep her elbow closer to her body and use a shorter stroke, which she did easily. With that alteration, her forehand volley became as good as her natural backhand volley.

On the backhand side, she needed topspin just as badly as she had on the forehand side, and for the same reason—to effectively pass her opponent. Martina's backhand was the typical slice backhand that all of the great Eastern European players used to learn on the clay courts of Hungary, Poland, Romania, and Czechoslovakia. It's a good shot if put to the right purpose, but you can't use it to pass effectively. She had to learn to come over the ball in the backhand, giving her the ability to drive the ball with a safety margin.

Another area of concern was her serve, which did not take advantage of the fact that she is left-handed. When serving to a right-hander in the ad court, a left-hander should use a slice serve to the righty's backhand. Because the ad court is across the net on the server's right, a lefty's slice serve will bounce with a lateral motion that pulls the righty off the court, a position from which it is hard to run down a cross-court volley from the lefty. Martina's serve was very like an American twist, which puts topspin on the ball and causes it to bounce nearly straight up, making a beautiful target for the righty's forehand return. So we worked on a slice serve, which came very naturally because of her left-handed delivery. In short order, the right-handed players on the tour had something new to deal with.

Martina's stamina also needed work, especially if she was to succeed in clay court tournaments. Clay requires patience. Martina could not get antsy and try to get the point over quickly. She had to put out of her head the pleasing possibility of a forty-minute match and prepare for the long haul. Though Nancy Lieberman was officially in charge of fitness training, my drills also contributed in that area. The most demanding, and my favorite, was the one that Martina hated the most: the corner drill. I would stay in a corner of the court and hit balls to Martina across the net. Martina had to run down each ball and hit it back to my corner. I would move her from one side to the other and from front to back until she was staggering with fatigue, whereupon I would show some mercy and hit a few in her vicinity, but after she had taken a couple of good breaths, I would begin stretching her again. We started with fifteen minutes for each corner, and when I called "Time!" she hung over the fence with her tongue out, just as I had done so many times when I was on the receiving end of the corner drill. In 1982, I told her that if she could do the corner drill for a half-hour in each corner without quitting or falling down, then she could win the French Open on clay. We gradually built up to fifteen, to twenty, to twenty-five, and finally to thirty minutes. At that point, I thought she was physically ready for the French. People don't give Martina enough credit for her work ethic. She worked like a dog to get better.

The physical training was only half of the equation. As Martina's coach, I had to address mental issues as well. It is impossible to entirely separate the two, and I have always stressed that a command of basic skills leads to confidence, which leads to a stronger mind. As Martina's fundamentals improved, her attitude did as well, but she continued to blame herself when things went bad. This was the negative side of what was in general a positive trait, her intense desire to win. But if she didn't prevail, if she lost a point, especially through an error, that situation might open the door to an emotional storm that could undo her.

One technique I used to overcome this tendency was to tell Martina that a person's brain could only hold one thought at any moment, and if that thought was a negative one about the last point, it would keep the vitally important thought about preparing for the next point from taking its proper place in her mind. So I emphasized that she should occupy her mind with a positive thought about the next point, rather than dwelling on the mistake she had just made.

"Remember, one thought in the brain at a time," I would repeat during our practice sessions.

Martina would nod, and eventually my tactic began to work. This simple trick of concentration made her more stable in difficult matches.

As Martina improved, finding hitting partners for her became a problem. Few women, including me, could give her a good workout, but I knew strong practice was critical, because Martina needed a challenge to invigorate her. This was never more clearly demonstrated than in 1987, near the climax of her career. She had just won Wimbledon and showed signs of a letdown during our first stadium practice at the U.S. Open. She gazed at the steel and concrete, probably remembering the cozy surroundings at the All England Club, and said, "I don't think I am up for it this year." We had wasted twenty minutes of precious stadium time when I heard someone behind me say, "Hey Renée, let me see if I can win a few points from Martina." There was no mistaking that voice. It was John McEnroe. Without turning, I replied, "Sure, John. Be my guest." I moved to the sidelines and watched as John and Martina began to play points. Martina went from dejected to fiery in an instant. The few workmen and stragglers in the stadium gathered around, aware that they were seeing something special: the two greatest left-handed serve and volley players in history going at it in the evening light. Martina was brilliant, and John did not hold back. I marveled at their intensity, but when John missed a volley and threw his racquet the length of the court where it smashed into the far wall, I said, "John, what's wrong? You just hit fourteen perfect volleys. You missed only the fifteenth." He turned to me with that famous pout and screamed, "That's the one I can't stand!" Martina subsequently played her best for two weeks and beat Steffi Graf in the finals.

For a player to be complete she needs not only talent and inspiration but also tactics, and Martina and I worked equally hard on that aspect of her game. I created a game plan for every match, and our daily routine at tournaments included two elements: a review of the match she had played that day, with some analysis of what she had done well and not so well; and intensive work on the plan for the next match. We did this work the night before and on the morning of the match. My game plans were extensive, involving not only tactics but also a general review of what strokes would work against a particular opponent. The morning session was especially involved, and I was often frustrated by Martina's seeming inattention. Many times, she would be distracted, most often by Nancy, and she would seem entirely disinterested in my laborious prematch routine. Once in a while, I would wave my hand in front of her to try to get her attention as she was watching television or kidding around, and I would say, "Martina, are you listening? Are you listening?"

"Yeah, yeah, I'm listening," she would reply, but I wasn't always so sure.

However, more often than not, she would show by her performance in the next match that she had heard me, though I was never comfortable with the distractions that boiled around her. If they had not been there, she might have been even greater, but we'll never know. When I thought the distractions were potentially harmful, I took a hand, as I did at Hilton Head in 1982.

The *Family Circle* Cup, played in Hilton Head, South Carolina, was especially important because it was the second part of my plan to get Martina ready for the French Open. I had already told her that if she could do the corner drill for half an hour, she could win on the clay at Roland Garros, but I had added a motivating proviso to my statement. She had to win on clay at Hilton Head, the premiere clay court event in the United States. This gave Martina something to point toward, and I knew that she would be supremely confident for the French if she won the *Family Circle* Cup.

Sea Pines Plantation at Hilton Head is a beautiful resort where players are housed in the luxury condominiums that are scattered around the grounds. The night before the finals, Martina and Nancy had a bunch of their friends over for a barbecue. It was the usual collection of familiar faces and local groupies, and they were all having a wonderful time when I realized that it was ten o'clock at night. I held my tongue for a few more minutes, but finally I couldn't stand it anymore. I rose, walked to the door, and opened it.

For most of my life, I have wished that I was more diminutive and had a sweeter, more feminine voice. About my height, I can do nothing, but in my incarnation as Renée Richards, I have tried to cultivate the habit of speaking softly; however, when I need it, I can call up something like Dick Raskind's old voice, which usually causes heads to turn. On this occasion that voice came in very handy.

"Ladies, the party is over," I said, opening the front door. "Good night."

I saw a lot of jaws drop. And then, one by one, each of the partygoers marched out the door. When the parade ended, the only people left in the condo were Martina, Nancy, and me. Judging by the expression on her face, Nancy was a bit shocked.

"Martina, you've got a big match tomorrow," I said, heading for the door. "Get some sleep."

She went out the next day and won the finals.

"Let's go to France," I said as I congratulated her.

At the French Open, we thought Martina would meet Chris Evert in the finals, but Andrea Jaeger, a nineteen-year-old meteor, beat Chris in the semifinals. While the world saw this as a mismatch, I knew better. Andrea could run like a deer, catch up to anything, and hit great passing shots. In spite of her youth, she had great tennis instincts. I worked out an appropriate game plan, just as I would have if Martina were scheduled to play an established star, and we went over it in our usual way the night before and the morning of the match.

The first set verified my concerns when it went to a tie-breaker, which Martina barely managed to win 7–6. I was gratified that she seemed to be using my one-thought-at-a-time technique, remaining poised through some testing situations. The first-set win gave her the confidence to execute the game plan perfectly in the second set, which she won 6–1. As I had predicted, she was the French Open champion. I wish this were the end of the story, but what happened next is an extreme example of the sort of extra duties I was sometimes called upon to perform as Martina's coach.

As usual, I skipped the postmatch press conference. I was a subject of media interest on my own and tended to draw a lot of attention, and I felt that the emphasis should always be on Martina. The press conference was attended by hundreds of international reporters. It should have been the stage on which Martina could take her well-earned bows, be generous to her opponent, and say all the usual things. I had no idea that anything else was going on as I sat waiting in the players' lounge, but suddenly Nancy came running in with a frantic expression.

"Renée, Renée! You have to come in. Martina's crying."

"What for?"

"Andrea says that you and I were coaching Martina during the match. She says that she couldn't play against all three of us."

This was ridiculous. None of us had done anything illegal during the match. My hunch is that Andrea's father, Roland Jaeger, who had never gotten along with Martina and Nancy, had told her to explain her loss in this way. It could be that he even believed it.

"Renée, what are we going to do? What are we going to do?"

It was obviously time for Moose.

I got up, brushed myself off, and went into the press conference. As I entered, all heads swung in my direction. The majority of the media people were French, so I made a strategic decision and addressed the throng in French. I said that Andrea's charge was absurd. Martina's coaching had gone on only before the match, actually for the whole month prior to our arrival in Paris. I emphasized that Martina was a great player who had won Wimbledon before Nancy and I had ever come on the scene. I concluded by saying that it was unfortunate Andrea had chosen to make such an accusation. That statement defused the whole affair and was especially effective because it was made in the language of the country hosting the tournament.

Andrea may have been unduly influenced by her father in this matter. She was a great player who should not have been making excuses. Her eventual maturity and true nature are best illustrated by her creation of the Silver Lining Foundation, which aids children with cancer. Sadly, her playing career was cut short by a shoulder injury.

THERE WERE MANY MOMENTS of triumph in coaching Martina, but also many trying ones, partly because full-time coaches were a new phenomenon at that time. Martina was among the first women players to employ one. Chrissie Evert had Dennis Ralston, Tracy Austin had Marty Riessen, Pam Shriver had Don Candy, and Hana Mandlikova had Vera Sukova, who used to startle callers by answering Hana's phone with a vigorous, "Sukova!" Before I came on board, everybody close to Martina seemed to have taken a hand in advising her, and they couldn't stop offering opinions. Virtually her entire family, including her grandmother, mother, and stepfather, played tennis, and they all had opinions regarding her game. Her stepfather, Mirek, would stand at the net post during practice and try to instruct Martina. When her mother, Jana, was on the scene, she would sit behind me during matches and tell me right in my ear what I should do with Martina. All of this was a little distracting, but I could have shrugged it off if it had come just from the family; however, other problems were more critical.

Martina's nutritionist, Robert Haas, is one example. I was resigned to his presence as long as he confined himself to planning meals and putting together tinfoil packets of food for Martina to take on court during matches, but he had bigger things in mind. Unbeknownst to me, he had created some sort of computer print-out on Martina's potential opponents, detailing their habits and game tendencies. This may have been forward thinking for the time, but I never saw this printout. I can only guess at when it was employed or how it tied into what I was saying. I thought then and I still think that it is rarely effective for players to be coached by committee, especially if the committee members don't collaborate. And when a coach is being aided behind the scenes by a "nutrition expert," the effect is definitely counterproductive.

But the most difficult coaching experience I faced involved Nancy Lieberman. Nancy's motives were good. She provided solid emotional support for Martina and did wonders for her fitness; however, she found it impossible to keep to those areas. I felt she wanted to coach tennis a little as well. This put me at a grave disadvantage. Martina was in love with Nancy, and when Martina loves, she loves completely. Martina respected me—I was clearly the tennis authority—but Nancy had the emotional edge. She and I banged heads regularly.

Probably the best example of the confusion caused by Nancy's presence came in 1983 at the French Open. By that time, I had returned to medicine but was called back to duty when Martina canceled her deal with Peter Marmureanu, the coach who followed me. That year, the French Open was especially important to Martina because she was the defending champion. My medical duties allowed me to attend only the second week of the tournament. Martina was scheduled to meet Kathleen Horvath in the round of sixteen, and I arrived the morning of the match, which gave us little time to do more than greet each other before I took my place in the stands next to Nancy.

Martina had played Kathleen three times before and won all of them, but those matches had been played on carpet. Clay was another matter, and though Kathleen was not nearly as good as Martina, she was capable of playing high-level tennis on the clay. Martina could beat her if she were patient and kept a positive thought in her head. Since there had been no time for strategizing, my main function was to encourage Martina to be steady. This called for no more than showing the proper attitude when Martina looked to the box for emotional support: I would demonstrate approval for the good things and wave off the bad. The match called for a lot of this emoting because Kathleen put up a great battle and strung together some shots that frustrated Martina. Still, after losing the first set 3–6, Martina seemed to right herself and won the second 6–0. In the third set, Martina lost her composure and with it the match at 3–6.

What made this defeat galling to me was that Martina did not receive the unity of support that might have made the difference in the match. At one point Nancy got up, left her seat near me, and went to a spot farther down in the stands, where she could better draw Martina's attention. Instead of being able to glance into the stands and see her coach and girlfriend sitting together rooting for her, Martina began to look confusedly from one spot to the other, uncertain of where to focus for support, and no doubt troubled by this split. Nancy may have had Martina's best interests at heart, but she should have known that the moment called for a united front.

In all, Martina played Kathleen eleven times and lost to her only that one time at Roland Garros, but it was the most important of their matches, and it brought my coaching relationship with Martina to a four-year halt. On that day, I didn't even check into a hotel. I left Martina a note saying I was sorry about the situation but couldn't coach her anymore, not if it meant competing with Nancy. There could be only one coach. I got on a plane and flew back to New York. I knew the score. It was resign or be fired.

Another problem in my coaching career was finances. Martina was a generous person in many ways. I once admired a Walkman while we were in Japan but returned it to the counter because it was too expensive for me. When we got back to Los Angeles, Martina pulled it out of her bag and gave it to me. On another occasion, in the dressing room of Madison Square Garden following a routine practice session, she gave me a Rolex watch, which I wear to this day. No special occasion, just boom, a gold Rolex. But these gestures did not offset the fact that I never made an amount of money that truly represented my value to Martina. I won't reveal my salary, but you can gauge what it was by the fact that I could not afford a Walkman. It is amazing to think that an athlete as successful as Martina would have to scrimp in the matter of a valuable coach, but her entire entourage had to be underwritten, and many times she was counting on winning a tournament so as to have enough money to pay the hotel bill. During my tenure as her coach, Martina won a million-dollar bonus. I thought I should have a percentage of that prize, but she held that I was entitled only to a cut of her tournament winnings.

To the outside world, my position must have looked enviable, but by the time Martina won Wimbledon in 1982, I was ready to switch to a job with better prospects. Full-time tennis had been rewarding in many ways, but I was more than $400,000 in debt and had no credit. In one more generous gesture, the most magnanimous of them all, Martina gave me the money to set up my new office, and she did it against the advice of her financial consultant. Why he was against it, I'm not sure, but Martina ignored him.

I was not entirely finished with coaching Martina, but from the point I returned to medicine, my career as a high-profile, full-time coach was finished. Still, we shared some wonderful moments when I was occasionally recalled for specialty duties, culminating in the summer of 1987 when Martina won both Wimbledon and the U.S. Open with me as her coach, a grand achievement that provided a fitting end to my professional association with the greatest player in the history of women's tennis.

In spite of the fact that we are sometimes linked in the public's mind, Martina and I see each other rarely, though we can instantly resume our friendship as if we had been in daily contact, as we did on one memorable occasion in the mid-1980s between the time I stopped coaching her and the time I came back for that wonderful summer of 1987. It was Labor Day weekend, and I was in Southampton, Long Island, enjoying the holiday at the beach. The phone rang. I thought it must be one of my friends, many of whom were on holiday in the area.

"Renée!" Martina blurted, not bothering to identify herself, "I have to play in the U.S. Open tomorrow, and my glasses are no good! I can't see a thing!"

And this on Sunday afternoon of Labor Day weekend. However, I left the beach at four in the afternoon and opened up my office at seven. Fortunately, the traffic was light, as could be expected. Who comes back to the city in the middle of a holiday weekend? Martina arrived soon after me. I examined her eyes, made the necessary measurements, and then called my optician friend Art Leonard, who arranged to have her new glasses made on Monday morning (Labor Day!) and delivered to Martina's hotel by noon. I'm not sure the president of the United States or even the pope could get a pair of glasses made in New York City over Labor Day weekend, but it was done expeditiously for Martina Navratilova, and she had fully expected Moose to make it happen.

"Thank you for coming back into the city and opening the office tonight," she said.

"No problem," I replied. And I smiled. "It's your office. You paid for it. Use it when you need it."

Whenever Martina and I meet, the years fall away. We come from separate worlds, but each of us has an appreciation of what the other has gone through. I have tremendous respect for her talent, intelligence, courage, loyalty, work ethic, and zeal for the underprivileged. She thinks of me as the coach, Moose, whose advice took her to another level, and though she has had other coaches, I was the one whom she wanted to present her at her enshrinement in the International Tennis Hall of Fame.

"Look, this is a big moment," I said when she called to ask me. "Why don't you get Billie Jean to do it?"

"No. You are my coach. You have to do it!"

This is how I concluded my remarks at the ceremony.

For a moment, close your eyes. Picture a grass court in the center of an old wooden stadium, filled to capacity—silent. The server stands at the baseline looking at the ad court with arms hanging down in front of her, racquet held loosely in her left hand. Both arms come up in unison, the right arm straight, the left arm bending, elbow up, racquet head behind her back. In perfect rhythm, her shoulders turn, her weight comes up onto her right side. She leans into the court, and then explosively propels herself upward. The racquet strikes the ball and rockets it over the net, a withering slithering missile landing in a cloud of chalk dust in the backhand corner of the service box. It slices out wide of the sideline.

The return is headed for the line. The server streaks toward the net and reaches the ball before it drops too low. Hardly breaking stride, in perfect balance, knees bending, shoulders turning slightly to the right, she crushes the volley into the open court for a winner. The stadium erupts.

Magnificent Martina!

A champion for all times.

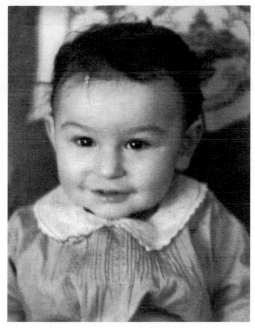

Richard Henry Raskind at age one.

With Uncle Albert Raskind shortly before
he went overseas with the 62nd Fighter
Squadron. He designed and fitted a bomb
rack for the P-47 Thunderbolt that turned
it into a bomber as well as a ferocious
fighter.

My father, Dr. David Raskind, with
his children at Deer Lake Camp.

Sister and brother at ages 16 and 11.

My mother, Dr. Sadie Muriel Baron, in her "foxhole." The bookshelves behind her desk contained *Psychopathia Sexualis,* the pioneering work that fascinated and horrified me.

At my graduation from Yale University, an important moment in my life. To this day, one of the chief ways I think of myself is as a Yale graduate. "Transsexual" is far down the list. I am with my mother and my girlfriend, Barbara Ehrenwald.

In the officer's mess aboard a submarine in 1963. This was Lieutenant Commander Raskind's only sea duty during his tour as a Navy surgeon.

Richard Raskind, speaking at my father's 75th birthday celebration. A year later Richard Raskind was Renée Richards.

At the 1977 U.S. Open. (Photo by June Harrison)

At the U.S. Open in 1976. I was still on the outside looking in. The following year, I won the right to play professionally as a woman. (Photo by Richard Drew)

The women's doubles finalists at the 1977 U.S. Open at Forest Hills. From left: Martina Navratilova with her partner, Betty Stove, and me with my partner, Betty Ann Stuart. (Photo by June Harrison)

Playing at the 1978 U.S. Open. (Photo by June Harrison)

With my mixed doubles partner, John Lucas, at the 1978 U.S. Open. When we played World Team Tennis together, John was instrumental in giving me the nickname "No Way Renée." (Photo by June Harrison)

Celebrating Martina's 1987 Wimbledon title with Joe Breedlove (on the left) and boxing great Sugar Ray Leonard.

With Nick, age 11. Two years later he ran off to Jamaica to become a Rastaman.

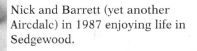

Nick and Barrett (yet another Airedale) in 1987 enjoying life in Sedgewood.

My dream home in Sedgewood, created with the aid of eccentric handyman/architect Wodjak.

With Dr. Harry Benjamin, the grand old man of American transsexualism, on the occasion of his 100th birthday in 1985. He died the following year.

My present home in Carmel, New York, a small, one-level cottage with much warmth and charm.

Nick with Arleen Larzelere in 1988.

My father with Billie Jean King at a super seniors tennis event in 1995.

Holding the trophy commemorating my induction into the Eastern Tennis Hall of Fame in 2000.

With Virginia Wade, the last Brit to win a Wimbledon singles title, at my induction into the Eastern Tennis Hall of Fame.

With Martina Navratilova. (Photo by
June Harrison)

At Martina's enshrinement in the International
Tennis Hall of Fame in 2000. On the far left is Pam
Shriver, who was Martina's most frequent doubles
partner. To the right of me are Craig Cardin, who
followed me as Martina's coach, Martina, and
Billie Jean King.

In 2001, I was the honoree at the Iris Ball sponsored by
the Manhattan League of the Helen Keller Services for
the Blind. I am with two of my former students, both
now eminent ophthalmologists: Dr. Lawrence Yannuzzi
(left) and Dr. Jack Dodick.

Nick in 2005. Martial arts
continue to be a big influence in
his life.

With my golfing buddy Kenny Piersa on July 4, 2006. With no prior consultation, we both showed up in red, white, and blue.

Playing doubles with Billie Jean King in 1977. (Photo by Richard Drew)

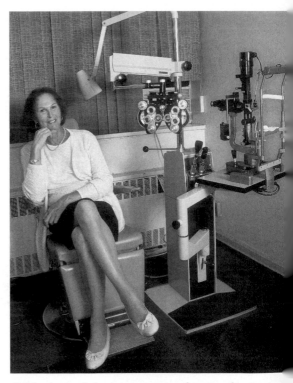

With my Airedale Tennis-ee in 1982, when I was training in Gainesville, Florida. (Photo by Hank Rowland)

With some of the instruments of my profession. At the age of 70, I still maintain my surgical practice. (Photo by Walter Iooss)

CHAPTER 7

The Doctor Is In Again

MY RETURN TO MEDICINE can be summarized in one word: terrifying. I was returning from a footloose adolescence to a world where the consequences of a mistake meant a great deal more than a lost point in a tennis match. When your business is invading people's eyes, you need to be up on the latest techniques, and I had been away five years. Even if I caught up, how many people would be willing to have their eyes treated by Renée Richards, internationally notorious tennis-playing transsexual? Trust is essential in my line, and I wondered if I could once again command that trust.

Half my former medical colleagues believed I had no chance, but the other half thought I could make it. I didn't know what to think. I imagined that I might go out to the North Shore of Long Island to a small community like Oyster Bay, buy a big old Victorian mansion, put my office on the first floor, and do general ophthalmology. This was a pleasant fantasy and one that was within reach but would require me to learn a broad range of recently developed techniques. Glaucoma treatment alone had changed radically in those five years, with new methods of management (especially daunting were the then-cutting-edge laser techniques), new corrective operations, and an increased multitude of medicinal drops. The idea of being a simple country doctor was attractive, but there was actually nothing simple about it. Perhaps it would be better to stick with my specialty. Strabismus was a tricky area, but it was at least well defined, and the surgical principles had remained unchanged.

My medical colleagues were not the only ones helping me ponder this dilemma. I was accompanied in this venture by one of the many people, often women, who have popped up in my life to keep me from drowning in a sea of everyday details. I am a great one for focus. I can do one or two activities very well, but when it comes to the basic support activities, I flounder. Going into an eye is in some ways less intimidating to me than going into an office supply store. Someone recently had to explain to me what a manila envelope is. I truly thought it might be an envelope made in Manila. It sounds silly, but this odd aspect of my character has prompted some of my close friends to laughingly refer to me as an idiot savant. Anyway, the job of keeping me in touch with ordinary reality was performed for several years by Melissa Hope Vinson, who accompanied me to New York as my personal manager.

I first met Melissa when I went to Gainesville, Florida, to learn tai chi. I had been training farther south in Port St. Lucie, Florida, with Frank Froehling, tennis coach and spiritual seeker. In spite of his odd techniques, which involved eating little and inhaling much, he had done a great deal for my fitness, my tennis game, and my personal finances. It was Frank who made me sit down and make a list of all my debts, and as I won a little money on the tour, pay one debt at a time and take considerable satisfaction in crossing it off the list. With his help, I was eventually able to afford an automobile. However, as is so often the case with coach and player, our relationship grew stale, so Frank put me in my compact Buick Sky Hawk and pointed me in the direction of Gainesville, where he knew a group of people who practiced tai chi. He was convinced that learning this discipline would improve my court movement and perhaps my spirituality. That I would head off on such an adventure was characteristic of my attitude at the time. I figured something good would turn up.

The most important thing to turn up was Melissa, who I was amazed to discover was probably the only person in Gainesville who had never heard of Renée Richards. She was a member of the spiritual group to which Frank had given me an introduction. Truthfully, I thought that I would stay a weekend, get introduced to tai chi, and return to South Florida, but that weekend stretched into three years, in large part because of Melissa, who volunteered to put me up for my stay in Gainesville. She could hardly have guessed how long that stay would be.

Melissa Hope Vinson is a distant cousin of Carl Vinson, for whom the aircraft carrier the U.S.S. *Carl Vinson* is named. Vinson had the longest tenure in the House of Representatives of any congressman in history. She is a distant cousin of a Chief Justice of the Supreme Court, Fred Vinson, as well. In addition to these admittedly distinguished connections, she is also the granddaughter of a high priest of the Ku Klux Klan. She has been trying to live that down all her life. On the in-law side, her first marriage was to the red-bearded grandson of Ike Clanton, the head of the family who fought it out with Wyatt Earp at the OK Corral. Melissa seems to be naturally drawn into eccentric circles, but on that first night in Gainesville she had no idea that the eccentricity level had risen sharply with my arrival.

Melissa took me to her house, a simple frame rental with no drapes, no shower curtains, and nearly no furniture. I was not surprised: Frank's old plantation house in Stuart was also sparsely furnished. In fact, I was pleased to learn that we would eat dinner at Melissa's from a coffee table, which was more convenience than we had at Frank's house, where he insisted we eat standing up in the kitchen so as not to give eating much importance. In Frank's spiritual system, which reflected the precepts of the Russian mystic philosopher Gurdjieff, eating was a low priority, drinking was slightly higher, and inhaling was highest of all.

Anyway, sitting on floor cushions and eating off a coffee table was a rare luxury. We were joined in this meal by Melissa's boyfriend, Billy, a physicist on the faculty of the University of Florida. He was a friendly fellow with a diamond stud in his ear. Our meal began with bread and broccoli, and as I enjoyed this simple food, eaten in a relatively conventional manner by comparison with Frank's standup technique, I commented, "This is good, a very nice hors d'oeuvre." Neither Melissa nor Billy responded, but when the bread and broccoli were gone, Melissa cleaned off the coffee table and said, "Let's go for a walk." My heart sank. I knew I was again among people who had little interest in eating, and I began plotting how I could do what I had done periodically in Stuart: sneak out of the house in the wee hours and head for the IHOP, where I would devour a stack of pancakes and sausage with a cheeseburger chaser. Those were hungry times.

Putting aside the food issue, I found Melissa, tai chi, and Gainesville to my liking. I spent the next three years training in a somewhat surreal atmosphere, learning tai chi at one hour of the day, running the bleachers in the Florida Gator stadium at another hour, hitting balls at the Devil's Run Tennis Club at another, and in my off hours mixing with a band of Aricans, an eclectic group of free-living souls whose goal was to reach enlightenment. In those days, Gainesville was a countercultural hotbed, famous for its Gainesville Green, judged by many connoisseurs to be the best pot in the nation. We had Gainesville Green growing conveniently in our neighborhood.

In Gainesville, Melissa was continuing a free-form life that had begun in Tarpon Springs, Florida. I take it that she passed her childhood in a shoeless nature-girl fashion which she continued as much as possible as an adult. She seldom put on footwear other than Birkenstock sandals unless the occasion demanded, such as when she found it necessary to find employment. When I met her, she was working at the University Medical Center transcribing dictation tapes in the psychiatry department, a job she eventually lost due to her habit of taking too many extended coffee breaks and devoting an excessive amount of time to solving the problems of everyone in the office. However, if she was interested in what she was doing, she could be a reliable and competent worker. That was the case when she became my personal manager, though she never lost her will-o'-the-wisp personality or her chameleon-like capacity to appear plain on one day and beautiful on the next, as Billie Jean King observed at the 1982 Wimbledon Ball when, upon seeing Melissa dressed formally for the occasion, she exclaimed, "Wow! Is that you, Melissa?" This then was the person who arrived with me in New York City to manage my medical practice, if I was ever to have one.

Melissa and I stayed temporarily in my father's Forest Hills house. Dad was appalled to learn that in coming with me to New York, Melissa had interrupted perhaps the longest matriculation in the history of the University of Florida, having started college at the age of eighteen and still not having graduated by the time I met her—when she was thirty-one. This was incomprehensible to a man who honored education above practically everything else. He was unimpressed when I pointed out her long and honorable record of attendance. After observing Melissa padding around his home barefoot, he took to calling her "the cracker." Nonetheless, he liked her and, as always, he enjoyed having a woman on the premises.

Though I was uncertain what medical path to choose, I knew that whatever I chose, there were many things I would have to catch up on, so I began poring over medical journals to survey the recent developments in ophthalmology. I began to learn once again a medical language that I had not spoken for more than five years. I also enrolled at Harvard Medical School for a postgraduate course that is given every year for two weeks, primarily to prepare graduating residents for the exams given by the American Board of Ophthalmology, though there were other attendees like me who just wanted to brush up on the latest techniques. These measures were a good start, but I knew only so much could be gleaned from journals or classes. I needed hands-on experience under the guidance of a competent mentor, but who?

As a young man, I had studied with three of the top four professors in the world in my subspecialty. The fourth was Dr. Marshall Parks, the dean of pediatric ophthalmologists in the United States. I hardly knew him, though he had once heard me deliver a paper for the Squint Club, perhaps the most hallowed of ophthalmologic organizations. That was the sum total of our contact. How I summoned the courage to write him, I will never know. He possessed the characteristics that intimidate me most: absolute expertise in my medical field and a completely natural self-assurance. By contacting him, I was exposing myself to potential humiliation on both a professional and a personal level, but somehow, I managed to start the letter. "Dear Dr. Parks: I am coming back to practice medicine in New York." Here I stopped, thinking of the man who would read these words: tall, white-haired, dignified, prepossessing. Why would such a man want to play host to an oddity like me? He was the professor among professors—esteemed by colleagues and patients alike. He might view me as nothing more than a well-known nuisance who had thrown away an honorable medical career in pursuit of a frivolous dream. But I finished the letter in spite of my misgivings.

I spent the next week in nervous anticipation, half-expecting a terse note from Parks' secretary explaining that her boss was a busy man with an important practice who could not take time to reeducate a medical dropout, but such thoughts did not do justice to either of us. His letter of reply generously invited me to spend as much time as I needed observing and participating in his Washington, D.C., practice. That was the beginning of a marvelous six weeks, a period that built my confidence and reminded me of what being a fine doctor means in the world. Every morning at 6:30 A.M., I arrived at Dr. Parks' home, a stately mansion on Massachusetts Avenue with an adjoining office. His wife, Honey, ran the show and escorted patients in and out to him all day long, usually about forty-five of them, most young, a few needing relatively little treatment. For most, Dr. Parks was the instrument that would determine their quality of life for the rest of their days. I hadn't been exposed to this sobering aspect of medicine for five years, and the gentle yet expert way that Dr. Parks went about his ministrations was a good reminder of the critical role physicians play in people's lives. Dr. Renée Richards would need an attitude quite different from that of Renée Richards, tennis player and coach.

I also admired Dr. Parks' skills as a teacher. In the beginning of our association, he would ask me very basic things like "What would you do for this patient with exotropia?" And I would reply, "I would do a bilateral lateral rectus recession." Having received the correct answer, he would continue, "How much would you do?" Now, these were simple issues to Dr. Parks, an expert in strabismus who had practiced continually since leaving medical school, but they weren't so simple for me, who had not pondered such matters for years. Before answering, I would have to reflect for a few moments. At no point did I ever have the sense that he was thinking, "She's supposed to be a specialist, and she can't immediately answer a simple question?" Quite the contrary—Marshall instinctively brought me along at just the right pace, and he had the compassion to do it without making me feel like the class dunce. When he saw that my command had started to come back, his questions grew more complicated, but he never jumped ahead to anything so difficult as to undermine my growing confidence. By the end of my time with Marshall, I was like someone who hadn't been speaking French for a long while but after spending time in Paris was fluent again.

Marshall and I never discussed my sex change. He was too tactful to mention it, and I was too respectful to bring it up myself. However, he accorded me a degree of solicitude that he might not have shown Dick Raskind. Once on a severe winter's day, the electricity was out in his home and consequently in his office. Though we were inside, everyone, including the patients, was bundled up against the cold. The linoleum floor in his examining room was freezing, and he had a rug put under my feet so that I wouldn't suffer while we did the exams. Marshal did without a rug.

He deferred to me in other ways. We used to take just a short break for lunch by opening the examining room door and going into the private part of his home, where the cook would put out a nice meal for us in the dining room. Marshall would take about five minutes to eat his, but he would encourage me to stay longer.

"I'll get started on the next patient. You take your time."

When I had finished my lunch, I would join him.

Marshall was courtly to everyone, except incompetents, and I always felt he was treating me like a lady. His easy masculinity was reassuring and even comforting, though I never abused this solicitude and I certainly did my share of work. Believe me, even if I had been a striking beauty, Marshal would have had me out the door in an instant if he had decided I was a halfhearted or mediocre physician.

My six weeks at the side of such a doctor revitalized my passion for medicine, but where I would practice was an as-yet-unanswered question. Though I was now well-prepared to resume my career, I still lacked two of the things necessary for a top physician: a hospital association and a practice of my own. To remedy the first need, I applied to be reinstated at the Manhattan Eye, Ear, and Throat Hospital, where I had discovered through some discreet inquiries that Dr. Renée Richards would be welcomed. I was pleased because I considered MEETH, as it was known, to be my home and its staff my family.

However, my return was not universally approved. Two of the surgeon directors objected, citing the very problems that I myself feared: the crippling effects of a long hiatus from medicine and the possible nervousness of patients at being treated by a notorious transsexual. They were also concerned about my stability. Could I stand up under the physical and emotional strains of a medical practice? Worst of all, they worried that putting me on the staff would draw criticism or even cause a scandal. I heard that there was some heated discussion at the meeting of the board of surgeon directors (a board I myself would serve on years later); but the majority ruled that I should be accepted after a thorough check into my credentials.

I didn't mind a working over by the credentials committee. In this regard, all Dr. Richards asked was to be treated like anybody else.

The second prerequisite, a practice, was still in doubt. I could not indefinitely continue working as a part-time physician in friends' offices, though doing so had been helpful in reintroducing me to the demands of treating and caring for patients. At this point, I was still contemplating life as a country doctor, though most of my associates thought I belonged in the city. I felt so, too, but was afraid I couldn't make it work. Then, out of nowhere, an opportunity presented itself. Sadly, Dr. John Hermann, a leading specialist in strabismus, died, putting the future of his Park Avenue office in doubt. His was a desirable practice and many specialists made it known that they would love to take it over. I was not certain that I wanted to enter such a high-profile world, but when a trusted colleague of John's recommended me to his widow as the best choice to succeed him, the fates seemed to be speaking. When my father also gave his approval, I concluded that the country doctor notion had been overruled by a higher authority. After some soul-searching, some legal conferences, and $50,000 from Martina, I became a Park Avenue doctor.

These developments were fine as far as they went, but buying a practice and being approved by a couple of committees couldn't entirely restore my reputation, and the split vote of the board of surgeons proved that there was some resistance to my joining the Manhattan medical community. As I walked the familiar halls of MEETH, clad in a no-nonsense skirt and blouse, I sensed certain people casting furtive glances at me, trying to find the imposing Dr. Richard Raskind in the figure of Dr. Renée Richards, probably as deeply confused by the similarities as the differences. A few on the staff were quite distant, acting almost as if I were a stranger. One I remember in particular, the wife of a fellow doctor, who hardly acknowledged that she knew me. And she and I had been friends! However, she was the lone exception among the women of the medical community, who were otherwise uniformly happy to have me back, whatever my name or gender.

Colleagues who in the previous era had been Dick's friends reacted to Renée as they had to Dick, with the exception of substituting the pronoun "she" for "he," a challenge they handled almost flawlessly. Others, who had not been close, struggled mightily with the pronouns and would occasionally refer to me as "he," which always stung. The oblivious offenders were the easiest to take because they would just make the mistake and move on. The well-meaning ones sometimes stopped with a horrified look on their faces, which was bad enough, but then might launch into an agonizing apology. It isn't easy keeping your dignity in a hospital hallway under those circumstances, especially when you know that everyone within earshot is tuned in. I found the best strategy was to say, "That's okay," and retreat if I could. The only positive result from such an encounter was that it was so anguished that the same person seldom did it twice. I never sensed that anybody was purposefully mixing the pronouns to be hurtful. If that had happened, I would have made it my business to see that he or she was looking for another job. Some things you just can't let go by.

The only person at MEETH that I gave any latitude to in

the matter of my sex change was Izzy Goldstein, an operating-room orderly who had been there for twenty-five years. Izzy was stout of limb and good-hearted, but he was not . . . well, let's just say he was not inclined to intellectual pursuits. He loved ice skating in Central Park, and a friend and I used to kid him about it.

"Just because your name is Izzy Goldstein," we would say, "you think you are the world's greatest ice skater."

"How did you know I was an ice skater?" he would ask, his gravelly voice full of surprise.

We made this comment probably a hundred times, and he always responded in the same way and with the same wonderment. He called me Dr. Raskind until the day he died, and I would never have thought of correcting him. The fact that I was wearing a skirt never seemed to make an impression on Izzy, which somehow made him all the more lovable. Once when he was on the Hospital Workers Union picket line on a brutal winter day, I stuck a hundred-dollar bill in his shirt pocket as I went by.

"Thanks, Doctor Raskind," he said.

Izzy apparently saw no difference between Dr. Raskind and Dr. Richards, but others felt that the change in me went deeper than the physical. One was Cheryl Kaufman, one of the residents who had been under my direction before I left New York. She had climbed high and was now in charge of the Friday-morning eye muscle clinic, in which she invited me to participate. The hospital had such a clinic every weekday, and it was an interesting experience to be at least technically under the authority of one of my ex-students. Cheryl had ample opportunity to watch me work and was forthright about the changes she saw, claiming that Dick had been something of a hard case, especially with the women students and residents. She used the word "sexist," but I reminded her that Dick was the first to start training women at the hospital.

"Dick was tough on everyone," I would say. "Medicine is a demanding field. Residency is supposed to make you strong."

"No," she would say firmly, "you are much more tolerant of frailty these days."

I can only trust her observations. I suppose Renée was a little gentler, but a bumbler is a bumbler and even Renée would abruptly take a case away from a resident if the bumbling got out of hand. The good of the patient is always the top priority, with the feelings of the residents running a distant second. They knew enough to be on their best behavior with Dr. Richards, though a compliment on her hair wasn't a bad start.

One difference that I did notice in myself was in locker room behavior. (Yes, they have locker rooms in hospitals as well as tennis clubs.) Dick Raskind had always treated a locker room, whether in a hospital or athletic facility, as a transitional area to be moved through at top speed. Renée was inclined to hang around a bit more and chat. By the time I returned to the hospital in 1982, the operating rooms were in a new building, and the women's O.R. dressing rooms were luxurious, with each surgeon having her own wooden locker. As a senior member of the staff, I enjoyed one that was fully seven feet tall. It was quite a departure from the no-nonsense steel locker Dick had shared with another surgeon in the old days. However, the improvement in luxury could not wholly explain my change in behavior. Though I didn't spend extended periods hanging around in there, I often had a cup of coffee, a muffin, and a bit of chat with one of the other doctors before going into surgery, something the driven Dick Raskind would never have done. But for Renée, it seemed the normal thing. I think it must reflect a biological tendency; something about safety and privacy pleases the female.

My first operations went well, though as a safety measure I asked one of the respected older staff physicians to assist me; however, that lasted for only a short period. It was obvious to me and everyone else in the hospital that I had regained my form. However, building my new reputation involved more than good surgical technique. Top doctors must be able to pass along their expertise. It is a professional obligation that physicians accept when they take their Hippocratic Oath, so I began to participate in grand rounds, a central event in a teaching hospital.

The turning point in my acceptance came when I made a presentation on Duane's Retraction Syndrome to the assembled staff of ophthalmologists. To the average person, a discussion of this eye muscle abnormality would seem an arcane topic, but for doctors who have to treat the disorder, it is riveting, and I gave a good performance on that day, speaking without notes and covering the history of the condition from its first description around the turn of the last century to the present day. After this tour de force, I think any doubters were convinced that the mind they respected in Richard Raskind was still at work in Renée Richards. Soon after, physicians started to refer difficult strabismus problems to me. I was back.

The office on Park Avenue posed a separate set of problems that were aggravated by a severe cash-flow problem. Melissa was managing the money, and despite her apparent unconcern with the material world, she was unyielding in the matter of personal responsibility. She had decided that I owed Martina the price of the office and would not let us live decently until the debt was paid. Consequently, this Park Avenue doctor spent several months sleeping on the couch of her office and running out to her father's house in Forest Hills for showers. Melissa, having lived as an impoverished student for thirteen years, was unfazed by this arrangement; I, however, had hoped for something more from my life as a top physician. Our office camp was not only undignified, it was also illegal and unthinkably plebeian for the Park Avenue neighborhood. Luckily, the setup was never discovered by either the police or the area's social arbiters.

While I saw patients and waited for the day when it would be only a few steps to the shower rather than a few miles, the already-large office staff I had inherited from the previous doctor had been growing at an alarming rate. The only good thing about this buildup of staff was that it brought Arleen Larzelere into my life. When Robin, who was then my office manager, found that attending to her managing duties cut into the time she could spend in the back watching soap operas, she decided to hire an assistant, who turned out to be Arleen. Arleen had been working in a New Jersey ophthalmologist's office and felt that moving to a Park Avenue office would be a way to better herself. From the outside this might have seemed sensible, but I'm surprised she did not run away screaming when she got the

insider's view. At that point, she could not guess the adminis-
trative chaos she was being drawn into nor predict the major
role she would eventually play in bringing order to my business
and to my life in general.

At first, Arleen was nothing more than Robin's gofer, but
it was not long before she became a roommate. The commute
from New Jersey was two hours each way and went through
some rough neighborhoods. I invited her to stay at Camp Renée
until she could find a place in the city, so after closing, the staid
doctor's office took on the aspect of a women's dorm, with various articles of clothing hanging from the fixtures and the walls
ringing with exchanges over who was taking too much time
in the little restroom. It was during this comic period that my
relationship with Melissa began to fray. What had worked well
in bucolic Gainesville was proving impractical in Manhattan.
Melissa remained unperturbed. When I would criticize her for
some mistake in the office, she would just look at me with an
enigmatic smile and say nothing. The strain increased when
I discovered that she had ignored the chance to get us into a
rent-stabilized apartment one floor above the office, thus pro-
longing our nightly agony on the office couch. Poor Arleen was
sleeping on the floor. I was furious.

Then again, Melissa had a new boyfriend in Connecticut,
who was the primary focus of her attention. She was very anxious to join him in Connecticut, and I think the only thing keeping her in Manhattan was the conviction that my life would fall
to pieces without her guidance. I think she saw very quickly that
Arleen was an able replacement, and soon afterward she took a
convenient opportunity to make her escape. As I've made clear,

I am content to have the daily details of my life managed by someone else. I am not good at it, and I will even submit to living in the back of the office if instructed to do so, as long as the person who instructs me will pick up the laundry. However, I am the ultimate authority in the matter of my specialties, tennis and medicine. One day, Melissa contradicted me in a medical opinion concerning one of my patients. I wanted to put contact lenses on him, and she flatly said I couldn't.

"I'm the president of this organization," I said menacingly, "and you have to do what I say."

"I have no intention of doing what you say," she replied with no further explanation.

"In that case, you're fired."

It was just that simple. The airy Melissa was off to Connecticut, and I later remembered that we had already tried contacts on the patient and found he couldn't tolerate them. If she had only communicated that information, we would not have clashed, but I'm convinced she wanted to leave, and with her went most of the last vestiges of Renée's adolescence.

Melissa's departure brought many changes. For one, Arleen and I did not hesitate to grab a studio apartment that opened up in the building that housed my office. It was nothing more than a large room with a Pullman kitchen on one wall, but at least we could eat in and take a bath on the premises, which was quite a step up in convenience. As I looked around appreciatively at the amenities I was now enjoying after nearly a year on the office couch, I decided that this was just the beginning. There was no reason why Dr. Renée Richards could not have the good life; however, I would have to take some steps to clear up the employee mess in the office so I could make enough money to finance that good life. By now, I was sure that Arleen was capable of managing both my personal and business needs. This meant that the soap-addicted Robin could be shown the door, and while I was at it, I made a list of all the other employees I was tripping over and the next day called them into my office.

"You're fired, you're fired, you're fired, and you're fired."

This housecleaning included my cousin Philis, who in a moment of insanity I had hired to work for us. Once the crowd at the office had been thinned to manageable proportions, I could concentrate on doctoring, though I was to learn that the acceptance of my new incarnation had limits.

While most of my old patients eventually found their way to my new office, there were exceptions. One memorable example stands out. As Dr. Richard Raskind, I had been a favorite of Chief Rabbi Teitelbaum, head of one of the powerful Hasidic sects in Brooklyn. How I got to be favored by Rabbi Teitelbaum, I never figured out. I was never *frum*—religious and observant—but the chief rabbis were smart and consequently knew who the "tops" were in every field, and they made sure their followers got treated by the best. In the old days, Rabbi Teitelbaum sent numerous little children to me, many of them cross-eyed or myopic, probably a consequence of strict rules against marrying outside the sect; the resultant marriages between first cousins collected recessive genes. Anyway, I would say, "Yes, your little *bubbala* needs an operation." The child's father would respond, "I have to go back and ask Chief Rebbe Teitelbaum." This would require a trip to the Williamsburg section of Brooklyn, where Rabbi Teitelbaum would tweak his beard and inquire, "Who wants to operate?" When the father would say, "Dr. Raskind," the chief rabbi would say, "Okay. Get the operation." This went on for years.

My Hasidic clientele followed Dick Raskind into some unlikely places. When I was a professor at Cornell Medical School, as gentile an outfit as they come, I still retained my mystique. I remember operating on a pair of twins at the Cornell Medical Center and later striding into the hospital room to find their father keeping watch in a nearby chair, his long beard almost obstructing his prayer book. He looked up and nodded toward one of the kids.

"Okay?" he muttered.

"He's fine," I answered.

Then he nodded at the other one.

"Also fine," I said.

With no further comment, he returned to his prayer book. We went through this routine every time I entered the room. They were the only words we spoke.

My shift from Dr. Richard to Dr. Renée brought my Teitelbaum referrals to a halt. On rare occasions at present I am referred a child from a chief rabbi in Brooklyn, but the case has to be so serious or so complicated that a "last word" consultation is required. It seems only in that circumstance can my history be, if not forgotten, at least momentarily ignored. Ironically, when I gave up my Park Avenue office in 2003, I joined the practice of the Rosenblum Eye Centers, an outfit so orthodox that it sees patients on Sundays in all three of its offices. I now have another little group of orthodox patients who don't seem to care who I used to be. You lose some, but you win some.

However, my farewell to the Park Avenue office was many years in the future as I settled into New York life in the early 1980s. My years in Gainesville had been charming and uncomplicated, but I found myself relishing the Manhattan pace and the perennial thrill of life in the city I had known so well. There is nowhere else like New York City, with all its good and bad.

Without question one of the good things about living in New York was being near my son. During my absence, I had spoken to him almost daily by phone and had made frequent trips home, but living in the same city with him was quite different and made for some continuing challenges. Almost immediately, the question of whether I was his mother or father became an issue. This confusion was compounded by the fact that Nick had inherited some of my tendency to be oblivious to my surroundings, and he often created situations that could have been avoided with a bit of discretion. I remember when he was only about eight or nine (not the most discreet of ages, even in conventional families), we were in the supermarket, and from one end of an aisle, he screamed to me at the other end, "Dad! Come down here by the meat department." At the sound of this ear-shattering command, my fellow shoppers naturally looked to see who was on the receiving end, but their annoyed expressions were immediately replaced by ones of confusion, dismay, or apprehension. All I could do was shrug my shoulders and try to appear nonchalant as I pushed my cart toward the meat department, flanked by people either pretending to be intensely interested in the canned peas or staring unashamedly at the most unusual dad they had ever seen. Either way, it was a disconcerting scene, and it occurred over and over in various permutations.

Most of my patients were children, and I felt good about their acceptance. In general, I was perceived by them as a female, though over the years, some little kids have come in the office and commented to their mothers, "Wow, is she big!" I never feel too badly about a remark like that. They're right: I am big. Probably the most devastating childish comment was made by a five-year-old during my first year back in the city. I feel it must have happened because of my voice. I try to modulate it, but sometimes I sound like Dick Raskind. I never know when I am going to have a bad voice day or even a bad five minutes. I must have spoken to the child's mother in that voice, and her daughter asked in all innocence, "Mommy, why is that man wearing a dress?" Hearing this from a child somehow pierced my heart more completely than any of the vicious insults hurled at me when I was a public figure. The child's mother was horrified.

"Think nothing of it," I said, but I couldn't take my own advice.

After they left, I cried a little and took a time out. Over the next few days, I repeatedly relived the moment, and I still remember it occasionally. Luckily, I never suffered through another such obvious incident, but I must have missed a great many subtler cues, thanks to my capacity for self-deception. I'm sure that what I see in the mirror is different from what others see, but a little self-deception has helped me preserve myself and move through life largely unaffected by insights that might have devastated me.

My tunnel vision, and a little naïvety, extend to matters other than comments about my sex change. On one occasion, I saw a young woman with an eye muscle problem. When she came into the office, I was told, "She's an actress," and nothing more. As I examined her, I noted that she was certainly attractive enough to be a leading lady. She had long curly hair and was wearing a T-shirt and blue jeans. She seemed down to earth, and I assumed that she was nothing more than another struggling young actress. You see them on the streets of Manhattan many times in the course of a day. I have always had a soft spot in my heart for them. Long ago, Dick Raskind had wistfully considered becoming an actor.

I thought she was probably strapped for cash, so when I finished the exam, I said to my office manager, "Give her a discount."

"Give her a discount? She makes twenty million dollars a picture!"

I suppose my staff assumed that I would connect her name with her fame. Like millions of moviegoers, I had seen her on the screen, but I never made the connection.

MY RETURN TO MEDICINE was not entirely a matter of day-to-day doctoring. One of the projects that I worked on for years was the development of an electrical pacemaker that could be implanted in the orbit near a paralyzed eye muscle to stimulate the muscle. By today's standards, it was crude, but I think it was the first such attempt. My collaborator in this research was Yu Quon Chen, a visiting scientist from the People's Republic of China. He was a pleasant young man, recommended to me by a colleague at Case Western Reserve University in Cleveland, where Yu Quon was temporarily on the staff.

When he was in New York for our project, Yu Quon stayed over by the Hudson River in an old Holiday Inn that the Chinese government had turned into its New York City embassy. There was no outward sign that it was the Chinese Embassy, and when I dropped Yu Quon off at the end of a day's work, he would walk to the door and a slot would open up and two little eyes would peer out. Once Yu Quon's identity had been verified, they would admit him. Occasionally I would take him to dinner, and he would have to make a prior arrangement with the embassy to let them know not to make a meal for him that night. What the penalty for not notifying them would have been I never found out. The whole situation gave me the creeps, and though I was curious about how the Chinese might have transformed the Holiday Inn to fit their needs, I never asked to see the inside. It seemed the sort of place that you might not come out of.

However, Yu Quon himself was the picture of geniality and diligence. With my instruction he developed a small implantable plastic and wire stimulator about the size and thickness of a quarter, and we set out to find an appropriate laboratory animal on which to try out our invention. The key requirement was human-like binocular vision, and that meant primates. There are only a few so-called "primate centers" scattered around the country. In those days, one of these was located in southern New York State. I made the necessary contacts and, after some negotiation, was given the green light to perform this first-of-its-kind operation. On the appointed day, I drove out into the country with Yu Quon, Arleen, and a car full of equipment. We found no sign on the rural road indicating the whereabouts of the primate facility. It seemed a very hush-hush operation. By carefully following instructions, we were able to find the complex, down a dirt road deep in the woods. It was an un-prepossessing collection of four single-story cement buildings containing the chimpanzee area and a few operating rooms.

Assisted by an interested young resident I had recruited, I implanted the first stimulator into a primate eye muscle, with Yu Quon Chen standing by, tending to the big box of electronic equipment he had built to feed data into the electrode. We dis-covered that our principle was correct. We could make the muscle contract and turn the eye, which held promise for hu-mans with paralyzed eye muscles. It was a satisfying moment. Along with the stimulator, we implanted the quarter-sized bat-tery pack, which we located above the floor of the orbit, just be-neath the eyeball itself. Afterward, the chimp made an unevent-ful recovery from anesthesia and tolerated the implant with no adverse effects.

Our research went on for the better part of a year while we monitored our implantable electrode and determined how the eye and orbit behaved with the additional hardware added to it. We presented our findings in a preliminary report to the Inter-national Conference of Electrical Engineers. Though we never put it in an ophthalmology journal, I did present the work one year at the annual meeting of the American Association for Re-search in Vision and Ophthalmology.

Once the research was over, I thought my exposure to the

chimps was also finished. Frankly, I felt relieved. Using such animals for research had evoked some conflicting feelings in me, but growing up and becoming a player in the high-stakes world of medicine requires hard choices. I saw no evidence of neglect at the lab, and Arleen, who takes a backseat to no one in her love of animals, was also impressed with the care the primates received and the devotion of those who gave it. Though I didn't know it at the time, I would soon be intimately involved in this care. In a few months, I received a call from one of the lab staff, who asked if I would come to the center to look at a couple of chimps who were not doing well. Both had eye problems.

"Sure," I said. "You've been very accommodating to me. It's the least I can do."

"Yes, but there's one other thing."

"Oh?"

"Both chimps have been infected with AIDS."

"Well, then . . . "

"Yes?"

"We'll have to be careful, won't we?"

In the mid-1980s nothing was scarier than AIDS. It was poorly understood, and even medical professionals were unsure just how communicable AIDS was. The general public was in a near panic, leading to the suspension of activities like religious communion and mouth-to-mouth resuscitation. All this underscored the potential importance of the chimp research. Arleen and I went back to the woods. After an initial round of greetings, I was ushered into a preparation area and helped into something like a spacesuit, complete with cloth helmet. As

I looked out of the Plexiglas eyepieces and listened to myself breathe, I felt as if I were in a science fiction film. But there was more. I was prompted to put on a pair of gloves that came up to my elbows and then a pair of paper overshoes that covered not only my footwear but rose up to my knees. After putting on a second pair of gloves, I was deemed protected enough to have a look at the eyes of the center's biggest and most dominant primate, Howie.

Howie was sedated, of course. The chimps of the larger variety can be very aggressive and have ten times the strength of a human. Even if the chimps can't attack directly, they will sometimes spit at the doctors and attendants or urinate or throw feces at them. Howie, I found, had a bad corneal ulcer on one eye, which he may have incurred in a fight with another chimp. I cauterized the base of it and injected an antibiotic just beneath the outer layer of the eye. Ordinarily, I would have skipped the injection and prescribed frequent applications of antibiotics, but that would have meant putting Howie to sleep several times a day, which would have been dangerous for him, and trying to administer the drops when he was awake would have been even more dangerous for his attendants. Howie was not one to let you go near him, much less touch his eyes.

Then I was asked to look at a baby chimp, almost like a human baby, very affectionate and responsive to touch, even if the touch came through a double layer of gloves. His optic nerves did not seem healthy, and he was feverish. It did not look good for the little fellow. After I had struggled out of my protective gear, I regretfully told the attending doctor that I was not optimistic about the baby's survival. The man looked stricken but attempted to maintain the appearance of professional detachment. I said I was sorry, and Arleen and I left the center for the last time.

The baby chimp had meningitis and only lived for a few more days. During that time, the attending doctor called me every day with a report on his status, and when the baby died, he was clearly bereft. Medical research is not done by robots or sadistic monsters. It is often done by people who love their charges and are in despair when they suffer or die. But they are professionals, too. The same doctor called me weekly to give me a report on Howie's progress. He recovered from the eye problem. How he coped with the AIDS, I never found out.

This then was the world that Renée Richards returned to after her adolescence in tennis. It is a world where the stakes are high: light or dark and sometimes life or death. You have to be like the doctor at the research lab, compassionate but resolute. You have to believe enough in what you are doing to make tough choices that others don't want to make. You get glory when it goes right and hatred when it goes wrong. And you get Wednesday afternoon off for golf. How can anybody begrudge us that?

CHAPTER 8

Country Retreat

M Y LIFE IN NEW York City was exciting and full of satisfactions. It was a continuing thrill to walk out of my office onto Park Avenue and glance uptown and down, both familiar but somehow refreshed by my reclaimed career. I loved it. Yet to feel a complete person, I had to be able to get away.

I suppose my love of the rural life started years ago at Deer Lake Camp, where every summer I escaped the turmoil of the Raskind house. Those endless hours of woodcraft touched me at a deep level. Even before my operation, I couldn't live a full life in a largely concrete and glass environment, and in the early 1980s, having just come from three years in leafy Gainesville, I was used to lots of foliage. I needed a country house, and not just for me but for my two dogs as well. And then there was Nick. He was an energetic twelve-year-old, and I wanted a place where he could whoop and holler and safely shoot a rifle. I figured we could catch up on lost time tramping in the country. It would make a nice counterpoint to the pressures and temptations of big-city life, which may afflict a kid even more heavily than an adult, especially when the kid's father is frequently mistaken for his mother. That perplexing problem was far less likely to occur in the woods. With these thoughts in mind, I set out to find a country house.

This quest was possible only after a rocky early period in the Park Avenue office, when the referrals were not coming as fast as they did later. My type of medicine runs almost completely on referrals by physicians who identify a need for my specialized surgery, so I am seldom the first doctor to see a patient. At first the referrals dribbled in, but they increased as I proved myself. After a year or so, when they were coming in a steady stream, I felt I could afford a weekend retreat.

At this time, Melissa was still with me, and together we started to look for an appropriate house. What we found was something Melissa thought was perfect. I sort of stood there with my mouth open, but in the end I agreed to rent it mostly because she was so enthralled. Perhaps it was her Florida roots that caused her to love a house situated on a swamp. The Plaster House, as it was called, had been built in 1600 by Dutch settlers and had reputedly served as a stagecoach inn on the route between Boston and New York during revolutionary times.

It had changed little since those days. Air-conditioning? Forget it. The place hardly had heat, just a few big Dutch ovens and open brick fireplaces scattered around, one in each of the bedrooms. These were all we had against the Connecticut winter. Perhaps this setup was considered cozy in the eighteenth century, but it was sadly lacking two hundred years later. The Plaster House was the last such Dutch-built house remaining in the area. That alone should have raised a red flag. All the others of its type had disintegrated or been torn down in disgust years before. However, with its steeply sloping roof and plaster walls, it had an Old World appearance. A stork's nest would not have seemed out of place on the chimney top. And to be fair, the place came with its own waterfall, located at the front of the house. It was fed by the Jeremy Swamp and emptied into a sparkling stream that ran alongside the house. We would paddle around in the small pool below the waterfall at the beginning of the stream. It was delightful on a hot day.

The swamp, however, was the subject of varying opinions. Some, like Melissa, thought it a mystical place of great power. On the other hand, Wallace Nutting in his *Connecticut Beautiful* recalled it with the words, "And what a dismal place it was." I tentatively agreed with Melissa's mystical assessment until I was attacked by voracious mosquitoes, at which time I retreated to the house, leaving her to sit by the waterfall and drink in the mystique. She drank it in for about two months, but after meeting Quincy, she abruptly decamped, leaving me with a year's lease on a house I hadn't wanted in the first place. Nick and I soldiered on. Melissa, by the way, ended up living in Quincy's mother's garage, while Quincy continued to live in the house with his mother. Mom was not inclined to allow her unwedded son to enjoy a conjugal relationship under her roof.

Melissa's abdication paved the way for the rise of Arleen Larzelere, who has gradually become truly indispensable and the single most important factor in stabilizing my crazy existence. She has been my best friend, housemate, confidante, keeper, critic, advisor, and censor for twenty-plus years and will undoubtedly continue as such until I die. When Arleen first entered my life, she knew nothing about Renée Richards except that in 1976, near her hometown of East Orange, there was a big ruckus at the tennis club in South Orange, with cars parked all over the place for miles, down to South Orange Avenue. She thought it was absurd that some surgically altered person was playing in the women's tennis tournament there. She has never been interested in sports or games of any sort, not just because she has been working to survive since childhood but because she hates the winning and losing aspect of games. She does not understand competition, and though she would deny it, she barely knows to keep score in tennis, golf, football, or baseball. Yet, if I do not win the senior golf tournament at my club, Arleen will be more upset than me, though she will never show it.

Why does she care? I'm not completely sure. I think she saw from the start that we have both been scarred by our childhoods, though the particulars differ greatly. Arleen was the daughter of an alcoholic father who regularly beat the daylights out of her and her little brother until at the age of fourteen Arleen called the cops and had him thrown out of the house. He was only occasionally a resident father thereafter. Her mother, who was beaten even worse, was afraid to leave her husband for fear of rendering herself and her children destitute. He was handy with machines and made a good enough salary for the family to live in a middle-class suburb of Newark, though his binges continually interrupted his working life. When Arleen was a child, her father kept her with him at all times, even in the bars where he caroused. Arleen's mother tried to reason with him, but he paid no attention. Arleen managed to make it through high school, though her controlling father tried to undermine her education by taking her books away from her. Nonetheless, she learned to love books and to this day reads several every week. Arleen's childhood environment was the polar opposite of the intellectual Jewish household in which Dick Raskind was raised, but every year when my sister visits and Arleen has a review of our brother-sister dynamic, she never fails to say, "Your childhood was worse than mine."

Our life together somehow works for both of us. She is completely devoted to me, and her driving force is to take care of Renée—which, I must admit, makes it pretty hard to find fault with her, though we do have our differences. I dislike the radio and always turn it off when I come into the kitchen in the morning, though I can still hear it from Arleen's room, where she also has it on. In fact, she has the radio on twenty-four hours a day. She is a good manager, taking care of our banking, correspondence, appointments, taxes, home maintenance, cooking, and shopping, and she is a gourmet cook. I would rather eat one of Arleen's meals on a TV tray in the den than sit down for dinner at the Four Seasons. Her cooking is that good.

Having lived with me for so many years, she is by now one of the world's authorities on transsexuals, and she thinks they are all nuts. The idea of a transsexual playing in women's competition strikes her as completely cuckoo because she does not consider them real women; however, she goes berserk whenever anyone uses the pronoun "he" when referring to me. Arleen has a wonderful sense of style, and she buys all of my clothes for me. As a group, transsexuals tend to dress like your Aunt Mitt from fifty years ago, but Arleen keeps me fashionable. She jokes that she should go into business dressing transsexuals, and she could probably make a good living at it. I sometimes go further than merely having her choose my clothes; I often wear Arleen's jackets and even her dresses. When I presented Martina at her enshrinement in the International Tennis Hall of Fame, my dress drew a lot of compliments: it was Arleen's. When I ask her what I should wear for an occasion, she always says, "You are Renée Richards. You can wear anything you like." But she never lets me out the door in anything that is not attractive and in good taste.

Arleen is the person who knows that the emperor wears no clothes. She keeps me honest. I certainly can't believe my press releases or the cheering from my friends when Arleen is around. She will puncture that balloon in a second. My dependence on Arleen in day-to-day matters has grown to the point that I simply turn over my weekly earnings to her and placidly accept whatever cash she gives me on Monday. I don't even know how much it is. I just put it in my purse and move on. If I run out, she gives me some more. Things go better that way.

Arleen was married and divorced before we met. She still has some gentleman friends, but these days she seems happiest to spend her free time at home with just an occasional foray out to her book club. Arleen does not analyze the nature of our partnership, but in a rare moment of reflection she once said, "I know I would never have been part of Dick Raskind's life in

the old days." But she knows that she has become the most important woman in the life of the person Dick Raskind became.

If I ever had any reason to wonder whether or not Arleen
had the grit to stick it out as my manager general, those doubts
were dispelled when I saw how she reacted to the Plaster House.
In the winter, the place was so freezing cold that we sometimes
had to sleep right next to the fireplace. On New Year's Eve, Arleen and I were sleeping next to the fire and the pipes burst in
the basement, sending the population of mice into a scurrying
panic. Arleen hardly batted an eye. When she was a child, her
family had lived for a while in a house with no running water
and plenty of mice. She probably thought the Plaster House
was a step up because at least it contained water pipes to burst.
Arleen simply moved our bedding to higher ground.

The Plaster House proved equally daunting in the summer,
when it was so sweltering that we were driven outside to brave
the mosquito swarm. When the heat grew especially intense,
Nick would drag his mattress into the cellar, where he claimed
it was cooler. I might have tried it myself if I hadn't been discouraged by the memories of all those mice after the pipes
burst. Nick, however, enjoyed the mice, or at least he enjoyed
dispatching them. He used to lay a trail of cheese crumbles
from one room to the next and then hide in the second room.
When the exultant mouse turned the corner, Nick would send
him into oblivion with one shot from his BB gun.

Nick invited many friends up from the city, and the Plaster
House was an eye-opening experience for them. One of them
got out of the car, listened for a moment, and then announced,
"It's raining here." This in spite of the fact that the sun was

shining and there wasn't a cloud in the sky. He had never heard a waterfall. City kids!

Before Arleen started coming up and running the house, I used to cook for the youngsters, mostly spaghetti. Nick says we ate a lot of it, and I won't dispute his word. I am no homemaker, but I can boil spaghetti. Luckily I don't bake, because it would not have occurred to me to shoo the mice out of the oven as Arleen later had to do. We once played host to a young woman who was being considered to write the screenplay based on my autobiography. She went into her upstairs room and found a dead bird on her bed. Arleen and I considered this a bad omen, and she didn't get the writing job. Besides, she wanted to change too many things about my life. What for? It's been weird enough.

Despite its drawbacks, the Plaster House was an ideal distance from the city, a very manageable hour-and-a-half drive into New Haven County, which was not as toney as Litchfield County. It was a simple country spot, for most people just a place to pass through on their way into the upper reaches of New England. And, whatever one's opinion of the Jeremy Swamp, the area in general was quite beautiful. In those days, there were only a few vacation homes in New Haven County. Most of its people were year-round residents, and among them were Hal and his wife, Midge, the couple from whom I rented the Plaster House.

Hal and Midge seemed more or less trustworthy at first. They were free-living types, but they were landowners and presumably married. And compared to the guy in white robes who used to camp out by the stream near the house, they were positively conventional. The white-robed man had some sort of fish-shaped wooden symbol tacked up between two trees. The fish suggested Christianity, but Nick says he was a Druid. I'm not sure how he came by this information, unless he disobeyed me and went close enough to the man to ask about his beliefs, which is quite likely. I did my best to ignore the alleged Druid, but I know that he performed occasional religious rites at the site. I am no stranger to eccentrics, and I assumed he was harmless, though late at night with no neighbors nearby he seemed more threatening, and he was one of the reasons I was glad to have guns in the house. However, when the guns were stolen I grew increasingly apprehensive about the Plaster House.

Nick and I traded theories as to who among our neighbors might be the culprit. I suspected the ones who had offered him pot, which he had refused (his involvement with drugs was to come later). I had forbidden him to see them anymore, though I doubt he minded me. Nick thought it might be one of his young friends from the area, but we never solved the mystery. All this made the Plaster House more interesting for Nick, and he didn't mind the loss of the guns because he got upgraded to new weaponry. I had insisted that he take the state firearms safety course before I gave him his first .22 rifle and later a twenty-gauge shotgun, which he used effectively on supervised bird-hunting trips in the area. He scored a 99 on the test. I could only wish that he had been as motivated in his academics, but at least I had the satisfaction of knowing that he could handle a gun properly, and it also proved that he could study a subject when it interested him. However, with stolen guns in the area, Druids in the swamp, bursting pipes, and pot being offered to my son, I decided that I would look for a more conventional vacation spot.

I cast my eye on Putnam County, New York, recommended to me by Felice Early, a former landlady from Dick Raskind's era. Felice is a longtime New Yorker and was once a Ziegfeld Follies girl. The apartment I had rented from her was a jewel, the most magnificent bachelor pad on the Upper East Side, so I trusted her taste in real estate. In exploring Putnam, the smallest county in New York State, Arleen and I came upon the Sedgewood Club, a collection of eighty homes scattered around two pristine lakes. It is definitely a spot for people in a certain income bracket, but not as exclusive as the nearby Gypsy Trail Club, where you have to be approved by a homeowner's board before you can purchase land there. At Sedgewood, the prices and amenities pretty much dictated the type of person who could buy: It contained a beautiful golf course, two red-clay tennis courts, and an old Adirondack-style boathouse on China Lake.

I knew this was where I wanted to have my home the first time I drove up oak-lined Kittredge Drive. Everything seemed so crisp and airy by comparison with the close, humid atmosphere at Jeremy Swamp. I was even more inclined toward Sedgewood when I found that the little red cottage we eventually rented was owned by Tom Dee, a classmate from my Horace Mann days and the editor of the yearbook the year before me. In my junior year, I used to have to do his bidding and run all of his errands to make sure that I would be selected as the editor in my senior year.

At Sedgewood, I felt nothing like the mild dread I had experienced before signing up for the Plaster House, and as we settled in on the gorgeous shores of Barrett Lake, I looked forward to a comfortable existence without mice or pot-smoking gun thieves. Incidentally, the Plaster House was subsequently bought by the actress Barbara Hershey. I think she suited the house much better than I, and maybe she managed to make it livable. In 1993, it was put on the National Register of Historic Places.

Our rented cottage in Sedgewood stood no chance of making it onto the National Register, but that fact did not bother us at all. We were happy to trade history for comfort and reputable neighbors. The people who made up the Sedgewood Club were an eclectic bunch of families, mostly from New York City, who didn't want to be out in the high-toned Hamptons in Long Island, or who had already lived that upper-crust existence and no longer found it appealing. It was a community in transition. The older members were dying off or leaving for nursing homes, making way for a younger group, many of whom had children they sent to school in New York City and brought to the country on weekends. Only a few families lived all year round at Sedgewood. Half of the population was Jewish and half Christian and many were professional people—lawyers, doctors, writers—who I felt would accept me as a citizen of the community.

And Nicky liked it. Sedgewood was home to deer, skunk, opossum, raccoon, coyote, hawks, American bald eagles, otter, fox, and even an occasional bear. The foxes have stolen many a good tee shot over on the golf course. I wanted Nicky to enjoy the wild in the same way I had as a youngster, and he reveled in all that the country offered, especially fishing in the lakes and deer hunting in season. This was what I had been hoping for, a comfortable retreat, where I could enjoy my son and get him away from the Southampton lifestyle he had experienced while living with his mother, with its excessive emphasis on status and money.

At Sedgewood, Nick was exposed to responsible, down-to-earth people. They were prosperous and accomplished, but they weren't snooty. They judged you on your personality and what you had accomplished, not on your lineage or the wealth you had accumulated. If wealth had been the yardstick, I would not have been accepted, because even though my practice was picking up, I had not nearly retired my debts or reached my maximum earning power. So, though I was delighted when Nick urged me to buy a home in Sedgewood, I was not certain I could swing it, even though I had been looking across the lake from our rented cottage and thinking how perfect the land over there would be for a home. I knew financing would be tough, but I decided to try, and in doing so I learned the benefits of doing business with a local bank. In Manhattan, Renée Richards probably wouldn't have stood a chance of borrowing the necessary cash, but Merritt Ryder, who owned the local bank in Putnam County, okayed my loan and enabled me to build the house of my dreams. Without him, I would never have been able to do it. Merritt's own home was directly across the lake where he could watch over his investment as it went up.

By this time, Arleen had become an integral part of my life, and together we planned the new house. We wanted it to complement the beautiful property and reflect our woodsy lifestyle. What better than a log home? Back in 1984, this was not as trendy an idea as it is now, and many people were leery of the problems entailed in building with logs. Yet the romance of the idea outweighed such concerns. But where to start? Along about then, for better or worse, Wodjak (pronounced "Voytak") entered our lives.

Wodjak was a Polish man who was doing handiwork in the area, mostly in Sedgewood and often for my friend Mike Gibbons. He was a handsome fellow with a brushy mustache and a head full of long dark hair. Mike thought Wodjak could probably build an entire house for me, since he had been an architect in his native Poland. My eyes lit up. If this were true, I could save a lot of money by becoming my own general contractor, purchasing logs cut to my specifications, and having Wodjak build the house using some of his Polish compatriots as low-cost labor. I sought him out and asked, "Can you build a house for me?" and without a moment's hesitation he answered, "No problem." In fact, he had never built a house before, but I didn't know that, and even if I had, it probably would not have made a difference.

As we toured the area, looking at the various homes in Sedgewood, some entirely of logs, some of logs and stone, and some of rough-hewn wood, Wodjak seemed knowledgeable. He exuded confidence, giving the impression that he could easily put up any of the types I might choose. Eventually we settled on a combination of logs and fieldstone. Much of the fieldstone could be gathered right on the eight acres of land I had bought from Mr. Beman, whom I kidded for years afterward as we enjoyed drinks on my deck overlooking the lake. "Mr. Beman,"

I would say, "you just sold me a bunch of old rocks up here." And, he would reply as if scandalized, "Oh no, Renée. This is a beautiful piece of land." I was never sure he got my joke, but he was right about one thing. It was indeed a beautiful piece of land, with ledges overlooking seventy-five-acre Barrett Lake, full of bass and pickerel, wonderful for fishing, swimming, sailing, and calming the soul.

Wodjak drew up the design for the house, and after paying a New York architect to sign off on Wodjak's blueprints, I sent them to American Lincoln Logs in North Carolina where they began to cut our logs. As planned, I acted as my own general contractor, though I knew nothing about contracting. How hard could it be? I discovered how hard about the same time I realized that my property lay half in the Town of Carmel and half in the Town of Kent. Permission had to be obtained from the Town of Carmel for the tennis court and from the Town of Kent for the house. And to further complicate the process, the County of Putnam issued the health permit and the permit for the overall project. I learned more than I wanted to know about health-related permits, well-drilling permits, electrical permits, plumbing permits, and on and on. They seemed endless, and this does not touch on the inspections that seemed to come every other day.

As I previously mentioned, the property was largely rocks and sloped steeply down to the lake. However, contractors must build houses and tennis courts on level ground. The way you level craggy property is to drill into the rock, put dynamite in the holes, and set it off with a bang that rattles windows a mile away. I never thought I would have much to do with blasting, but as general contractor, I arranged for both blasting and logging, which are expensive, and as I signed the checks for these preliminary activities, I congratulated myself on having been smart enough to hire Wodjak. I would save a ton of money there. But you might not be surprised to learn that though the choice did save some money, it created issues that I had not anticipated.

In short order, I found myself smack in the middle of a series of labor-relations problems. The tradesmen who did the electrical and plumbing work were from families who had been in the area for generations, and they were not keen on working with the recently arrived Wodjak and his merry band of Polish men. I heard complaints from both sides, some expressed in a Hudson Valley early American twang and some in a thick Polish accent. I grew increasingly sympathetic with the old-line tradesmen as I tried to build a fire under Wodjak, whose progress had slowed to a crawl. One morning, I arrived at the site to find Bronco, one of Wodjak's men, slowly spackling a wall.

"Bronco, what are you doing? That wall has already been spackled."

Bronco replied with remarkable naïveté.

"Wodjak said, 'Make like work.'"

Apparently, it had gotten around that Wodjak was building a house for Renée Richards and on the basis of my notoriety, he had been offered a lot of other jobs, which he accepted in spite of not having enough men to do both my work and the new work. Instead of cutting his profit margin by hiring new men, he started to make a show of working on my house while sending the bulk of his crew across the lake to fulfill other contracts.

When he wasn't busy on the other side of the lake doing another neighbor's renovation, he would sit and watch while I trained one of my junior protégés on a nearby tennis court. Meanwhile, Arleen and I were living on the land in a tent, though in retrospect that was the best part of the whole process. We experienced complete tranquillity: no phone, no radio, no intrusions. However, we could not camp out forever, and eventually I got so mad at Wodjak that I had to get my friend Sig Nagorski, who in his distinguished career as a bona fide Polish statesman had dealt with Khrushchev, to negotiate between Wodjak and me. I could no longer speak to him without blowing my top.

The dream house took a long time to finish, but when completed it was so beautiful that we forgave Wodjak his sins. Together, we had created a gorgeous stone and log home. In fact, it was considered several times as a movie location when the script called for a country retreat at the border of a lake. We chose not to allow it because the compensation the companies offered was not worth the inconvenience of vacating the property during the shooting, not to mention the damage such invasions usually cause.

Once the house was done, we put in the extras that made it a perfect pleasure retreat. By the lake, we built a dock where we kept not only a small boat for fishing but also a beautiful twelve-foot fiberglass sailboat, which Nick and I took turns capsizing on the lake. As might be expected, the tennis court received special consideration. It was built by my ex-coach and friend Frank Froehling, who had years before sent me to Gainesville to study tai chi. He came up from his Florida home and drew his crew from the local laborers who used to congregate around the railroad station in Brewster looking for work. We held the inaugural party for the court just after Martina won Wimbledon in 1987. The guests, mostly tennis friends from New York, played on the newly constructed synthetic grass court, celebrating the crowning detail of our home. I felt we had made the most beautiful tennis court in the area. It was surrounded by a fine black wire fence so transparent that it gave the impression that the court was open to the pine forest bordering it. For both the spectators in the small wooden reviewing stand and for the players on the grass-green court, the effect was enchanting, tennis in a woodsy glen. Finally, we were done with building, and though the process of creation had been trying, it produced the jewel of Sedgewood.

So began fifteen years of the good life. Arleen and I settled in with our "extended family": the three dogs, the cats, and the birds. Our devotion to these creatures is one of the most powerful bonds between us. In fact, Arleen is seldom off our property because she won't leave the dogs alone and refuses to put them in a kennel. I stop short of that degree of commitment, but not much. I am especially attached to my young Airedale, Travis, who is ever at my side, but all the animals are dear to both of us. Our Sedgewood years were heaven for humans and animals alike.

I was hoping that this beautiful setting would have a good effect on Nick, who was beginning to rebel in a variety of ways, though he was good in an emergency and had already shown his resourcefulness at the Plaster House, when he and a friend were sleeping by the fire one winter's night. The cold had not yet driven me out of my bed and downstairs to the fire, so the boys were alone. At some point, a flaming log rolled out of the fire and onto the wood floor, where it threatened to set the house ablaze. Roused from his sleep, Nick did not run screaming for Dad; instead, while his friend slept on, he got buckets of water and extinguished the log. In the morning, as I listened to his recounting of the night's adventure, I could only say, "Good work. You probably kept us from being burned alive." That sort of potential disaster was unlikely in our modern Sedgewood home, but Nick may have saved my life in a different way during our time there.

Though our house had all the amenities of modern life, getting to it required us to negotiate a two-mile dirt road winding around Barrett Lake. This was a wilderness road in the true sense, and nature often created obstacles such as fallen trees and washouts. It was on this road that Nick once again showed his best side. Arleen, Nick, and I were returning from a party in Manhattan at about one o'clock in the morning. February can be brutally cold in rural New York, and I realized that the temperature was dropping as we drove north. I was hoping to reach the house before it dropped low enough to freeze the approach road, but I watched the thermometer go from thirty-eight degrees to thirty-six to thirty-four, and before we got home, the temperature had dropped below thirty-two. We were all dressed for a Fifth Avenue party, which means to the hilt. I was in heels and a cocktail dress. Arleen's outfit was similarly chic, and even Nick had dressed up a little. We were quite comfortable in my Audi station wagon, but that comfort was to be rudely interrupted halfway down the road to our house.

As I feared, the road had frozen over, creating a crust of black ice. The Audi's wheels began spinning on this slick surface and our progress halted. It was frustrating to be stopped so close to home, so I got out of the car and tried to walk forward. I don't even know why I got out of the car. The details of this episode are hazy for reasons that will soon be obvious, but I guess I was trying to see if we could clear some of the ice so that the car could proceed. But high heels plus ice is a bad combination, and my foot went out from under me as I was picking my way in the darkness ahead of the car. It happened so fast that I had no time to reach out a hand to break my fall. I slammed into the icy ground nose first. My eyeglass frames lacerated my brow and sent a stream of blood over my face. Arleen and Nick didn't see me go down, so I lay alone on the ice and took stock of my injuries. I explored the three-inch gash in my eyebrow and realized that the frontal bone was exposed. My nose was displaced at least half an inch to the right. I crawled back to the car and opened the door. Arleen and Nick looked on in horror as I turned on the overhead light and, using the rearview mirror, took my two thumbs and put my nose back where it was supposed to be. At that point, I suddenly felt very cold. I started to shiver and went a bit glassy-eyed.

The next thing I knew, Nick was out of the Audi, heading down the road to the house, while Arleen did her best to keep us comfortable, huddling with me under our coats. After a few minutes we saw lights coming toward us from the direction of our house. It was Nick, driving the four-wheel-drive Pathfinder that we kept for just such weather conditions. I rallied when I saw him drive up, but I still had to be supported by Nick on one side and Arleen on the other while we switched cars.

If I had been in a state of mind to diagnose myself, I would

have said I was in the first stages of shock, but I was not thinking clearly, as is proven by what I did next: I insisted on driving. Nick and Arleen protested, but I would not get in the Pathfinder unless it was on the driver's side. I was too much for
them to handle and time was of the essence, so they let me
drive, resolving to keep a close eye on me as I drove down the
icy road holding a glove against my wound, a measure that did
little to stop the blood from spurting out of my head. We had
hardly started before I turned the Pathfinder over. By the time
we extricated ourselves from the vehicle I was pretty much out
of it. Arleen and Nick got me back into the Audi. There was no
point in trying to go forward or back in that car. The ominous
black ice would not allow it.

So once more Nick trudged off into the blackness, this time in
the opposite direction, toward Ron Wilson's house, which was the
first one on the other side of the lake from ours. He tells of trying
to avoid the black ice by feeling for the crunch of snow beneath
his feet. The clouds shut out any moonlight that might have helped
him see, so he was navigating in almost complete darkness, but
he found his way to Ron's house and pounded on the door.

"Ron! Dad's hurt. We need your Jeep."

Minutes later Ron and Nick got to us, bundled Arleen and
me into the Jeep, and brought us to the warmth of Ron's home.
While we were recovering, Ron called the Putnam Hospital. I
could vaguely hear him talking.

"She needs an ambulance. Don't you have anything that
can get through? All right. I can make it. Be ready for her."

The black ice that had foiled me had also foiled the ambulance. All of Sedgewood was frozen in. After a couple of hours of

rest, I felt well enough to make the drive to the hospital, where my friend and associate Hal Farquhar spent an hour sewing up the gash in my eyebrow. My nose was in surprisingly good shape for having been self-adjusted in the front seat of an Audi. Hal didn't have to touch it, except for some cleaning and antiseptic. I came out of the incident with only slight scarring, but if it hadn't been for Nicky's dramatic trudge through the woods for help, I might have gone into shock and died. He was a hero that night.

Not all of Nick's Sedgewood moments were so heroic. One night I looked out the window and spotted a searchlight shining over the tennis court. I stepped outside and thought I heard voices. Wilderness solitude is great most of the time, but it turns a little scary when persons unknown are encroaching on your property. I called the Kent police, checked the guns, and waited for developments. Shortly, a patrol car arrived and two officers gave the property a thorough going-over. When they had completed their investigation, they returned to the house and made a report.

"Well, Dr. Richards, the searchlight you saw is the moon."

"The moon? Are you sure?"

"Yeah. It's real bright tonight. You're not the first to make that kind of mistake when it's low in the sky."

"What about the voices?"

"They probably drifted over from the golf course. Local kids hang out there. We chase them off, but they come back."

"That's over a mile away."

"Sound travels on these still nights."

"Well, I certainly hate to have brought you out here on a wild-goose chase."

While they made the usual think-nothing-of-it-just-doing-our-job remarks, a thought struck me. I could reward these public servants by giving them a tour of the house, which was the subject of a lot of local interest. And as a proud owner, not to mention a general contractor, I was anxious to show it off. I ushered them in. Arleen said, "Hello," and left the guided tour to me. I showed them the living area with the random plank chestnut floors and the double-sided fireplace rising to the ceiling, the spectacular kitchen with the electric induction stovetop, everything. I even took them outside to have a look through the window at the special suite I had built for Nick, his private area, with a beautiful bedroom and a loft up above it, and a private entrance to the outside as well as a separate entrance to the wraparound deck. The policemen shined their flashlights into the area, the better to appreciate its appointments. The beams played over the furniture and came to rest on Nick's pot plants. They hesitated for a moment and then switched off their lights. I suppose that the deputies deduced from my horrified expression that I did not know the marijuana was there. They said nothing, only reassured me that Arleen and I were safe and left with no more than some pleasant compliments about the house. We have a small police department in the Town of Kent, near Carmel, and they take good care of us. One time I was speeding on Peekskill Hollow Road and got pulled over. The cop looked at my license and said, "Oh, Doc, I can't give you a ticket. You take care of my kids. Please slow down and stay safe."

Sedgewood was entertaining in many ways. A lot of interesting people lived near us: Itzhak Perlman, the famous violinist, and Jim Wolfensohn, who was then president of the World Bank. In previous years, Willis Reed, the great basketball star for the New York Knickerbockers, was easily picked out on the weekends as he walked Sedgewood's country lanes in a purple warm-up suit or fished in China Lake, which offers the best bass fishing in the county. I was in Willis Reed's house occasionally, and I expected it to be tailored for his size, but I had to duck to avoid hitting my head on the doorjamb. I don't know how he managed. He must have loved the area to stay in a house that didn't fit his height. He finally sold his home when he got busy as the general manager of the New Jersey Nets.

One of the most colorful of Sedgewood's residents was Geoffrey Bell, the famous economist, who was an especially good friend. Geoffrey, a self-made zillionaire Englishman, often played golf with me on Saturday morning, and more than once announced, "Gotta go! Having lunch with Tony Blair in the city!" His home was directly across Barrett Lake from ours. The golf course was a mere five-minute drive from his house, but that did not bring golf close enough for Geoffrey. He had a net suspended by a wooden frame on his lawn so that he could hit practice shots while at home. One night, Geoffrey's wife, Joan, called and grimly reported, "Renée! Geoffrey is hurt. He is bleeding all over!" I drove around the lake and found that a ball had hit Geoffrey's net frame, rocketed directly backward, and struck him between the eyes. Joan was holding an ice pack over the gash. We took Geoffrey to Putnam Hospital, and I put ten sutures in the laceration, which was deep enough that while I worked, I thought I caught a glimpse of his brain. Not much was going on in there that night. Geoffrey invests funds for Argentina and Jamaica, among other nations, which just goes to show that even a financial genius is not immune from an occasional boneheaded maneuver.

WHEN I READ OF writer Spalding Gray's suicide in 2004, I recalled the many times I saw him in Sedgewood. I socialized with him at a few parties. He did a monologue at one of them. It was a good performance piece, but I found it depressing, dwelling as it did on his mental, physical, and family problems—the types of things I was trying to forget. He suffered from macular degeneration and asked my advice. I advised him to see a specialist friend of mine, which he did, but he also tried every kook treatment in the phone book. I don't want to minimize his suffering, but he had the condition in one eye only and so many people have the deterioration of two eyes to deal with. Yet he wrote of his condition as if he were the only one in the world to have it. I kept thinking he should take up golf. If you put your mind on your putting stroke, you don't have much time for crippling self-examination, but that's an athlete talking.

I often found Spalding walking the Sedgewood lanes on weekends, but I seldom recognized him as I drove up behind him. Consequently, I identified him as a stranger and feeling rather possessive about my environment, I would say, "Excuse me! Can I help you?" My tone of voice suggested that my real meaning was, "Put your hands up and freeze!" The poor guy would turn around and say, "Renée, Renée! It's me, Spalding!" This happened repeatedly, and each time he seemed hurt that

I hadn't recognized him, but I simply could not keep an image of Spalding in my mind.

Though Arleen and I had no inkling of it, our days in Sedgewood were numbered from the beginning. A force was gathering that would eventually evict us. If my life were a movie comedy, the source of our problem would have been some grumpy narrow-minded neighbor with a grudge against transsexual, tennis-playing surgeons. However, the force that drove us out of Sedgewood was much less entertaining: money. Through 1993, my income continued to rise, but when managed medical care came in, it started to go down faster than it had gone up. I found myself dealing with reams of paperwork and a bureaucracy that does not compensate doctors in accordance with the good they do or the risks they take. Managed care has caused doctors to see more patients just to break even or to join medical groups where the overhead is spread out. Many older doctors with years of priceless experience have just retired rather than endure the situation. Others, like me, have had to give up their dream houses. In my case the equation was straightforward. Because Sedgewood is New York City reservoir land, and there's little commerce in Kent, the area taxes are very nearly the only source of civic income, which means they are high. The tax collector used to say, "If you want to live in Shangri-la, you have to pay for it."

Unfortunately, we could no longer afford Shangri-la, so we sold the dream house and moved across to a cottage on the reservoir road, where we can live comfortably on what a doctor can make in the new century. I'm still a member of the Sedgewood Golf Club, and I play regularly with my treasured friends. However, I can no longer live in Sedgewood in my dream house. Still, I am not unhappy. Our present home is beautiful, though small, with only one level. Yes, it has a tennis court!

Sedgewood and all that went with it is terribly important in the story of Renée Richards because that is where I found something like normality and overcame nearly fifty years of upset and transience. My situation with Arleen is unconventional, but it has given me what a home should: commitment, caring, continuity. I have carried those with me out of the physical confines of Sedgewood, and though I was sad to leave my beautiful home, the move has been satisfying in one crucial regard. It showed me that my peace of mind is not connected to a piece of property. It comes from inside me.

CHAPTER 9

The Physical Side

I HAVE ALL THE PROBLEMS of a middle-aged man and those of a middle-aged woman, too." This is how Christine Jorgensen characterized her health upon turning fifty.

Everybody knows in general how sex reassignment affects an individual's anatomy. If you are a woman, the surgeon transforms you into a man. If you are a man, it's the opposite. However, the average person has little comprehension of how precisely this seemingly straightforward goal can be accomplished. They may imagine the result as a rough approximation of natural genitals, like something Dr. Frankenstein might come up with. Luckily, in the case of reputable sex-reassignment surgeons, a bad result is rare, especially in the United States and Europe, where rigorous standards are enforced. Still, the operation can go wrong resulting in a variety of bad outcomes such as shallow vagina, incontinence, genital numbness, and pelvic cancer.

However, if properly fashioned the new equipment will look right and function correctly, though some would-be transsexuals face an uphill battle because they lack what I call general somatic compliance: their bodies are too masculine to make a believable woman. I dislike saying this because it is judgmental and maybe arbitrary, and it precludes some very distressed people from seeking happiness, but I am convinced that no matter what the psyche desires, some men should not try to live as women. I was lucky because, in spite of being tall, I had several physical features in my favor: good skin and complexion, high cheekbones, good legs, and a face that aged slowly. My head was not too large, and my facial bones and the muscles connected to them were not extremely prominent as in some males. I did not become a beauty, but I was attractive and that helped.

I have a friend, a gentler guy you would never meet, but his face is like a bulldog's. He looks so mean that men feel like either running or getting in the first punch. Thankfully, he is no transsexual. Years ago, I had a transsexual patient who was six feet six inches tall. She wore miniskirts and two-inch heels. Maria, my office assistant, once observed, "She wouldn't last five minutes in the South Bronx." Maria was right. In the wrong part of town, my patient would have been noticed, despised, and possibly targeted. Much is made by some transgender advocacy groups of the frequency of violence toward transsexuals. Accurate figures are hard to find, but some supposed experts estimate that a male-to-female transsexual is sixteen times more likely to be murdered than a member of the general population—three times the frequency for African American males, the next highest group. Others have noted that the transgendered are strangely susceptible to certain types of murder: twice as likely to be stabbed, three times as likely to be bludgeoned to death. I have no idea how valid these claims are, but they do not surprise me. When I was playing tennis, my life was threatened several times, and I remember well the special heat with which some people confronted me. It was irrational and scary. I'm sorry to say that one health risk you must accept if you choose sex reassignment is the possibility you will be brutalized. So it's no wonder that so many transsexuals prefer to go in "stealth mode." But without somatic compliance that is a chancy enterprise.

Maintaining a sexual identity that is the opposite of the one nature provided is an undertaking that brings with it a series of lifelong medical issues that any transsexual must accept as the price of his or her new body. The transformation begins long before the scalpel comes into play. Once approved for the process, a transsexual must begin a course of hormone therapy to bring about as much physical and mental adjustment as possible prior to surgery. In my case, that program started with a series of shots. Dr. Harry Benjamin injected me in the buttocks every other week with the female hormone Delestrogen. The injections did not hurt even though the needle was large, because at the same time as he thrust the needle into me, he slapped me on the back. He learned that trick in Germany's Tübingen Medical School, from which he graduated in 1912. Eventually I went on Premarin, first in pill form and much later in life using an estrogen skin patch.

It took five weeks of treatment for me to notice any physical change: an increased sensation in my nipples. Initially, I treated this development just as most people would. I ignored it. If it registered with me at all, it was only to note it and dismiss it as one of those aches, itches, or twitches that come out of nowhere and eventually disappear on their own. I spent a couple of days absently shifting the fabric of my starched shirt away from my nipples before it dawned on me that the chafing might be connected to my hormone therapy. With this realization, my interest increased, and a little rubbing and tweaking demonstrated that something new was indeed happening. Dick's nipples had never been an erogenous zone, though I knew that many men got a good bit of tingle out of theirs. I had never envied them. What we've never experienced, we don't miss, but my nipple experiments strongly suggested that there were some good things in the future. For the present, I experienced too much unaccustomed sensitivity to be entirely comfortable, but I took satisfaction in the subtle hints of erotic sensation. As I became more expert, I started feeling a response in my groin, little bursts of sensation, not profound but definitely sexual.

So far so good. There is nothing like improved nipple sensitivity to make one optimistic about the path one has taken, but there was a great deal more to my attitude than this or any other physical change. The hormones seemed to induce in me an uncharacteristic sense of well-being, even though my emotional swings increased markedly. I had laughing fits and crying jags, but they seemed natural and even therapeutic. In part, this sense of well-being may have been the result of my having at long last started to make myself into the person I had always desired to be. If I had not been repeatedly thwarted in my attempts to transform myself, I might not have experienced so great a sense of peace, but I really think the hormones played a big part in it. I also experienced a notable increase in my level of personal interest in the people around me, which was quite a change in demeanor. As Dr. Richard Raskind, I had cultivated aloofness, in part because it fit the role of the great healer and in part because the great healer had a secret life that he could not afford to have people poking into. And let's face it, at that point in my life I was not really interested in what somebody's kids did at school on Monday. Hormone therapy altered that. Domestic details seemed somehow more worthy of my attention. I apologize to the feminists if this sounds stereotypical.

Very soon after I discovered my more sensitive nipples, I began to see changes in the texture and appearance of my skin. Frankly, it was already so good that I hadn't expected to experience any improvement. My mother had given me her fabulous complexion, a bequest that I had been thankful for on many occasions. If it hadn't been for my accursed whiskers, I wouldn't have needed much makeup at all to pass as Renée. So, when I glanced in the mirror one morning and noticed that I was looking especially good, I leaned in closer to my reflection. The grain of my skin had definitely started to tighten. The pores seemed not only smaller but also more regularly sized and distributed. When I ran my palm over my forehead, I was delighted to feel how smooth it was. This was more like what I had in mind for myself.

The skin improvement was soon followed by alterations in the shape of my face, which became less angular as my muscles softened. The muscles in my arms and legs lengthened and lost a lot of the knottiness that males develop through exercise. I could no longer flex a very impressive bicep, but I could wear a sleeveless dress without feeling self-conscious about my arms. I started to accumulate fatty deposits in my ass, resulting in a more feminine outline. All of these changes were welcome, though during 1965, my last year in the Navy, I certainly began to look out of place in my commander's uniform. Luckily, I had given up my military crew cut before I started my hormone therapy. As my hair grew finer, it would not have been able to stand up as the crew cut required, but it was well suited for my longer style. As for the hair on the rest of my body, it grew finer or fell out. Dick had never had a lot of body hair anyway, and when the hormones had done their work, he was quite smooth. In this he was lucky. Some transsexuals must have electrolysis not only on their beards but, poor souls, on arm, chest, back, and leg hair. In all, it took me three years of pain to get rid of my beard. I can only imagine what torture the truly hirsute endure.

Meanwhile, Dick's abused genitals began to react to the hormones. His testicles shrank to the size of marbles and became increasingly pliable, taking on the consistency of Silly Putty. If mashed, they would deform and then slowly come back to their original shape. Dick's penis could still grow erect, but it had lost the rod-like stiffness of the past. Even at full erection it could be bent into a right angle. As for ejaculations, Dick could still have them, but their old force and quantity gradually diminished. As the hormone therapy progressed, his orgasms became less and less satisfying. After a few weeks, they were actually uncomfortable. During climax the ejaculate seemed drier and more granular than normal, though when examined it did not look or feel any different. All this seems rather sad, but actually, this was a good period for Dick's genitals because Renée was feeling optimistic. As a result, she was much less inclined to the violent measures she had previously taken in minimizing Dick's masculinity. A simple panty girdle was enough to satisfy her, thinking as she was about the more complete life she had ahead of her.

As it turned out, Renée was overly optimistic. The doctors handling my case discontinued my treatment, fearful that surgery on a prominent doctor would be seen as irresponsible. I went cold turkey off the hormones, the beginning of an on-and-off cycle that went on for years. Each time I went off the hormones, my body would regress, but I always kept some of the physical femininity that had been induced by the most recent round of hormones. By the time I met the woman who would become my wife and the mother of my son, I was a rather androgynous being with a very smooth body and considerable breast tissue. With all good intentions and considerable hope, I entered into marriage, and for a while my wife Meriam and I actually enjoyed the impact we made when we walked around together. We were an exotic, head-turning couple. But as time passed, the breast tissue proved increasingly embarrassing, so I underwent breast reduction surgery.

This procedure was carried out on me in exactly the same manner as it is done on a woman. A small incision is made in the areola, which is composed of a distinctive form of tissue that does not scar. This areolar opening gives the surgeon a way to access and cut away the unwanted breast tissue and provides the portal through which it is drawn out. My surgery was done by a friend and noted plastic surgeon, Dr. Tom Rees, and went smoothly. When I was healed, I could go topless on the beach without calling attention to myself. Maybe my nipples were a little larger than most men's but easily within the average range. I thought perhaps my breast problems were over. I could not know that in a very few years I would be on the surgeon's table again, this time for breast implants.

After my marriage failed and a brief try at more analysis proved fruitless, I finally had my surgery done by one of the best men of the time, Dr. Robert Granato. When I asked him about the operation, he replied, "It's a hell of an operation. You'll be on the table for four hours. Some people cruise right through it and others have a rough time." Actually, my operation took only three and a half hours, and if I did not have a rough time, I would not like to be in the body of somebody who did.

Basically the operation goes like this. An incision is made extending from the base of the penis down to an inch above the anus. It is deepened in preparation for forming the vagina. All this requires the usual clamping of blood vessels and dissecting of muscles that attends most operations. Specialized structures like the urethra and erogenous tissue are prepared for future use. Elements that will no longer be needed, such as the seminal vesicles, are removed and discarded. The connective tissue and pelvic muscles that are occupying the space where the vagina will be located are moved aside. There is more than enough room in the body cavity for everything. The penis and testicles are removed, but the penile skin is retained and used in forming the vagina. In my case, additional skin from my right thigh was needed. This skin is wrapped around a plastic mold and sutured in place. When healed, it forms the vaginal walls. The most sensitive erotic tissue is located in the position of the clitoris. The urethra is oriented properly and secured. Scrotal tissue is used to form the vaginal labia. The last phase of the operation is to insert packing around the vaginal mold to hold it firmly in place.

Anyone who wants to see illustrations and even photographs of this procedure can easily find them on the Internet. Frankly, I can't stand to look. Before the operation, Dr. Granato gave me some material containing color photographs showing the stages of the surgery. I glanced at the first one and hastily put them away. I have never looked at anything like that again and have no plans to do so, though I do occasionally hear of advances in technique. I understand that in recent years the surgery includes the creation of clitoral-like tissue taken from the resected penis. Though I have erotic tissue in that area, I do not have any structure resembling a clitoris. But before you feel too sorry for me, I'm pleased to say that after my operation, I discovered with much relief that I could have an orgasm. It is not clitoral in nature, but it is nice. I have even heard of surgery to create tissue to resemble a cervix by inserting a rubbery device at the end of the vagina. I guess that might be useful in case somebody bumps in that far. These advances tell us about the evolution of surgical skills and, more important, about the terrible compulsion of some patients to retool their bodies in search of the impossible. Surgery cannot undo that Y chromosome or insert functional ovaries—not yet, anyway. What the future holds is anybody's guess, and I must admit that I would not know whether to cheer or boo if such adjustments were possible. The mind boggles at that degree of control and the ethical questions it raises.

But after my own surgery, such issues were far from my mind. I was too busy shaking uncontrollably and getting acquainted with several types of pain all at once. I had everything: aching pain, shooting pain, sharp pain, dull pain, burning sensations, icy sensations. I could go on. Even my penis and testicles hurt, and they were in the trash somewhere. Phantom pain, they call it, but it was excruciatingly real to me. Unfortunately, the fact that I was shaking suggested that I might be in shock, which meant that I could not be given any painkillers for fear they would further lower my already low blood pressure, which would have been very dangerous. So, for a while anyway, I just had to hang on. I have always had a high tolerance for pain, but this tested my limits. I look back on this as Renée's birthing pain, and in retrospect it seems somewhat appropriate; but if it had been a conventional birth, I would have been begging for an epidural. The pain was better later in the day, but for the first forty-eight hours I felt as though I was being stabbed between the legs if I moved my pelvis or even coughed.

But I got through it, and when I healed I had the best female body modern science could provide. As Doctor Granato so eloquently put it when he was interviewed about me after I hit the news, "She's a woman. She has a vagina. She has orgasms. That's a woman." He never stopped trying to improve his work. Years after my surgery, he saw me and said, "Renée! I've figured out how to make your labia perfect. Let's go!" I was grateful for his interest, but I declined. "Nobody's taking any pictures," I concluded.

I don't know exactly what improvements Dr. Granato had in mind, but his work was good enough to earn a nice compliment from the man who became my primary gynecologist, my dear friend Don Rubell. Don had played a lot of tennis with Dick Raskind, and Dick had been a sort of role model for him. Both went into medicine, as a good number of eastern tennis players did, and I can only imagine his feelings as he contemplated his first examination of Renée. I had been in his Manhattan office before, but never as a patient. It was nice, nothing extravagant but with a good professional feel. His receptionist greeted me in a pleasant fashion and sent me down the hall to an examining room, where I donned a paper gown. I sat there twiddling my thumbs and staring at the examining chair with its stirrups. I can truthfully say that I was enjoying most everything about my new womanhood, but the chair with the stirrups and the speculum that I knew would soon be hauled out were not on my list. I very quickly developed the same distaste for these items that virtually all women feel. Dr. Granato had introduced me to the speculum during my recovery. It serves the same purpose for me that it does for any other woman, and it has the same uncomfortable effect.

After a few minutes, Don entered the room. This was a guy with whom I had lounged around the locker room on many occasions, but he was now Dr. Rubell, slightly formal and anxious to put Miss Richards at ease. Of course, there were the usual preliminaries, listening to the heart and all, but finally the moment of truth arrived. Don glanced at the nurse, who had been called in for propriety's sake, and then at me.

"Please get in the chair."

"Sure."

I settled in and put my feet in the stirrups. Out came the speculum. I thought I saw Don take a deep breath, but beyond that he showed no anxiety. While he carried on, he made the conventional encouraging remarks about everything looking good. He was very composed, but I'm sure he was as relieved as I when the speculum came out. Soon after that, we were done, and as I dressed I wondered what Don's report would be like. It turned out to be a perfect reflection of our relationship and a tribute to Dr. Granato's skill.

"Renée, you look like an ordinary woman who has had a hysterectomy. But stay off the tennis court. One look at that crazy windup you do on your forehand, and the whole world will know who you are." He was so right. Ultimately, the thing that immeasurably complicated my life as a woman was tennis, not surgery.

However, I did have two more operations to endure: one voluntary, one not. During my last round of hormone therapy, my breasts had not enlarged satisfactorily. The breast reduction I had undergone during my marriage had left too little tissue for a significant response. Tom Rees had retired, but his partner, Dr. Gary Guy, performed an augmentation, inserting silicone implants to improve the size and shape of my breasts. The result was acceptable and served me well for many years, including my time as a tour tennis player. However, years after I retired from tennis, the capsule of the implants hardened. Dr.

Sherell Aston, who took over after Tom and Gary, replaced the implants.

The day after the procedure, I had to take Nick up to St. Bernard's to meet with the headmaster to try to convince him not to kick my son out of school. It was pouring rain. I held an umbrella over us against the rain and wind as we marched up to the school's entrance. The strain on my arm and shoulder was too much for some of the blood vessels near the breast tissue. I started to hemorrhage. By the time I got home, I had a massive hematoma on the side of my chest. So I went back to the operating room for four hours of revision, evacuating blood, and closing off bleeding blood vessels. That was my last operation. Today, my breasts look okay, but so much surgery has had a sad effect. They are not really soft, and the size and shape of my nipples are not as feminine as when I first went on hormones so many years ago.

Even though I have so little breast tissue due to the original reduction procedure, I do fear breast cancer, which is a big concern for most transsexuals because breast cancer in males—and my DNA is male—is particularly virulent. Estrogen increases the chances for breast cancer, and I have been on estrogen without a break for more than thirty years. My aunt Esther died of breast cancer, so regular mammograms are essential, and I am faithful in going for them, but mine are difficult to read properly because of the implants. When I leave the radiologist's office, I cannot be completely sure that I am clear, but then mammograms aren't perfect, even for women with natural breasts.

I continue on estrogen therapy to maintain the appearance of my face and figure and for the emotional well-being it promotes. I know the medical profession is divided about estrogen treatment for older women. It is beneficial for bone density, but may increase our risk of breast cancer. Opinion is mixed on its effects on the heart and cerebral blood vessels. I am hopeful that estrogen protects my heart as it seems to in natural-born women, who have far fewer heart attacks than men, but it can also create a sort of "sludge" in the blood, increasing the possibility of a stroke. I take a daily baby aspirin to counteract this effect.

I was on Premarin for quite a long time, but when I started getting frequent migraine headaches, I thought it might be connected to the pill form of the medicine. I switched to Estraderm, the skin patch, and the headaches became fewer. The hormone is absorbed through the skin and does not reach the liver, as the oral form does. I do feel that the patch is not as effective as the pill. I see it in my face, but maybe that's only because I am getting older. I have some friends who are plastic surgeons, and they would love to do a Botox treatment on me or even a face-lift, but I am not in the mood.

I have never been very interested in knowing the exact hormone levels in my body, but my friend Jack Geller was. He did the research that led to the development of Proscar, the treatment for enlarged prostate. For years, Jack and I played once a week at the county tennis club in Westchester. Nobody else would play with us because we were notoriously unreliable, prone to showing up late or not at all, which we suffered in each other because as doctors we understood how demanding and unpredictable our profession is. Jack kept promising to do some lab tests on me to check my testosterone and estrogen levels, but nothing came of his promises until one day when he showed up with a syringe and needle that could have been for a large horse and proceeded to relieve me of about a pint of blood right there in the locker room. Week after week went by, and each time we played I would ask, "Jack, what were the results of all that blood you took from me?" A few months later he admitted he had lost the syringe. So much for studying my female-male hormone levels.

Whatever potential health problems I might have suffered from estrogen therapy were made considerably more dangerous by my smoking, which I continued for ten years after my sex reassignment surgery. When I was nearing my fiftieth birthday, my friend Marcia Storch said, "You have a keg of dynamite ready to go off in your head: estrogen, migraines, smoking!" She was a brilliant gynecologist who for many years took care of half the women in Greenwich Village, so she knew what she was talking about. I decided to quit in honor of my fiftieth birthday. At ten minutes to midnight, I asked my friend John Poster to light me up for the last time. Instead of complying, he grabbed the cigarette out of my mouth, threw it in the wastebasket, and exclaimed, "You don't need that one, either." I haven't put a cigarette in my mouth since.

Marcia Storch, who was so forceful on the subject of my smoking, died of a uniquely female ailment, ovarian cancer, something that I don't have to worry about. For that matter, I don't have to worry about testicular cancer or prostate cancer, either. In the end, the positive and negative health effects that come with transsexuality probably just about balance out, and we are left to consider what genes nature gave us. In that regard I'm glad to say that for the most part my family is long-lived and relatively healthy. My mother did die of colorectal cancer, so I have regular colonoscopies, though I hate the vile stuff they make me drink beforehand. I eat pretty much as my father ate: ice cream, bacon, eggs, sausages. He lived to be a hundred, so maybe I will do the same, but under any circumstances I intend to enjoy my life, not make it an experiment in the effect of health food on transsexuals. I do avoid foods that exacerbate the migraines, like too much vodka, but there will always be a certain amount of vodka. A drink or two in the evening is a pleasurable thing.

On the whole, my life is full of pleasures. I have good energy, which I attribute to sleeping nine hours a night and not worrying. Sometimes I tell Arleen how depressed I am, and she retorts, "You don't know the meaning of the word!" I suppose she is right as usual. The greatest source of depression in my life is probably losing a few pennies in my weekly golf game. And speaking of golf, I have gained and lost in that area as well. At seventy years of age, I am still quite flexible, which is a possible effect of my estrogen regimen. In this area, I seem to have the edge on my male friends, especially my old tennis-playing pals, most of whom have had surgery on their knees, hips, shoulders, backs, and combinations thereof. I play a lot of golf and suffer nothing more than an occasional sore muscle. Oh, I have had a little Achilles heel problem and a torn knee miniscus, but in general, I can bend, twist, and uncoil with no worry. On the other hand, I am not as strong as my male friends. Dick's muscle mass was long ago reduced by the absence of testosterone, and it irks me that some of them can outdrive me on the golf course. I have one pal who always says, "Atta girl!" when I hit a good drive, but he always waggles his finger at me if I head for the ladies' tee. Where's the fairness in that?

In the morning when I look in the mirror, I am satisfied with what I see. Maybe there are a few pounds and a few wrinkles I'd like to lose, but overall I see a woman who is healthy in body and in contentment, which is quite a change from what I saw so many years ago when Dick was staring back at me. He may have radiated physical health, but there was a look of desperation in his eyes. That's gone now.

CHAPTER 10

Sex, Love, and Romance

I FIND THE TOPIC OF romance daunting because many people think romance must be impossible for me. Romance is associated with sentiment, hearts, and flowers, none of which is consistent with the creepy feeling some people still get when they hear of a sex change, even though many thousands have by now undergone the procedure. Because the decision to change seems so strange, the public assumes the relationships that emerge after the change must also be strange. Worse yet, they tend to conclude that strangeness is desired, when the opposite is true. For me, and I think for most true transsexuals, the goal is normalcy, the fullest possible playing out of the new gender role—and in my case that included romance. Not that I wasn't interested in the other possible roles: coquette, libertine, and so on, and I played them enough to get my fill, but the one thing I have always desired is a great romantic love. Unfortunately,

I have not had a great love as Renée Richards, but I have had some exciting sex and some pleasant romances.

Many people will be surprised to hear that I have been a romantic all my life. As Dick Raskind, I deeply desired a meaningful connection to a woman. It was more than a desire; it was a need. Maybe that was part of my "problem." In the America of that era, and most especially in my family, women were put on a pedestal. For good or ill, they were seen to embody virtues and noble emotions that were impossible for men. If they did not rise to that standard, they were discounted, though many men (including Richard Raskind) took the favors of less-than-perfect women. The right sort of woman was thought to be beautiful on both the outside and the inside. Of course, she was chaste, though in liberal circles flirtation could blossom into sex with a virtuous woman if it were an expression of love. No man I have ever known was more sexually attracted to women or had more respect for them than Dick Raskind.

By age ten, I had a girlfriend. At age fifteen, I had my first orgasm with a girl, the outcome of which demonstrates the burden that females of the time bore. We didn't even have full sex, but the next day, in an agony of guilt, she called to tell me that she never wanted to see me again. She had compromised her status as a "good girl." I was stunned. My purpose had been to express love, admittedly a fifteen-year-old's love, but love nonetheless. In the vernacular of the day, "I respected her," and she reacted as if I had been thinking only of body parts. This rejection significantly strengthened the hold of Renée on young Dick Raskind. Perhaps at some level he decided that if he could not connect with the mysterious female in another human being, he would actualize the female in himself, but this is the sort of Freudian conjecture in which I have lost interest. I can honestly state that none of Dick Raskind's significant relationships were solely sexual. After thirty years of being Renée Richards, I am still friends with all but one of the women who had romantic ties to Richard Raskind.

Dick Raskind's best chance at life as a normal male was associated with a romantic relationship. This occurred during my long therapy with Dr. Bak. Gwen, my girlfriend, was beautiful and womanly, and she put her relationship with me first in her life. She gave my masculine ego a tremendous boost, but not just because our sex life was stupendous, which it was. There was something more, a very fulfilling personality connection. Dr. Bak was surprised by my sexual connection with Gwen and did nothing to discourage it. "Sex is the best thing you kids do," he would say, but he flatly refused to consider my marrying Gwen. To this day, I rue my weakness in not standing up to him. At that point a marriage might have worked. In fact, many thought we were married. We gave so much the impression of being a settled couple that a teenage Arthur Ashe once called Gwen "Mrs. Raskind." It seemed natural to do so.

Our involvement was so strong that it survived Gwen's finding out about my secret life. When this happened, I decided my deception had gone on long enough, and I confessed that the women's clothes Gwen had found were used by my other personality. Gwen knew I was seeing a psychiatrist, so it was simple to hold up a female garment and say, "This is the reason." She accepted my explanation and asked me almost no questions about my problem. The most she ever said was, "Why don't you get rid of those clothes?" To which I would reply, "You know why." Sometimes when she was leaving the apartment, she would say, "You're not going to do any of that *stuff* while I'm gone, are you?" I would tell her that I wasn't, and often I would abstain, but I became Renée frequently enough to make my stability a constant worry in an otherwise warmly romantic relationship.

Gwen argued that we should be married so she would be with me more and thus give Renée fewer chances to emerge. On the surface this seemed to make sense (I wondered if Renée emerged when Gwen was absent because I missed Gwen). However, I feared that if I suppressed Renée entirely by marrying Gwen, Renée might demand to come out somewhere other than the apartment, like at the hospital. Just imagine it! Virile young Dr. Raskind caught strolling along a hospital corridor in a dress. The mind boggled. My medical career would be over, and so would my life as a respectable member of society. Yet, as far-fetched as it seemed, I could not dismiss the possibility. Renée was that strong.

And there was an even more disastrous scenario. If denied existence, Renée might grow despondent and kill herself, taking a most promising young physician with her. That would be the pinnacle of humiliation. I could imagine the news coverage: *Manhattan Eye, Ear and Throat resident Richard Raskind took his life Monday evening. The corpse was discovered wearing a tailored skirt and blouse with low-heeled pumps. A matching handbag was found nearby.* Gwen understood my concern. We hung on for a long time, six years in all, but gradually our relationship withered away. However, I have never been sure that a marriage to Gwen would not have succeeded in smothering Renée for good. Gwen and I were so deeply in love that I would have braved the consequences and tried marriage if Doctor Bak had not objected so strongly. Had I married Gwen, I might still be Dr. Richard Raskind to this day. I have previously mentioned that one important woman in Dick's life has not remained close to me. Sadly, Gwen is that woman. Since our breakup, she and I have not spoken a word.

For many years, Richard Raskind was the only one of the two personalities inhabiting my body who could exercise his desire for romance, which accounts for Renée's many abuses of Richard. However, Renée was always on the lookout for her opportunities, and she did drag Dick Raskind into some humiliating situations in her search for romantic validation. A few times she demanded that Dick go to seedy transvestite revues at a cabaret called Club 82 in Greenwich Village. Dick hated the place, but Renée could fantasize there. Dick still had enough control to keep from entering the club dressed as Renée, which would have been asking for big trouble, but he could reconcile going there as a young man. The college kids of the day sometimes sought out such offbeat entertainment, and if Dick had been caught, he could have claimed to be slumming. Even Renée recognized that the Club 82 shows were tacky, but they represented the one area of American culture that came closest to legitimizing her. But neither she nor Dick was prepared for the effect of a similar, much superior show that seventeen-year-old Dick attended at Harlem's Apollo Theater, which in those days was not an entirely black venue. The show was called The Jewel Box Revue, a glossy, highly professional entertainment that Renée found enthralling. Here were beautiful performers who seemed to have triumphed over their male bodies and come to life as real women. It looked like a chance for Renée, and she insisted on exploring it. So after the show, Dick was compelled to go, like an unwilling husband, backstage.

The producers of the show were a homosexual couple named Jimmy and Clyde. Clyde was sick and seldom seen, but Jimmy had personality enough for both. Renée had asked to see the director of the troupe, and Jimmy came out all sharp creases and a carnation in his lapel. He was a well-built man of about fifty, with a square, pleasant-looking face and a tidy mustache. When Renée announced that she wanted to become a performer, he obligingly looked me over, commented favorably on my bearing and complexion, scribbled an address on a card, and said to bring some clothes to his house the following night after the show. Renée said she would. Of course, Dick had no idea of ever becoming a transvestite performer, but for Renée, this flirtation with an activity through which she could live, and perhaps even thrive, was exhilarating.

The next night found me on the way to the address on the card, carrying a suitcase containing a complete woman's outfit plus wig. My route took me through a rough neighborhood, and Dick nearly turned back a couple of times, but Renée would not have it. When I finally reached the address, located near the theater district in a then-forbidding section of Manhattan's West Side known as Hell's Kitchen, I was surprised to find a rather charming courtyard with several town houses. One was Jimmy's. He came to the door in a kimono, greeted me warmly, and sent me upstairs to change.

When I came down, wearing one of my sister's flower-print dresses, Renée was in full bloom. Jimmy told me how pretty I was and fussed a bit with my makeup before ushering me to a sofa strewn with pillows. It was deep and comfortable and the icy orange drink he handed me went down easily. At that age, I hadn't tasted any mixed drinks and only in later years realized I had gulped down a screwdriver, a potent combination of vodka and orange juice. Soon everything began to glow, and Jimmy's voice was so soothing that Renée began to think she had found love at last. She confessed that she was a virgin, but Jimmy was most reassuring. Not long thereafter, her clothes started to come off.

Up to that point, Renée had been in exclusive control, but as the trappings of womanhood were removed, Dick regained awareness, though only through the fog created by the screwdrivers Renée had drunk. This half-Renée, half-Dick state of mind created a most complicated situation, since Renée was heterosexual, Dick was heterosexual, and Jimmy was homosexual. The only person not confused was Jimmy, who continued on his course, kindly agreeing to Renée's request that they use the missionary position. After his climax, Jimmy uttered a few endearments and then actually fell asleep, leaving both Renée and Dick mortified. But as I dressed and gathered my things, it was Dick who was most in command, and he was sickened by what had happened, angry at himself, and guilt-ridden. As he made his way home in the early hours of the morning, wincing from an occasional pain in his backside, he resolved as he had so many times before to somehow conquer his demon.

Renée's evening with Jimmy was really the only one of my

sexual experiences that could properly be labeled gay, since I was fully a man on the physical level, even though I was made up as a woman. In later years, before my sex change, I was intimate with men on a few occasions but only when I was on hormones and was physically and emotionally more female than male. The most meaningful of these encounters involved an ironic twist that effectively sums up the romantic dilemma that haunted me for so long.

My affair with Sam was very exciting. He had an important position in the medical field, a wife, and three children. Though he lived in Philadelphia, he had business in New York and made frequent trips to the city. While there, he would sometimes visit The Baths, New York's famous meeting place for members of the gay community. In spite of his homosexual proclivities, Sam was very much the macho man in appearance; no one would have guessed his orientation. If he had been swishy, I would never have been sexually interested by him. By the time I met Sam, the hormone treatments had softened the contours of my body, developed my breasts, and enlarged my hips. My skin was smooth and hairless. I was quite feminine, though I had not yet had the operation that would complete my transformation. My appearance was extremely attractive to Sam. I was an exotic creature, somewhere between the masculine and feminine, and he was a married man, apparently able to appreciate women but more interested in men. Where exactly he was on the sexual-preference spectrum, I don't know for sure. We did not discuss such things.

Sam was a physically powerful man, which was to my liking, not conventionally handsome but with regular features and a level gaze that could freeze you in your tracks if he put it on you in earnest. Away from the hospital, I had become increasingly soft-spoken and even reticent under the influence of estrogen, but Sam was confident and at ease in the male role. He was cultured and serious, though he had a quiet sense of humor that was attractive. (I usually don't enjoy raucous men in social situations, though they can make athletics fun.) Sam and I would meet for dinner, where we would talk about music, theater, medicine, friends, and family. I was a little nervous about being seen at restaurants in Manhattan where Sam's sexual orientation was known in some quarters, but Sam cared little about what happened in New York City since he lived in Philadelphia (though he was very careful in his home environment).

However, even if some of our acquaintances had seen us sitting there, they would hardly have guessed that we were romantically involved. Putting aside my unusual appearance, which had admittedly set rumors flying at the hospital, there was nothing to mark us as different from any other professional colleagues having a meal together. We did not even indulge in the secret gestures that go with such rendezvous, the seemingly accidental brushing of hands or the loving remark spoken too low to be heard at the next table. When we went to my apartment after dinner, it was a different story.

I was turned on by the differences between us. Where I was soft, Sam was hard. Where I was smooth, he was hairy. And he was ardent as he made love, which was very exciting. In bed Sam was not talkative but he did compliment me, especially my breasts, which he found very stimulating. I loved his strength and his passion and the feel of him, every part of him. I loved being a "woman" with him, although at that point I could not perform fully as one. Even so, we never tried the alternative, anal sex, but we did everything else. The greater part of our lovemaking was oral and mostly me pleasuring Sam. By this time, my male genitals were shrunken and not capable of producing intense gratification, so I found my greatest romantic reward in being an object of desire and in satisfying my lover.

In a stroke of irony that rivals any I have experienced in a life full of ironic twists, Sam gave me $1,000 toward my sex-change operation. He was one of two well-off friends who contributed to the project. But after I had recovered and could have an orgasm through conventional male-female intercourse, Sam lost interest in me. He tried, but I could tell he had to work at it. Gone were the days of unbridled lust. Eventually, he dropped me as a lover, though I would have gladly continued indefinitely as his mistress.

But that was not the end of my relationship with Sam. There was unfinished business between us. Sam wanted his $1,000 back. When we would occasionally meet, he would remind me quietly and forcefully of the money I owed, and he did not stop until I had paid him back every dime, even though I was not flush for many years after we broke up. For him, money meant business, and in this area he was very tough-minded. This characteristic was one reason I did not fall in love with Sam. He was a good lover, but aside from the passions of the bedroom, he was an extremely controlled individual, a trait that had a certain attraction but not one upon which I could base a long-term loving relationship. For me to have fallen in love with him, Sam would have had to show more empathy. Maybe he saved it for his wife and family. I know he was concerned about them. Anyway, at times I found his toughness a little scary: You would not want to cross him. Better to repay the $1,000.

AFTER MY SEX-CHANGE OPERATION, I relocated to California and tried my hand at "woodworking," which is the term transsexuals use for living as a woman without acknowledging one's past. The idea of an anonymous life appealed to me since I hungered to be accepted as a woman without reservation. With Sam, I had already seen how confusing the issue could be, and I wanted the chance to enter into some uncomplicated relationships. The ethics of woodworking can be debated endlessly (does a lover have the right to know?), but that is not my purpose here. I did it, and that's that. I was in this "stealth mode" (yet another term for keeping the past a secret) when I met Mike, the first man with whom I had a completely heterosexual relationship.

I was practicing medicine in California and was a member at the John Wayne Tennis Club. Only three people in the area knew of my previous identity. To my other associates, mostly members at the tennis club, I was just another youngish professional woman, a bit tall and a bit mysterious about my past, though somehow the rumor circulated that I was recovering from a tragic love affair. I don't remember who started it. Maybe me, but anything that helped explain my retiring attitude was to the good. The one completely clear thing about me was that I was a damn good player and my talent drew more notice than anything else. Good players are in high demand in tennis clubs. That was how I met Mike.

We became friends and doubles partners at the club soon after I joined there. He was an émigré from South Africa and ran a successful sports equipment business. He had that good-natured masculine self-assurance such as you find in South African golfers Ernie Els and Retief Goosen. I would have loved it if he had been as big as the two men I have mentioned, but that was not the case. I used to kid him about his height, and he would comment, "Big guy—big cock. Little guy—all cock!" In his case, this was true. And what he lacked in height, he made up for in strength. When he held me, there was no doubt about who was in charge. For him, I was just a normal, willing female, and I relished being the focus of his unforced masculinity. With Mike in those early days, when we would have intercourse I would sometimes fleetingly see his penis in me and almost not know whether it was my penis in him or his penis in my vagina. I bet there are not too many people who could have a thought like that, but it was among the odder perceptions I experienced as I adjusted to being female.

Though I was a compliant sexual partner with Mike, I did not play that same role as his tennis partner. The same easygoing manner that made him so enjoyable in social interaction was sometimes irritating on the court. Once I got fed up because he would serve and then just saunter up to what he considered an adequate volleying position. I told him in no uncertain terms that he was not close enough to the net to hit an effective volley. He shrugged me off. This could not be tolerated. I took my racket and scratched a line on the cement court halfway to the net.

"See this line?" I said menacingly. "I want you to get to this line before you hit your first volley!"

He went back to the baseline, served, and came running as fast as he could toward the net, but he slipped and fell on his face.

"What happened?" I asked, looking down at him.

"I slipped on that line you drew!" he replied, gazing up at me with his good-natured South African smile.

Everybody enjoyed seeing Mike and me compete. We made such a contrasting partnership: a tall, willowy woman and a short, powerful man. People kidded us about that all the time, and they never let Mike forget about that invisible line he once tripped over. In fact, Mike became my unofficial tennis booker: if you wanted to play with Renée, you had to clear it with Mike.

Sadly, it was tennis that ended my anonymous life and convinced me that woodworking is more a romantic fantasy than an attainable reality. This was especially true in my case because of my high-profile past, but I think that any transsexual will encounter problems similar to the ones I did. Having a sex change is huge, but it is minuscule compared to all that is left over from your former life, and so many of the leftovers are things you don't want to give up: friendships, family ties, career aspirations, personal interests, and on and on. Donny Rubell, my gynecologist, had been correct when he cautioned me to stay off the tennis courts. How I wish I had taken his advice!

I thought that my unmasking in La Jolla might cause some consternation for Mike, but I found that I had been living in a dream. He had discovered my past months before when an athlete with whom Dick had participated in the 1973 Maccabiah Games showed up at the club and recognized me. I assume she felt it was her duty to go privately to Mike and reveal my past. Mike said nothing to me about this and became even more solicitous. It was about this time that he took over the management of both my tennis and social calendars, becoming a short, South African guardian angel.

Truthfully, the romance part of my relationship with Mike had cooled by then, and it had been fun, though not carried out in quite the stealthy way I had thought. However, there was another man in Newport Beach who was caught by surprise. I couldn't properly call my encounter with Billy a romance. It was one of those casual flings that most forty-year-olds have gotten out of their systems years before; however, you must keep in mind that Renée was playing catch-up. I met Billy at my apartment complex. He was working out, and I stopped to admire his technique and the results: a very muscular body. He apparently also liked what he saw when he looked at me because shortly thereafter we started a short but satisfying sexual relationship. He was physically powerful, which has always appealed to me, and though intelligent, he was not given to intellectual pursuits. Here again, I found myself drawn to an uncomplicated man. Perhaps this is because my own psychology had been so convoluted, and I had been forced through years of therapy to explore its every aspect. I found it refreshing to be with a man who was not given to self-examination, whose primary interests were physical. Billy and I enjoyed some lovely physical times together, and the fact that he hadn't a clue about my past added to my pleasure. He disappeared out of my life following my unmasking but not without a last courtly gesture.

I had not seen Billy for some time. He was supposedly away on a business trip, but I suspected that he was avoiding me out of embarrassment. One day, I was standing outside my apartment when a large group of paparazzi had cornered me. They wouldn't let me pass unless I answered their questions, which were coming in a confusing torrent. I was doing the best I could but was flustered. Suddenly, Billy appeared and came toward me, clearing his path by roughly casting aside reporters left and right. When he reached me, he looked me in the eyes for a moment and then turned to face the reporters.

"Would you like me to throw these guys in the ocean?" he asked.

The reporters shifted uneasily. They knew Billy could do it.

"No, Billy," I said. "That won't be necessary."

"You're sure?"

"Yes."

He walked away, and that was the last time I saw him. We weren't in love, but he treated me with respect, which is one of the most important components in a good romance.

Once my picture had been plastered across the front pages of the world's newspapers, the type of stealth relationship I had enjoyed with Billy became difficult to find, and I went through a period during which I didn't much care if my partner knew about me or even if my past were the source of the attraction. Some of my liaisons were highly transient and showed questionable judgment. I found some of them through David Buffum, who later became my manager after the blow-up in La Jolla.

He had another job when we started together and was trying to build up his management business by taking on struggling personalities on a part-time basis. Through him, I was introduced to the fringes of show business. That was how I met Jason, the drummer for a rock band that never quite jelled. He was a dynamic person, and physical as drummers tend to be, though slight of build and not at all my type. I detested the music his band made. All I can remember was that it was cacophonous and played at a deafening level. I can't even recall the name of the band. His main attraction was that he liked to screw me and was good at it. The feeling of being desired as a woman was still new, and I enjoyed it immensely, but my time with Jason was brief. One day he went home and put a bullet through his head. It had nothing to do with me, and I never found out exactly what the problem was. There were a lot of drugs around. Maybe he was stoned when he did it. Those were crazy times.

Sometimes people remind me of incidents from that era that I hardly remember. Once I visited Rosie Casals at her home in Sausalito. I stayed overnight, and Rosie threw a big party. The guests included Patty LaBelle, though this was before she became famous. Adjacent to the swimming pool, Rosie had a hot tub so deep that you could stand in it and still be in water up to your chest. Rosie still reminds me that she saw me furiously making it in the tub with one of Patty LaBelle's roadies. If I concentrate, I can vaguely recall it!

Later in my tennis career, I found myself training in Stuart, Florida, under the guidance of Frank Froehling. His eccentricity and strong ideas about everything on earth were at once irritating and attractive. As a coach, he was a tyrant. If, after a training session, I didn't look like I couldn't take another step, he felt he hadn't done his job. Then, as I was staggering through the ninety-degree heat, he would hop in his car and say, "See you back at the house," expecting me to jog several miles back, which I did.

Frank was highly sexed and once told me that when he was married he had screwed his wife several times a day. This struck me as an unromantic way of putting it, but Frank had a blunt manner and prided himself on being above the niceties practiced by conventional people. Though short on tact, he was nonetheless a tall, strong, assertive man, the type I found attractive, and I did occasionally fantasize about sex with him.

During Frank's tenure as my coach, I had a sexual experience that shows Frank's tough approach. It was the antithesis of a romance, but I will include it here for what it's worth. The incident involved massage, which is a continuing part of any athlete's regime. For many people massage has sexual overtones, but for athletes it is welcome therapy for bodies pushed beyond normal tolerances. Long before I trained with Frank, I was having massages, and most of them I can't remember, though a few have been notable.

Here is one example. In 1977, I was in my first year on the women's tour, and I was playing in the Virginia Slims tournament in Kansas City. It was February, and the Kansas winter was at its most brutal. After one grueling match, I couldn't have felt worse if I had been run over by a truck. This was in the era before the WTA hired full-time trainers, so when I got back to my hotel I looked in the phone book for a masseuse. I saw an ad for "Massage," and I called for an appointment.

"This is Dr. Renée Richards," I said (You usually get improved service if you say "Doctor."). "I would like to come for a massage."

"Sure, sure, *Doctor* Richards," said the voice on the other end of the line, dripping with sarcasm. "Come right over."

With the address in hand I marched out into the cold and headed down the street. As I traversed one block, then another and another, I saw a subtle change in the neighborhood. The closer the numbers on the buildings got to the number of the address in my hand, the less I seemed to be in midtown Kansas City and the more in midtown Sleaze City, but I had been in far worse spots, so I pushed on, intrepid as always. Eventually, I arrived at my number, a one-story storefront with a solid wood entrance door. There was a peephole in the middle. I knocked and the peephole opened. I heard a gasp.

"Jesus Christ! It *is* her!"

The door opened, and I was ushered in by a small man with sandy hair. The place was decorated very much like the French brothel I had visited in 1954: mirrors on the walls, heavy velvet drapes, a huge plush massage table, and an elaborate bed. I looked up and saw that there was also a mirror on the ceiling.

"I thought this was a massage parlor," I said.

The attendant nodded agreeably.

"I need a massage," I added.

"Oh! I see," he said, the light dawning. "Actually, this is not that kind of massage parlor, but in order to keep our license we do have one of our staff who is a licensed masseuse."

"Is she here?"

"Yes, she is."

"Then go get her."

In a few moments, my masseuse arrived, wearing net stockings and a purple corset. She put me on the cushy "table" and proceeded to give me a first-class massage. I've never had better. When she was done, I paid twenty bucks and walked back up to the Radisson Muehlebach feeling like a new woman. The trappings had been a little unusual, but the massage had worked as expected.

So there was nothing strange about Frank Froehling's sending me for a massage during my training in South Florida. Our exhausting workouts had taken their toll. A rejuvenating massage would be a nice reward but even more important would put me in shape for further training. I was looking forward to it as I drove to the prescribed address, which turned out to be in a respectable business area of Port St. Lucie. The building was undistinguished but well-kept, and the interior was what I expect in a legitimate massage parlor: clean, white walls, no nonsense, except maybe a plastic tree in one corner of the waiting room.

My masseur was a short Italianate man of about sixty, dressed in a white T-shirt and white pants. You would not think twice about being naked in his presence. I certainly didn't, and I had the usual towel for modesty's sake. The process went as expected while he did the backside. Then he asked me to turn over for the front, which I did. That was when things got crazy. Before I knew it, he had pulled me down to the end of the table, spread my legs apart, and climbed on me with his pants around his ankles. He was fast for a sixty-year-old, and it was over right quick. I was in a state of shock.

I hurried off, like so many women in similar circumstances, feeling numb and wondering what I might have done to provoke such an act. Could I have sent some signal without knowing it? I kept mulling the incident over, trying to put a rational face on it, but I could not come up with a plausible explanation. Even so, I was hesitant to use the word "rape" with regard to myself. I was no choir girl. Yet I felt I had to tell someone, so I went to the person who was most influential in my life at the time, Frank. When I got to his house, I found him standing in the kitchen.

"Frank, the masseur screwed me!"

He laughed. He had a silly laugh, and it never struck me as sillier than upon that day.

"The masseur screwed you?"

"That's what I said."

"You let him?"

I didn't know how to respond to this, so I said nothing. Frank just laughed again and went about his business. That was the end of it. I was highly susceptible to Frank's reactions at the time, and if he laughed it off, I guessed I would too.

Even though Frank exercised a sort of Rasputin-like influence over me, I had my limits. One evening during the Christmas season we were practicing at the only indoor court in Palm Beach, and I blew up at him, which was my first step in ending his dominance over me. He was unhappy with my forehand, and he kept asking me how it should be hit. And no answer I gave would satisfy him. He fancied himself a Zen master, asking a riddle of his disciple. According to his rules, he could confront me, but I could never confront him. His badgering went on for about an hour, during which I demonstrated my forehand with variations a hundred times, and each time he would say, "That's no way to hit a forehand!"

Finally, something snapped.

"You think you are so fucking good?" I yelled. "The hell you are! Second place is your spot! You lost to Osuna in the final at Forest Hills; you lost to Connors in the final of the U.S. indoor; you lost to Richey in the final of the U.S. hard court. You stink, and your forehand stinks, too! The only thing you ever won was the U.S. father-son, because your father could play! I could beat you myself! I'll play you right now for a hundred dollars."

This was a crazy challenge. Frank was eight years younger than me and probably the best man for his age in the country. He was also an inveterate competitor, so at almost midnight we played a one-set match, with a "pro set" tiebreak at eight all if necessary. It was necessary. We both played like maniacs in the solitude of that barn-like building, surrounded by darkness, with only our court lighted. We reached eight all, and Frank won it in a tiebreak, seven points to five. Soon after this match, I moved on, and he was my coach no more. Twenty years later I saw Frank in the players' lounge at the 2002 U.S. Open. During a rain break we reminisced about his time as my coach.

"You remember that time we had it out over my forehand?"

"In West Palm," he replied without a moment's hesitation.

I have included this incident in the romance chapter because when I left Frank's sphere, I also left behind a tendency to place myself at the command of powerful male figures. I still love strong men, but self-assurance, charisma, and talent are no longer enough. My psychiatrist, Dr. Bak, was a man next to whom I felt inferior. He dominated my life for years under the pretext of helping me, but he did far more harm than good. His ego and intellectualism were not moderated by empathy and compassion. My demanding and ascetic coach, Frank Froehling, to whom I am indebted for resurrecting my tennis game and bringing order to my finances, was like Dr. Bak, in some ways, not too aware of my emotional needs. I had to move on to another phase of my life wherein, ironically, I would return to women for the emotional support that I had hoped to find in men.

I do not mean that I went back to women sexually. I will say this loudly and clearly. If I had undergone a sex-change operation only to become a lesbian, I would really be a cuckoo! I am accused of being a cuckoo anyway, but if I am, at least I am a heterosexual cuckoo. I will admit, like many naturally born women, to some casual experimentation. I think going both ways is something that women handle much better than men because, by and large, they are more emotional and more willing to reach out, whatever the sex of the person toward whom they reach. Many straight women have significant relationships with other women without compromising their heterosexuality, but I must stress that such experiences for me have been friendly and very rare, just playing around. In fact, I haven't even received many offers, though you would think that having been on the women's tennis tour and having coached history's highest-profile lesbian athlete, offers would have come more frequently. Maybe they did, but I didn't notice. As strange as it may seem to the world at large, I wasn't looking for them.

When I say that I turned to women, I mean as partners in

life. After I left Frank, I found Melissa Vinson, who was my companion and personal and professional manager for several years. Melissa was followed by Arleen Larzelere, who has been my devoted helpmate for more than two decades. Both Melissa and Arleen have had to endure the knowing glances and wrong conclusions that a close relationship with me entails. However, these two have something in common. They are strong enough to shrug off the opinions of others. They know the real story.

But what, then, of romance? Has there been nothing of significance? Yes, but a little explanation is required before I get to that. For me, romance is associated with acceptance and deep caring. Perhaps that is why I have always wished I could have had a guy like one of my close male friends from my youth. They have all stood by me in their separate fashions, and though my sex change was unnerving, not one of them ran and hid. They adjusted because they loved me and continue to do so, though I am losing them one by one as the clock ticks. Recently, I attended the funeral of Larry Levine, perhaps the most idealistic of my gang. As I listened to the funeral remarks, I was astounded. I thought I was the only one who really knew him, but the speakers on that dreary day described vintage Larry: irascible, argumentative, competitive, outspoken, brilliant, generous, loyal, and concerned. If I had been capable of speaking myself, I could have added an anecdote that summed him up for me. My thoughts went back to my sixtieth birthday party. It was a dinner-dance held on a boat circling Manhattan. The skyline was lit up, making for a romantic scene. All my old pals were there. We were kidding around, just as we always had, when Larry suddenly made a startling request.

"May I have this dance?" he said, holding his arms out.

Before I could answer, he had swept me out onto the floor, where we circled and pirouetted to my great delight. Larry was a good dancer. He was good at everything, especially friend-ship. Though he would call me out in an instant for any infrac-tion of his moral code, I could never take permanent offense. He cared about me, and as he had done so often in his life, he proved a leader at that party, shaming all of my other male friends into dancing with me. As each of them took his turn, I felt loved. Not that I wanted any of my friends for a romantic partner, but I did want the unconditional acceptance that I felt in their arms. It is an acceptance that I came close to finding in only one romantic relationship.

Alexander was about as unlikely a lover for me as I could imagine. He was an elder in his Presbyterian congregation.

His business is hard to describe. I still don't fully understand it. He looked over people's books, sort of a freelance accountant. I never saw him dressed in anything other than a nondescript business suit, often under an overcoat with no belt at the waist, just hanging straight down almost to his ankles. He always wore a gray fedora. To my mind he was the image of Willy Loman in *Death of a Salesman*. He made his rounds in a gray Chevrolet sedan. You couldn't ask for anyone who gave more the impres-sion of being a bland, Republican member of the conservative herd, yet in his fashion he became my champion.

Alexander emerged at a time when I was the target of some venomous comment by *New York Daily News* sports columnist Dick Young. Young had asked to interview me before he wrote anything, but I never received the request, so I didn't respond.

I think he felt slighted and got mad because he wrote some horrible stuff, claiming among other things that I was an impostor, not even a physician. For some reason, Alexander was offended in my behalf, and he started writing letters to Dick Young refuting Young's claims. Alexander sent me a copy of one of his letters, and based on its content, which was sensitive and intelligent, I agreed to meet him for a drink. I must add that this is the only time I ever met anyone based on a letter, though I have received a multitude of requests over the years. There seemed to be an element of kismet in our relationship. He was an unlikely man to have written such a letter, and I was unlikely to have responded. Yet it happened.

We met at a stodgy mid-Manhattan restaurant. I was to find out later that it was his favorite place, and this preference said a lot about the man. It was as Old World as he was, decorated in heavy brocade curtains and featuring a big oak bar and sometimes a violinist or accordionist who would serenade the tables. The management knew Alexander and were attentive to him. He was completely at home there, but others felt differently. I went in once with my friend Herb FitzGibbon, who took a look around and sat down with his back to the wall as if he were expecting Mafia soldiers to start shooting at any minute. I do believe the mafiosi hung out there. From time to time, I saw some suspicious-looking guys at the tables around us.

Anyway, when I sat down opposite Alexander, what I saw was not exactly my type of man, though he was big, and that was in his favor. His Scotch-Irish face was not handsome, but it was kind, which is just as good as handsome and maybe better. He was about ten years older than I, sixty-plus for sure. I discovered he was a grandfather and that his family was more important to him than anything, except maybe the church. It was obvious from the start that we had little in common except sports. We both followed the Yankees and the Giants, and like true fans we would say "the Yankee game" or "the Giant game" as if the opponent were a matter of indifference. Alexander's main attraction was that he liked me from the start and later loved me, not in that dangerous or muscular way that had been my lot so often, but in a gentle, interested fashion. To go back to a word much bandied about in my youth, he was "sincere." And even in today's sophisticated world, women will tell you that sincerity has a powerful charm.

The sex was not that great. After dinner, we would some-times—not often, but sometimes—go back to my office and make love on the couch, not a romantic setting and not too comfortable, either. But Alexander would tell me how soft my lips were and how beautiful I was. That's the sort of approach that makes the office couch an attractive proposition.

The thing we both liked best was something more romantic than sexual, a day at the races. This was a rare but treasured event. On a beautiful spring day, he would take me to Belmont Park. I would get into my best afternoon dress and a picture hat, and Alexander would pick me up in his gray sedan, wear-ing as always his gray suit and gray fedora. We were the but-terfly and the moth, but I loved being on his arm and noting his pride as he squired me about. He was actually puffed up! And when we sat in the clubhouse sipping a cool drink, he would look across at me with eyes full of love and approval. In those moments I felt cherished. How can you not respond to a man who makes you feel that way?

Even so, the differences between us could not be overcome. We spoke of how we might go on, but eventually we had dinner less and less often and then not at all. But for years after, Alexander would call the office weekly. He and Arleen would have a nice conversation, and after he had made sure I was okay, he would hang up without speaking to me. Each year on my birthday I would receive a dozen yellow roses from Alexander. Eventually, however, he got old. The calls and the roses stopped coming. Soon after, a relative wrote me to say that he had died.

Now I am past the age for romance. There is much love in my life but not romantic love. I would not turn away from romance, but I recognize that my chances for a great one are fading fast. Still, like other women, I sometimes think back to the men who have desired me and those who have loved me. I think of the yellow roses, and I realize that I have had more romance than many women can claim.

CHAPTER 11

Was It a Mistake?

AUTUMN HAS ARRIVED. IN rural New York the leaves have turned and the winds blow cooler, but occasionally they are warm. It is an even greater pleasure than usual to walk my dog. He is a happy companion, nosing about and running just for the pleasure of being in motion. I'm delighted when he rushes back to check with me before darting off again. We are a team, Travis and me, living the moments together. Our courses may diverge, but our reunions are always joyous. Everything is straightforward. I ask him no questions about his doings, and he asks me none about mine. Our only concern is whether or not all is still good between us. With him there are no sidelong glances. He does not read my name in the newspaper. He never shakes his head ruefully. He cares only about now. He wants his pat on the head; he wants his smile; he wants his treat; he wants my presence in his life. To him I am perfect. In that way he is everlastingly refreshing.

Things are different in the human realm. Lately, it seems that everyone wants to know if Renée thinks her sex change was a mistake. I don't mean my friends but people in general. In a way, I created this problem myself. The roots of it go way back, but recently something happened that rekindled the public's interest in the subject: I agreed to give an interview. It's something I seldom do, but if the subject is sports, I usually try to oblige. In this case, the interview was to commemorate the twenty-fifth anniversary of my first playing as a woman in the U.S. Open. I didn't think much about it. The article was for *Tennis* magazine, which I myself read and contribute to through an occasional letter to the editor or opinion on matters ophthalmic. There seemed nothing to dread. Perhaps I relaxed a bit more than I should have as I discussed my career, family life, friends, and memories of playing on the women's tour. I felt good about what I had said. I looked forward to hearing the reactions of my friends in the tennis community, most of whom read the magazine. I thought it would go no further than that. I was wrong.

The article had not yet been published when I saw newspaper headlines saying, RENÉE RICHARDS REGRETS SEX CHANGE. The stories asserted that I had made this admission in an interview with Cindy Schmerler for *Tennis* magazine. Outraged, I called the magazine and was told that the content of the interview had been made available for publicity purposes. Somebody along the line concluded that I was remorseful about my sex change. In fact, I had said nothing of the kind, though I will admit that

I did utter the word "regrets" that day, but what I actually said was that I had some regrets about my campaign to play on the women's pro tour once I had been unveiled in that long-ago La Jolla tournament. I observed that it might have been better in many ways if I had just returned to my life as a woman ophthalmologist and let the publicity storm blow itself out. If I had done that, I might have been able to live something like a private life as a physician. The loss of that chance is in the main what I regret. In short, I have some regrets about my career path, but apparently the words "transsexual" and "regret" cannot appear in the same article without somebody shouting, "I knew it!"

Since those headlines appeared, I have received a stream of invitations to be interviewed on the subject of my regrets about my surgery. Producers want to put me into television documentaries about regretful transsexuals. When I say, "No," they ask, "Would you agree if it was a documentary about just you?" It appears that there is a deep need to get the word out: "Have your genitals altered at your peril! You may regret it. Renée Richards does. Take a lesson, fool." I detest being put in this position.

Yet I do have regrets, and yes, they do touch on my sex change, and however much I would like to keep them to myself, I will go over them one time for the record. But before I do this, I must make it clear that I do not take any pleasure in laying myself bare. I value my dignity. I consider dignity one of the necessities of life. It may come second to food and sex, but without it one is not a whole person, man or woman. In my family, pride was not considered a bad thing. Achievement was expected, and you were invited to feel proud of yourself and others in the family who achieved. I have a strong aversion to anything that degrades my dignity, yet for nearly all of my life, I have had to struggle with one of the most undignified of conditions. In American culture, it is low comedy or perversion for a man to wear women's clothes. It is even worse for Jews, who revere the Old Testament: "A woman must not wear men's clothing, nor a man wear women's clothing, for the Lord your God detests anyone who does this" (Deuteronomy 22:5). To be considered a joke, a pervert, and detested by God wounds my dignity.

Is it any wonder that Dick Raskind developed a sizable ego to compensate for the indignity that repeatedly forced itself on him over the years? Is it any wonder that he learned to ignore, discount, and forget? Is it any wonder that I am put off by the notion of airing my regrets and compromising the dignity that means so much to me? No, it's not easy, but I'm writing a book and apparently my regrets have to be included. Inquiring minds want to know—but whether out of jealousy, macabre fascination, or a desire to nullify my existence, I can't say.

When I think of my life, I am reminded of Yogi Berra's sage appraisal of the Yankees' performance after a losing game: "We made too many wrong mistakes!" Certainly, I have made my share of mistakes. I have never denied that, but now there is a rumor out there that Renée Richards is just a transvestite who went too far. If that were true, I would truly have been guilty of a "wrong mistake," the kind that can eat people up and drive them to suicide. Back in 1962, when the transsexual movement was in its infancy, I knew a few who made that mistake and killed themselves. Even if you are a true transsexual, you have to be strong in order to carry through with a sex change. I recall that in classical myth, Hercules was once punished by being made to wear women's garments and perform women's tasks for three years. The strongest man on earth, mind you, experienced that transformation. He persevered, but when his task was done, he was allowed to return to his natural state. I wonder if his strength would have been great enough to endure living permanently as a woman. When one contemplates the surgeon's scalpel, what impresses are its simplicity and its keen edge. There is no doubt about its function. It is for cutting. Whatever one believes about one's psyche, that knife is the instigator of an irreversible reality. You need the courage of Hercules to face it and to live with the result.

Unlike Hercules, I did not have the luxury of finishing a term of service and picking up where I left off. The deed was done. There has been nothing to do but live with it. Could I afford regrets when even the healthiest mind has trouble dealing with them? I grew up watching my father swim in regrets. He was to all appearances a successful, relatively well-adjusted man. He made a nice living, did well by his patients, and was a loving husband and loyal friend. But he was also the greatest woulda-shoulda-coulda guy I ever knew. He should have sold his stock. He should have bought that house. He should have taken an orthopedic residency when he got the chance. His second-guessing went on constantly. Every decision he made was reviewed a thousand times, and if it was wanting, he relived the shame or loss a thousand times. I will not follow his example. If a stock sale or a house purchase can plague a person, how much more a sex change? What positive thing could come out of my dwelling on that decision and judging it wrong?

But suppose I did secretly think that I had done the wrong thing? What good would a public admission do? Whether I like it or not, Renée Richards has been a poster child for trans-sexuality, hailed as a standard bearer for the sexually disen-franchised of all descriptions, and described as a fighter for the rights of anyone denied legal or social acceptance in the United States. I have meant something to people. To turn my back on that by saying that the last thirty years I have spent as a woman were a mistake would constitute a betrayal of everything I have come to represent. I have freely admitted that my motives in standing up for myself were not completely idealistic or altru-istic. Very few people can claim such purity, but the effects of what I did remain, and I will not turn my back on them.

But what of those poor souls who might make a mistake? Don't you owe them something? Shouldn't you save them? To these questions I can only answer that I have done all I can for these people. I will say again that I do not think that there are a great many true transsexuals. I think that anyone contem-plating a sex change should view it as a last resort. However, if the psychologists and pharmacologists have done all they can for you, and you are still contemplating suicide, as I was, then I think surgery is a reasonable step. What other choice have you?

If being a transsexual were a matter of choice, I would be the first to say it is a bad choice, and if somebody with free will made that choice, I would say, "Big mistake!" But when I reflect on my own experience, free will does not figure in very heavily.

I cannot pinpoint a time when of my own free will, I could have made a choice that would have changed my destiny. How much free will did I have in the fateful decision I made thirty years ago? If I ever had it in the first place, a lifetime of conflict had essentially destroyed my free will. I was programmed by that time. As my venerable psychoanalyst Dr. Bak would frequently say, "These things tend to snowball." A drive like mine gathers momentum, and by 1975 I was not exercising free will.

So where were the mistakes? Did nature make the mistake in my hormonal makeup? Did my family make the mistakes during the imprinting phase of my growth? Or does it all fall on me? Maybe I was weak. Maybe I should have had more strength of will. If that is the case, I can sincerely say that I regret not having possessed that strength, but I refuse to dwell on it or let it spoil my days. When I walk the dog, I want to enjoy myself, not beat my breast.

I sometimes wonder what my life would have been like if hormone therapy and surgery had not been available to me. History is full of examples of people, sometimes great people, with a transsexual bent. Surely there has been a parade of undocumented others with my problem who lived out their lives as men, harboring their desire to be women. Most of them did not end up in state mental wards like the inmates described in *Psychopathia Sexualis*. They survived and presumably led productive lives, which I might also have done if no other course had been open to me, but to my mind these people lived as half-creatures. I applaud their bravery and their achievements, but I am too much of a purist to bear such an existence when a remedy, even a flawed remedy, is available to me. After thirty years of life as a woman, I realize that I had to do what I did. However hard I tried, I could not control the force that drove me, so I have no regrets on that score. It's like tennis. Sometimes you play somebody who is just too damn strong for you, so you lose. If you can't shrug it off, you get ulcers. If you can, you don't. I don't have ulcers.

But the public's interest goes deeper than the issue of whether or not I regret my sex change. There is a subtle variation: "Do you regret not being able to stay a man?" This question grants that I could not help myself and generously allows me to put aside regrets on that score, but it shifts the emphasis onto whether I was a better man or a better woman. It suggests that I was a very good man who was changed into just a fairly good woman, so the discrepancy must be at least a little galling. I must pine for the good old days when I was smack on. As my ex-wife has said, "Renée should have stayed a man. Dick was better looking than Renée."

Well, I must admit that I had better equipment to be a man from the anatomic, physiologic, and psychic standpoint. I could function sexually and reproductively. My orientation was heterosexual, and my sex drive was certainly strong enough to have a good sex life with female partners. I had the potential to lead the life of a husband, father, and family man. But even if I project myself back to the days before hormones and therapy, I cannot shake the sense that my life would have been awful. I would have had to live with my compulsion, sometimes great, sometimes minimal, but never knowing when it was going to rear its ugly head. Never knowing when I would feel the pressure to dress up as a woman, to mutilate myself, to expose myself to shame, social stigma, arrest, imprisonment, and violence. And maybe, having fought for most of my life, I might have finally caved in to my compulsion at an age when I had little chance to live any sort of fulfilling female existence, becoming an old woman who had missed the pleasures of youth. Yes, yes, but suppose none of that happened? Would you have liked being a man better?

Can't people see how impossible it is to answer that question? I don't hate Dick Raskind. He is part of me, but my idea of being a man is so tangled up with all the conflicts that Dick went through that I can't relate to masculine life under any other circumstances. I can certainly observe well-adjusted men, so I know that such a state exists, and for periods of my life as Dick, I feel I came close to it. But always there was the hidden threat, an anxiety that was never completely gone. So if you want me to say that I would have preferred life as a fully functioning man with no fears of the sort I have described, I can say, "In all likelihood, yes." But as long as we're speculating, I can also say that I would probably have preferred life as an angel. So what?

There is one further aspect of the regret problem that I am sometimes asked to ponder. As I have said, in 1975 I was too far gone to do anything other than have the surgery: The snowball described by Dr. Bak had reached the unstoppable stage. I took my chance at a life that would give me some peace. But what if there had been drugs to treat me? What if there were techniques to help mute the behavior, something other than analysis, which I had exhausted with years of fruitless therapy? Perhaps there might have been some form of behavior modification, or biofeedback, or who knows what else, to diminish the compulsion without rendering me unable to function as a man. Suppose these pipe dreams had been real? Would I have used them? The answer is that I would have used any method or methods that I thought might have worked. Given my experience with psychotherapy, I am doubtful as to their effect, and even now, in 2005, I don't know of any such therapy. Perhaps if something like that had existed I would now be a happy old guy contentedly scratching his balls. But no such fix existed in 1975. Even the seemingly all-purpose Prozac didn't go on the market until 1988. Do I regret that nothing but surgery was left to me? I suppose so, but only at an intellectual level. Emotionally, I don't sweat it. I sleep like a baby.

Maybe I've convinced some readers that I don't regret my surgery and that I had to do it for good or ill. And maybe I haven't. Either way, let's move on.

At the beginning of this chapter, I said I did have some regrets. For the first and last time, I am going to go through them, hoping that doing so will help lay them to rest. What do I regret?

I regret that circumstances turned me into a transsexual, whether through nature or nurture.

I regret that I posed such a threat to my sister that she contributed to my condition.

I regret that I developed the urge to start dressing as a girl and fantasizing about being one.

I regret that I couldn't fight off that urge.

I regret that I did not have the courage to go against family pressure and make a life for myself in athletics. It might have saved me.

I regret not pitching for the Yankees. A few scouts said I had a chance.

I regret that I did not reach my full potential in medicine. The psychic energy I might have put into medical research was spent coping with my personal problems.

I regret that I loved women, not men. I have been in love three times, each time with a woman. As Renée, I have never loved a man in the way Dick loved those three women, and no amount of "good sex" with a man can compensate for that loss.

I regret most deeply that one of those women had an abortion because I let my psychoanalyst talk me into allowing it. I might have succeeded as a man with this beloved woman if not for that abortion.

I regret that my marriage with another of the women I loved ended in a divorce that caused her so much pain. Meriam was left without a husband, without the financial resources to which she was accustomed, and, to her mind, without the father of her son. I regret the humiliation and embarrassment she endured because of my notoriety.

I regret what I did to my son. His pain was immeasurable, and he still suffers from the loss of his father as he knew him. The confusion and shame I put him through have been awful, and he will carry those scars for a lifetime.

I regret that I tested the love of my father so severely. He, too, valued his dignity. How he must have cringed when he learned of my sex change, but his love for me never wavered.

I regret my decision on religious grounds. I am a Jew. The Torah forbids the sorts of things I have done. I carry that guilt.

Though I am glad that I stood up for my rights and became an inspiration to many disenfranchised people, I regret many of the effects of that decision. I regret my loss of privacy, which was so much harder to endure than I ever imagined it would be. I regret the loss of my best earning years. So many of my friends have achieved the freedom that comes with wealth. I regret that I do not have that freedom. There are many things I would like to do for myself and my loved ones, but they are beyond my means. I regret the animosity and negativity I caused in the world of tennis. I, who had been the paragon of the amateur sportsman in the old days, became in the eyes of some a pariah and villain. That was hard to take.

Finally, I regret being a facsimile. I think I'm a pretty good one, but I will never be more than a fax, a woman with a Y chromosome: no ovaries, no uterus, no capacity to bear children. I can only add that I did the best I could.

Those are the regrets that come readily to my mind. I'm sure I have left some out. Certainly there will be people who will read what I have written and say, "My God, she doesn't regret such and such?" In their honor, I'll add one further regret: I regret that I may have omitted their favorites.

So where have I arrived, having gone through so many regrettable experiences? Certainly my life is more peaceful now. No incessant pressure to do something I felt was not right. No urge to go "haunting," as my dear departed friend Josh would call my dressing up and sneaking around town in women's clothes. I am a woman, the best I can be, with no pressure to be something I am not. I have no shameful urges to hold off.

Thankfully, I lack many traits that are often associated with "real men." I don't spit. I don't curse. I don't belch. I don't smoke cigars. I don't pick fights, but I might try to stop one. As my friend Herb FitzGibbon observed back in 1975 when he first heard about my sex change, "But Dick was the guy who would break up the fights in the bars." I still have Dick's toughness. At seventy, I am confident, strong, and unafraid, but in this I am no different than so many women of the twenty-first century.

I have made my living in what is often called a "giving" profession, which I love, just as Dick did, but for Renée there is more emotional involvement, less of the imperious distance and more of the human touch. I love art, music, and literature, all of which are fitting for both women and men. On the other hand, I am not into cooking, gardening, or flower arrangement, and I am grateful that the feminine role no longer requires a mastery of these skills. As I have grown older, clothes have come to mean less and less to me, though at one time they were quite important as a badge of femininity. However, once I actually became a woman, they made less difference. Don't get me wrong, I still like to get into a gown and attend a classy affair, but now the opportunity is strictly an occasion for fun, not for validation.

My dear friend Larry Levine used to argue with me about whether "personality" could be changed. A psychologist friend of his did a study suggesting that under the right circumstances it could be changed, but from my experience I argued that major changes were unlikely. I don't think Renée's personality is essentially different from Dick's, with perhaps the exception of some hormonally heightened emotionality. I don't regret that. Dick was in many ways a very sensitive man, despite his competitiveness and daring. As Renée, I am happy to have some traits that might be more admirable in a man and some that might be more admirable in a woman. I have the same politics I always had. I like the same Bach partitas for unaccompanied violin. I am not as sexist as Dick, but I don't think that reflects personality change. The change in our culture is as much responsible for that as the change in my sex.

Am I suited to this life? All I know is that I am comfortable in my skin. To my old friends who knew Dick, I have become Renée, and because I want to be a woman they treat me as such. To strangers, I am a woman. To small children, I know I am sometimes a confusing entity; they are so very perceptive and honest, so in the end I am what they want me to be, what they see me to be.

As a parent, I am not motherly in the physical or psychological sense. But I am caring and protective, even overprotective, of my son, and if I am ever blessed with grandchildren, who knows how I will see them or they me? That is an uncharted frontier. I hope that love will be the main component of the relationship and that nothing else will matter.

In the end, who can truly explain the choices he or she has made or plumb the depths of his or her regrets? Most of us can only stand mute or inadequately recount some unsatisfactory details, but sometimes a poet can come close.

> *Two roads diverged in a yellow wood,*
> *And sorry I could not travel both*
> *And be one traveler, long I stood*
> *And looked down one as far as I could*

To where it bent in the undergrowth;
Then took the other, as just as fair,
And having perhaps the better claim,
Because it was grassy and wanted wear;
Though as for that the passing there
Had worn them really about the same,

And both that morning equally lay
In leaves no step had trodden black.
Oh, I kept the first for another day!
Yet knowing how way leads on to way,
I doubted if I should ever come back.

I shall be telling this with a sigh
Somewhere ages and ages hence:
Two roads diverged in a wood, and I—
I took the one less traveled by,
And that has made all the difference.

—Robert Frost

Acknowledgments

*N*O WAY RENEE COULD not have been written without the contributions of the following people:

Dr. David Raskind, my father, and Nicholas Raskind, my son, both of whom stood by me no matter what.

Arleen Larzelere, who has kept me grounded and in one piece for the last twenty years.

Eugene Scott, who helped pave the way for my start in women's professional tennis.

Billie Jean King, who submitted the crucial affidavit in the historic court case that gave me the right to play women's tennis and then backed it up by playing doubles as my partner.

Martina Navratilova, who let me stand by as she won all four of the Grand Slams.

Dr. Lawrence Yannuzzi and Dr. Jack Dodick, who facilitated my return to my old hospital when I resumed the practice of medicine.

Allen Bomser, who gave me expert legal advice in getting *No Way Renée* started and found Jane Dystel to represent the project.

Jane Dystel, my literary agent. She's the best.

Sydny Miner, my editor at Simon & Schuster, who brought her enthusiasm and expert advice to the project.

Index

African Americans, murders of,
232–33
AIDS, 202–4
All England Club, *see* Wimbledon
American Association for Research
in Vision and Ophthalmology,
201
American Board of
Ophthalmology, 183
American Lincoln Logs, 218
American Psychiatric Association,
81
Andrews, Dana, 66
Andy Hardy movies, 61–62
Antonoplis, Lea, 31
Apollo Theater (Harlem), 253–54
Ashe, Arthur, 251
Austin, Tracy, 157–58, 170
Australian Open, 128

Bak, Robert C., 14–16, 19, 59, 70,
77, 251, 253, 270, 283, 285
Baron, Grandma, 10, 36
Baron, Joseph (grandfather),
35–38, 50–51
Baron, Molly (aunt), 10, 37
Baron, Sadie Muriel, *see* Raskind,
Sadie Muriel Baron
Baths, The (New York), 256
Beene, Kathy, 30

Bell, Geoffrey, 227–28
Bell, Joan, 227
Benjamin, Harry, 15–17, 20, 23,
78–81, 233
Benny, Jack, 62
Bergman, Ingrid, 52
Black Panthers, 29
Blair, Tony, 227
Bolsheviks, 44
Borg, Bjorn, 138, 140
Boston Lobsters tennis team, 152
Botox, 244
Breast cancer, 243–44
Breast implants, 238, 242–43
Breast reduction surgery, 22,
237–38, 242, 243
Brown, Knockout, 45
Bryn Mawr College, 37
Buenos Aires Lawn Tennis Club,
129–32
Buffum, David, 263–64
Buse, Enrique and Eduardo, 135

Cancer, 245–46
breast, 243, 244
colorectal, 41, 246
Candy, Don, 170
Carillo, Mary, 134
Carlson, Dick, 28
Carter, Lynda, 160

Casals, Rosie, 125, 264
Case Western Reserve University, 200
Charles, Lesley, 125
Chinese Kempo, 119
Churchill, Lady Sarah, 100, 104, 105, 110–11
Clanton, Ike, 180
Cleveland Nets tennis team, 32, 137
Club 82 (Greenwich Village), 253
Cohn, Roy, 33–34
Coles, Glynis, 125
Colorectal cancer, 41, 246
Connecticut Beautiful (Nutting), 207
Connors, Jimmy, 269
Cornell Medical School, 3, 196
Cosell, Howard, 2, 31

Dee, Tom, 214
Deer Lake Camp, 63–66, 205
Delestrogen, 233
Depression, 246
Devil's Run Tennis Club (Gainesville, Florida), 181
Diagnostic and Statistical Manual (American Psychiatric Association), 81
Dietrich, Marlene, 62
Donahue, Phil, 2
Druids, 213, 214
Duane's Retraction Syndrome, 191
DuPont, Laura, 125

Early, Felice, 214
Earp, Wyatt, 180
Eastern Tennis Hall of Fame, 4, 161
Elbe, Lili, 75
Ellis Island, 44
Els, Ernie, 260
Enola Gay (B-29 bomber), 66
Estrogen, 19, 243–46
  breast cancer and, 243
  presurgical, *see* Hormone therapy
  skin patch, 233, 244

Evert, Chris, 87–88, 123–24, 139, 150, 152–53, 155–57, 168, 170
Evert, Jeannie, 123–24, 134
Exotropia, 184
Eye surgery, 3, 49
  income from, 122
  laser techniques, 178
  see also Ophthalmology

Family Circle cup, 167
Farquhar, Hal, 225
Fibber McGee and Molly (radio show), 62
Fishbach, Joe, 131
Fishbach, Michael, 131–33
Fitzgibbon, Herb, 95, 273, 289
Florida, University of, 180, 182
  Medical Center, 181
Foerster, Josephine Baron Raskind (sister), 35, 50–54, 68, 101–2
  childhood and adolescence of, 8–10, 51–53, 286
  Nick and, 53–54, 100, 109
  and sex change, 17–18, 53, 59
  visits from, 54–60, 209
French Open, 129, 164, 167–69, 172
Freud, Sigmund, 10
Freudian analysis, 14, 15, 40, 76–77, 251
Froehling, Frank, 178–81, 220–21, 264–65, 267–71
Frost, Robert, 291

Gays, 72–73, 87
Geller, Jack, 244–45
Gender dysphoria, 80–81
Genderqueerness, 83–84
Gender reassignment, *see* Sex-change surgery
Gerulaitis, Vitas, 137
Gibbons, Mike, 217
Gifford, Frank and Kathy Lee, 160
Giscafre, Raquel, 129, 134
Glaucoma, 178
Goldstein, Izzy, 189
Golf, 246–47

Good Morning America, 2
Goosen, Retief, 260
Graf, Steffi, 166
Granato, Robert, 80, 239–42
Grand rounds, 191
Gray, Spalding, 228–29
Great Expectations (movie), 64
Great Neck Country Club (New York), 131
Gurdjieff, George Ivanovich, 180
Guy, Gary, 242, 243
Gynecological examinations, 241–42

Haas, Robert, 159, 171
Hair, changes in texture of, 236
Hamberger, Christian, 19
Harrisburg Hospital, 46
Harvard University, 45
  Medical School, 182
Hasidic Jews, 195–96
Head Hunters, 118
Health Channel, 61, 121
Heldman, Gladys, 31–32
Helen Keller Services for the Blind Award, 3
Henning, Basil Duke, 84, 85, 89
Hepburn, Katharine, 53
Hermann, John, 187
Hershey, Barbara, 215
Hillel Foundation, 87
Hippocratic Oath, 191
Hiroshima, atomic bombing of, 66
Hitler, Adolf, 66
Hollywood Production Code, 62
Hollywood Squares, 2
Homosexuality, 72–73, 87, 255–58
  cultural stereotypes of, 62
  Jamaican paranoia over, 108
Hormone therapy, 16–17, 94, 233–37, 242, 283, 284
  changes induced by, 234–36
  discontinuation of, 17, 20, 79, 237
  resumption of, 23
  sexuality and, 256
  see also Estrogen

Horvath, Kathleen, 172–73
Hospital Workers Union, 189
House of Representatives, U.S., 179

Ihlenfeld, Charles L., 23
Indiana Loves team, 142
International Conference of Electrical Engineers, 201
International Tennis Hall of Fame, 176
Internet, 73, 76, 239

Jaeger, Andrea, 168–70
Jaeger, Roland, 169, 170
Jennings, Waylon, 144
Jewel Box Revue, The, 253–54
Jews, 2, 8, 36, 37, 46, 52, 68, 133, 209
  attitude toward sex change of, 280, 287
  in Ivy League schools, 77, 44–45, 87
  Nazi atrocities against, 66
  orthodox, 195–97
  at Sedgewood, 215
John Wayne Tennis Club (Newport Beach, California), 25, 28, 259
Jorgensen, Christine, 15, 75–76, 231, 231

Karate, 119
Kaufman, Cheryl, 189–90
Kenpo, 119
Kennedy, Jacqueline, 21
Khrushchev, Nikita, 220
King, Alan, 33
King, Billie Jean, 32, 125, 147, 176, 182
Ku Klux Klan, 180

LaBelle, Patty, 264
Larzelere, Arleen, 102, 115, 207–11, 230, 246, 271, 275
  clothes sense of, 86, 210
  and Jo's visits, 54–56, 60
  and medical practice, 192–95

Larzelere, Arleen, *(cont.)*
  during Nick's runaway episode,
    103–4
  and primate research, 201, 202,
    204
  at Plaster House, 211, 212
  at Sedgewood, 214, 216, 220–24,
    226, 229
Laser surgery, 178
Leand, Andrea, 154
Leonard, Art, 175
Leonard, Sugar Ray, 160
Lesbianism, 270
Levine, Larry, 84, 271–72, 289
Levinski, Battling, 45
Levy, "Rolls," 48
Lieberman, Nancy, 158–61, 163,
  166–73
Little Women (Alcott), 67
Los Angeles Strings tennis team,
  139
Lucas, John, 138–39, 141–48

Maccabiah Games, 151, 262
Macular degeneration, 228
Madison Square Garden, 173
Mammograms, 243
Mandlikova, Hana, 170
Manhattan Center, 71
Manhattan Eye, Ear, and Throat
  Hospital (MEETH), 18,
  186–91
Man into Woman (Wegener),
  74–75
Marijuana, 181, 213, 226
Marley, Bob, 103
Marmureanu, Peter, 172
Martial arts, 119
Maryland, University of, 142
McCarthy, Joseph, 33
McEnroe, John, 165
Migraine headaches, 244, 245,
  246
Miller, Mary, 85, 88–90
Milwaukee Bucks basketball
  team, 147
Murders of transsexuals, 232–33

Murren, Patty, 115
Muscles, changes in, 235–36, 246

Nagasaki, atomic bombing of, 66
Nagorski, Sig, 220
Nastase, Ilie, 139
National Basketball Association
  (NBA), 138, 142
National Enquirer, 61
National Register of Historic
  Places, 215
Navratilova, Martina, 3, 88,
  126–28, 149–76
  in International Tennis Hall of
    Fame, 176, 210
  Lieberman and, 158–61, 163,
    166–73
  medical practice financed by,
    187, 192
  in U.S. Open, 154–58, 162, 165,
    174, 175
  at Wimbledon, 3, 152, 155,
    160–61, 165, 170, 174, 221
Navy, U.S., 2, 15, 17, 65, 236
  tennis team, 151
Nazis, 66, 133
Neubauer, Peter, 95, 96
New Jersey Nets basketball team,
  227
Newsweek, 1
New York Apples tennis team,
  147
New York City Health Department,
  29
New York Daily News, 272
New York Giants football team,
  274
New York Knicks basketball team,
  147–48, 227
New York Police Department
  (NYPD), 101
New York University, 3
New York Yankees baseball team,
  274, 287
Nicholas II, Czar of Russia, 44
Nicholson, Jack, 160
Nipple sensitivity, 234

North American Sport Karate
Association, 119
Nutting, Wallace, 207

OK Corral, gunfight at, 180
Old Testament, 280
Ophthalmology, 3, 18, 178,
182–99, 278, 279
animal research in, 199–204
private practice of, 187, 192–99
see also Eye surgery
Orgasms
in adolescence, 250
after sex-change surgery, 239,
240, 258
effect of hormone therapy on,
236–37
Orthopedics, 46
Osuna, Rafael, 269
"Outing," 81

Parks, Honey, 184
Parks, Marshall, 183–86
Pattison, Andrew "Iron-Arm," 138,
139
Patton, General George S., 67
Penis
effects of hormone therapy on, 236
phantom pain in, 240
removal of, 238
People magazine, 1
Perlman, Itzhak, 226–27
Phantom pain, 240
Pituitary hormones, 21
Plaster House (Connecticut),
206–7, 211–15, 221–22
Poster, John, 245
Premarin, 233, 244
Primate research, 200–204
Privacy, right to, 81
Proscar, 244
Prostate, enlarged, 244
Prozac, 17, 286
Psychiatry, 8, 38–40, 46, 286
Freudian, 14, 15, 40, 76–77, 251
Psychopathia Sexualis (Krafft-
Ebing), 69–70, 283

Purple Heart, The (movie), 66
Putnam Hospital, 224, 227

"Queer," attitudes toward term,
82–83

Ralston, Dennis, 170
Raskind, Albert (uncle), 58, 66–67
Raskind, Anita Litofsky
(grandmother), 26, 44
Raskind, Ben (uncle), 67
Raskind, David (father), 8–10,
17–18, 35, 40–50, 101, 182,
187, 246
death of, 54, 58, 120
during World War II, 66
early life of, 44
education of, 44–45, 86
medical training of, 46
Nick and, 99–100, 102, 109,
113–14, 119–20
photographs of, 58
regrets of, 281
and sex change, 17–18, 42–43,
47, 287
tennis and, 9–10, 47–49, 63
Raskind, Joseph (grandfather), 44
Raskind, Josephine (sister), *see*
Foerster, Josephine Baron
Raskind
Raskind, Meriam (wife), 2, 20–22,
29, 95, 98, 237, 284
divorce of Dick and, 22–23, 96
impact of sex change on, 94, 287
during Nick's runaway episode,
99, 101, 105, 109, 113
Southampton lifestyle of, 216
Raskind, Nick (son), 2, 4, 91–120,
226, 237, 290
birth of, 22
childhood of, 22–24, 28, 29, 34,
92–97, 197–98
clothing business of, 118
gambling by, 118–19
grandfather and, 99–100, 102,
109, 113–14, 119–20
impact of sex change on, 287

Raskind, Nick (son), *(cont.)*
 Jo and, 53–54, 100
 martial arts training of, 119
 Martina and, 160
 at Plaster House, 205–7, 211–14,
  221–22
 runs away to Jamaica, 100–114
 school problems of, 97–99,
  114–16, 243
 at Sedgewood, 215–16, 220–26
Raskind, Olga (aunt), 44
Raskind, Richard (Dick)
 adolescence of, 11–13, 68–75
 birth of, 7
 breast reduction surgery of, 22,
  237–38, 242, 243
 childhood of, 2, 7–11, 39–40,
  51–52, 61–68, 139, 205
 divorce of, 22–23, 94, 96–97,
  238, 287
 ego of, 280
 as father, 22, 23, 93–94, 287
 impact of conservative culture
  on, 61–63, 67, 68, 77, 79–80
 marriage of, 2, 20–22, 287
 medical practice of, 2, 18, 23, 80,
  188–91, 195–96
 and mother's death, 40–41
 muscle mass of, 246
 in Navy, 2, 15, 17, 65, 80
 psychotherapy of, 2, 13–15,
  76–77, 238, 251, 286
 reflections on life as, 284–85,
  289–90
 romantic relationships of,
  250–53, 287
 sex change of, 16–20, 247 (*see
  also* Hormone therapy; Sex-
  change surgery)
 sexuality of, 13, 20, 21, 236–37,
  250, 255, 284
 in support group, 77–78
 as tennis player, 2, 13, 14, 25,
  27, 73, 131, 135, 151, 241,
  262
 at Yale, 2, 13, 82, 84, 86–87
Raskind, Sadie Muriel Baron

 (mother), 8–10, 35–41, 50, 56,
  63, 65, 75
 confession to, 76
 death of, 15, 40–41, 59, 246
 early life of, 36–37
 family background of, 35–36
 gives birth to Dick, 7
 Jo and, 51–53
 medical training of, 37–38, 46
 photographs of, 58
 physical appearance of, 39–40,
  235
 psychiatric career of, 8, 38–40,
  46, 68, 69
 and sex change, 41
 during World War II, 66
Rasputin, Grigori Yefimovich, 36
Rastafarians, 106, 108
Reed, Willis, 227
Rees, Tom, 238, 242, 243
Reid, Kerry and Raz, 128–29
Richards, Renée
 adolescence of, 4, 121–22, 129,
  130, 137, 139–49, 204
 Arleen's relationship with,
  207–11, 216, 221, 271
 coaching career of, 3, 115,
  149–76
 during Dick's childhood and
  adolescence, 11–13, 64,
  250–51, 253–55
 and Dick's romantic
  relationships, 250–53
 Dick's transformation into,
  18–19, 23–24, 237 (*see also*
  Hormone therapy; Sex-change
  surgery)
 fame and notoriety of, 1–3, 27–31
 family background of, 35–39,
  43–46
 father's relationship with, 41–43,
  46–50, 287
 frustration and hostility toward
  Dick before sex change of,
  13–15, 237
 in Gainesville, 178–81, 193, 220
 health of, 241–47

medical practice of, 3, 25, 49,
82, 96, 121, 122, 174, 176,
177–78, 182–99, 206, 232,
259, 287, 289
moves to California, 24–25, 94,
121
"outing" of, 81–82
at Plaster House, 206–7, 211–14
primate research by, 199–204
reflections on past of, 279–90
romances of, 249–50, 253,
256–64, 271–76, 287
at Sedgewood, 214–30
sexual experiences of, 239, 250,
255–56, 258, 264–68, 270
sister's relationship with, 51,
53–60
son's relationship with, 4, 24,
91, 94–120, 197–98, 205–6,
215–16, 221–26, 287, 290
tennis career of, 2–4, 25–34, 49,
96, 121–44, 178–79, 204, 208,
233, 259–62, 268–70, 278,
288
Tennis magazine interview with,
278–79
Yale event honoring, 84–90
Richey, Cliff, 269
Riessen, Marty, 138–40, 157–58,
170
Ringling Brothers and Barnum &
Bailey Circus, 44
Rochester, University of, Medical
School, 13, 82
Roland Garros Stadium, *see*
French Open
Rolex Junior Championships, 115
Rosenblum Eye Centers, 196
Rubell, Don, 241, 261
Russell, JoAnne, 128
Ryder, Merritt, 216

Savitt, Dick, 104
Schmerler, Cindy, 278
Scott, Gene, 29, 30
Sea Pines Plantation (Hilton Head,
South Carolina), 167

Sedgewood Club (Putnam County,
New York), 214–30
Sex-change surgery, 23–24, 77–81,
94, 231–32, 238–41, 259, 270
in Casablanca, 18, 19, 79
early, 74–75
and friends from former life, 261,
271–72
preparation for, 15–17, 78–79
(*see also* Hormone therapy)
procedures in, 238–39
recovery from, 240
reflections on, 277–90
Shadow, The (radio show), 62
Shaw, Fred, 78–79
Shriver, Pam, 170
Siegel, Sari, 84, 88
Silver Lining Foundation, 170
Simmons, Jean, 64
Skin, improvement in, 235
Smith, Paula, 126, 127, 129
Smith, Stan, 131
Smoking, 245
Snyder, Tom, 2
Somatic compliance, 232, 233
Spirituality, 178–80
Sports Illustrated, 1
Squint Club, 183
"Stealth mode," 259
Storch, Marcia, 245
Strabismus, 18, 178, 184, 187, 191
Stratton, Jane, 134
Sukova, Vera, 170
Sunbelt Nets tennis team, 32–33,
137–47, 152, 158
Sunrise Tennis Club (Sunnyside,
Queens) 9–10
Supreme Court, U.S., 179

Tai chi, 178–79, 220
Teitelbaum, Rabbi, 195–96
Tennis, 3–4, 25–34, 73, 96, 121–37,
177, 242, 278–79, 284, 288
Arleen's indifference to, 208
coaching, 3, 88, 115, 122–23,
149–74, 178–79
death threats and, 121, 233

Tennis, *(cont.)*
  father and, 9–10, 47–49, 63
  home courts, 218, 220–21, 225, 230
  network of friends in, 102, 278
  rivalries in, 87–88
  satellite circuit, 122–25, 151
  sex and romance and, 259–70
  in South America, 126–27,
    129–37, 154–55
  team, 32–33, 137–47, 152
  at Yale, 85, 86, 151
  see also U.S. Open; Wimbledon
Tennis magazine, 278
Testicles
  effects of hormone therapy on, 236
  phantom pain in, 240
  removal of, 238
Testosterone, 21, 244, 246
Time magazine, 1
Tinling, Ted, 149
Today show, 2
Transsexuals, 4, 15–16, 62, 209, 283
  changing cultural attitudes
    toward, 80, 82–84
  early examples, 74–76
  medical issues for, 233
  psychiatric view of, 76–77, 81
  purported cures of, 59
  regretful, 279–82
  somatic compliance of, 232, 233
  violence toward, 232–33
  would-be, support group for,
    78–77
  see also Sex-change surgery
Trans*topia (website), 76
Transvestites, 70–73, 78, 280
  performances by, 253–54
Tübingen Medical School, 233
Turnabout magazine, 78
Turnbull, Wendy, 125, 139

U.S. Open, 269
  Dick in, 129
  Martina in, 154–58, 162, 165,
    174, 175

Renée in, 33, 34, 49, 131, 154,
  278
United States Tennis Association
  (USTA), 28–29, 33–34
United World Federalists, 55

Vagina, 240
  surgical formation of, 238–39
Vietnam War, 62
Villeverde, Susanna, 135
Vinson, Carl, 179
Vinson, Fred, 179
Vinson, Melissa Hope, 178–82,
  192–94, 206, 207, 271
Virginia Slims tournament, 265

Wade, Virginia, 125
Wegener, Einar, 74–75
West Point, U.S. Military Academy
  at, 73
Wilson, Ron, 224
Wimbledon, 131, 182
  Junior Championship, 31
  Navratilova at, 3, 152, 155,
    160–61, 165, 170, 174, 221
Wolfensohn, Jim, 227
Women's Christian Temperance
  Union, 36–37
Women's Medical College of
  Pennsylvania, 37
Women's Tennis Association
  (WTA), 28–29, 33–34, 137, 265
"Woodworking," 259, 261
World Bank, 227
World Team Tennis (WTT), 32–33,
  137–47, 152
World War II, 62, 65–67, 131

Yale University, 2, 13, 44–45, 90
  Medical School, 45
  Saybrook College, 84–90
  tennis at, 85, 86, 151
  Trans Issues Week at, 82, 84
Young, Dick, 272–73
Yu Quon Chen, 199–201